Wearing Wellies

Wearing Wellies

✦

A Year of Life & Love in London

Garrett Ellis Ryan

iUniverse, Inc.
New York   Bloomington

Wearing Wellies
A Year of Life & Love in London

The views expressed in this work are solely those of the author and do not necessarily reflect the views of the publisher, and the publisher hereby disclaims any responsibility for them.

iUniverse books may be ordered through booksellers or by contacting:

iUniverse
1663 Liberty Drive
Bloomington, IN 47403
www.iuniverse.com
1-800-Authors (1-800-288-4677)

Because of the dynamic nature of the Internet, any Web addresses or links contained in this book may have changed since publication and may no longer be valid.

ISBN: 978-1-4502-0860-4 (sc)
ISBN: 978-1-4502-0859-8 (dj)
ISBN: 978-1-4502-0861-1 (ebk)

Printed in the United States of America

iUniverse rev. date: 4/5/2010

This book is dedicated to Carol

If I had only known,
I would have made more of an effort to get to know you.

And to my wonderful and loving mother and father,
words cannot express the gratitude that I have for parents
like you.

Everyone should have a best year ever.

This was ours.

- *Preface* -

Let's begin.

The tears had been there all day, but they were getting worse. Teary-Eyed Sarah, the nickname I had given my beautiful wife for when she started to cry, was quickly making another appearance.

"What if something happens?" she whimpered through large sobs of tears, which streamed from her angelic blue eyes and dripped to her chin, before falling to the ends of her long sandy-blond hair.

"There's nothing to worry about," I said in an attempt to comfort her.

"If something happened to her, I could never forgive myself," she whispered back.

"Don't worry. She's a fighter. She has been through so much in her short life. If something happens, she'll find a way to survive. Plus, if something catastrophic does happen to her, it will also happen to us."

"What?"

Wrong words at the wrong time, I thought to myself. A man approached us, carrying a large white envelope that we had been patiently waiting for; it saved me from my insensitive comment and the need to elaborate on it.

"Are you Mr. and Mrs. Ryan?"

"Yes, we are," I said.

"Here is your final paperwork. She has received lots of attention from all of us and is doing great. She will be just fine. There is nothing to worry about. They will be checking on her throughout, and she will come through just fine," he reassured us.

"Thank you so much. You have no idea how much we appreciate it," I said.

"No problem. It's my pleasure," the man said as he smiled and walked away.

"Ladies and gentleman," the static PA system suddenly sprang to life, "on behalf of British Airways, I would like to be the first to welcome you to BA Flight 296, nonstop service from Chicago to London, Heathrow. Please take your seats as quickly as possible. We have an extremely full flight tonight with no empty seats, a full cargo hold, and even one dog on board."

Sarah and I smiled and laughed together as we gave a small cheer of acknowledgement that the dog somewhere deep in the large, dark cargo hold of the plane was our dog, our Sydney.

This is the story of a young couple who sold their car, rented out their home, placed all their belongings in storage, said good-bye to their friends and family, put their dog on a plane with them, and moved 3,963 miles to London, England, for a year to learn a little more about the world, themselves, their marriage, and what can happen when you find the courage to take a chance and do something great.

This is also a story about taking weekend trips to Paris, visiting Italian cooking schools, queuing at Wimbledon, walking through the Cotswolds while wearing wellie boots, running marathons, cooking spotted dick, learning to love the French, finding a long lost friend, greeting friends with a kiss on each cheek, living under the rule of a queen, and loving a dog named Sydney.

- Chapter One -

Liftoff

✦

It takes a fully loaded 747 airplane almost a full minute to gain enough speed for aerodynamic lift to take effect and lift the massive plane into the air. I have comfortably sat through many airplane takeoffs in my life without the slightest fear of flying, but this was the most important flight of all, and at that moment, my blood pressure could not have been any higher. The plane shook violently as it accelerated down the runway with its huge engines roaring, pushing the plane faster and faster.

My heart was beating with an intensity I had never experienced as I held Sarah's hand, smiled, and attempted to project an image of confidence and courage. But my efforts were feeble after such a long and exhausting day, and I could not hide my true feelings. The only thought on my mind at that moment was *Get this plane in the air, or I'm going to have a heart attack!* I pictured Sydney sliding to the back of her large plastic crate somewhere deep in the dark cargo hold of the plane as the nose of the plane finally lifted into the air, beginning its steep climb upward after what seemed a lifetime. After a couple of minutes, we achieved the desired altitude, the plane leveled off, and the roar of the engines softened.

I looked over at Sarah, who looked like she, too, was about to throw up, and smiled.

"We're on our way. No turning back now," I said to her, pausing for a second. "You really shouldn't feel bad about Sydney. She has much more leg room in her crate than we do in these seats." Sarah smiled, but I could tell that she did not appreciate my comment. She leaned back and closed her eyes.

We were on a five-thirty, red-eye flight that would have us arriving in London at seven o'clock in the morning local time. Because we were traveling east, it would only be a few short hours before we would see the sun rise. The flight crew served us drinks, dinner, and more drinks before dimming the cabin lights so passengers could get a couple hours of sleep before our arrival in London.

I have never had a problem sleeping on airplanes, especially red-eye flights, but I just could not sleep. Even after four large glasses of white wine, every small bump of turbulence sent my heart racing as I thought of Sydney. She always curled up and went to sleep when we put her in the car for a long drive. She did not like loud noises, and I was sure that where she was did not resemble anything like the backseat of our old car. Exhaustion was setting in for Sarah, and she rested her head on my shoulder, as she often did on our flights together. I desperately needed some sleep, and I thought about taking the sleeping pills I had in my bag, but I feared that, after all the wine I had been drinking, I might never wake up again if I took the sleeping pills.

Our day had started at three o'clock in the morning as Sarah, Sydney, and I tried to get some sleep in Sarah's sister's guest bedroom in the suburbs of Chicago. But I had been wide awake and unable to sleep. *Are we doing the right thing?* I thought. Had I convinced Sarah into chasing some wild dream of mine?

My career was going great and was right where I wanted it to be. I was working for a growing ad agency with a dream boss, dream clients, and a job description that allowed me to hang out and schmooze with my clients at fashionable photo shoots in trendy loft workspaces in cities like New York, Miami, and Chicago. My job was one of the few respectable jobs where writing phrases like "client feels the model's breasts are too large" (or "too small") in meeting reports was perfectly acceptable.

We had a beautiful condo in Chicago. We were surrounded with lots of friends and family. Our retirement funds and savings accounts were growing, and we had no debt. Our marriage was performing like a well-tuned orchestra, hitting all the notes at just the right time, and we even had a wonderful dog that we had successfully kept alive and used to "test the waters" before starting a family.

Was this the right time in our lives to be doing this? What would this journey do to us as a couple and as individuals? Would it strengthen us or reveal some deep fault in our marriage that we had not known existed? We were moving to a place where we did not have any friends; we would be spending a good amount of our savings; and we would be living in an apartment a quarter of the size of our home. *Are we doing the right thing?*

We had been required to arrive at the British Airways cargo drop-off five hours before our flight in order to drop off Sydney to prepare her for the flight. When we arrived at the cargo drop-off, Sydney jumped out of the car and meandered around the small grassy area in front of the British Airways cargo office and we encouraged her to "do her business" one last time. Sydney wagged her tail, happy to be on this adventure with us, until the first plane had taken off in the near distance, shaking the ground violently and sending Sydney scurrying for cover. Sydney did not like thunderstorms, and to her, it seemed as if the mother of all thunderstorms had quietly snuck up on her without warning. After a few tense moments, Sydney did her business, and we walked her inside the British Airways cargo building to check her in for the flight.

To take Sydney on the flight and bring her into the United Kingdom, we followed the long and strict set of rules and procedures that also had cost us a small fortune in expensive overnight FedEx fees to send blood samples for testing. We also had completed the required and seemingly endless progression of signatures, often checking, and rechecking to make sure we had followed all the proper procedures.

The final step before heading to the airport had been a flea and tick treatment by the veterinarian, along with a final stamp and signature by the United States Department of Agriculture within twenty-four hours of the flight, and then she would be allowed into the United Kingdom upon arrival. By accurately following the long and expensive procedure required under the Pet Travel Scheme (or "PETS") to bring a dog into the United Kingdom, we would avoid having Sydney placed into quarantine—a kind of purgatory for dogs for six months upon arrival in the United Kingdom. We had heard numerous stories about dogs actually dying from depression while separated from their owners for six months. We had no idea if any of the stories were true or not, but being told that Sydney would have to stay in quarantine when we arrived in London was a nightly recurring nightmare for us.

When we checked Sydney into the flight, we had been relieved to see how well the British Airways employees had treated her. In preparation for the move, we had saved up a small fortune that we were quite proud of and that we thought would be enough to help get us through the year along with Sarah's income from her job. We would no longer be "DINKs" (dual income, no kids) but single income supporting a student and a dog. Somewhere among the confusion of arranging for Sydney to be allowed on the flight, we had misinterpreted *a seventy-five-dollar handling fee that turned out to be only a* small portion of a larger fee for taking Sydney on the flight. The rules for taking a dog on the flight stated that the crate had to be large enough so that the dog's head did not touch the top of the crate while standing and that the dog had to be able to easily turn around in the crate as if chasing its tail. We had not wanted to take any risks, so we had purchased the largest crate we could find. After officials had weighed the crate with Sydney in it, we were told it would cost $1,500 to bring Sydney on board. There was nothing we could do but hand over our credit card and force a smile.

We had said our final good-bye to Sydney and left her to check ourselves into the flight. We had thanked Sarah's sister for dropping us off and waved good-bye to her one last time before turning and walking into the international terminal at Chicago's O'Hare airport.

It had not been easy deciding what we would need in London and what we should pack. Packing for the move had been a three-week process, and the final result was six extremely heavy and overstuffed bags and two ridiculously oversized carry-on bags that seemed to grow larger by the minute. When it was our turn at the check-in counter, Sarah had handed over our passports as I struggled to get the large and heavy bags onto the scales for weighing and tagging.

"How many bags will you be traveling with today?" the British Airways employee had inquired with her British accent.

"Ah, six," I had said with a sheepishly guilty Midwestern American accent.

"I'm sorry, sir, but each traveler is only allowed two bags and one carry-on." She had yet to see what we were trying to pass off as carry-on baggage. That was not good.

"But we were told that our dog was allowed two bags as well." I had handed the women our documents for Sydney, hoping the appearance of some official-looking paperwork would lend credibility to my flat-out lie.

"Who was it that told you this, sir?"

"They." I had been trying to use the faceless "they" often referred to in "Well, you know, they said … " but she was not buying it.

"I'm terribly sorry, sir, but whoever told you that was misinformed. You can bring the additional bags onboard, but we will have to charge you."

Again, I had handed over the credit card and forced a smile.

"Here are your boarding passes. I have upgraded you both. There is no need to worry about your dog; the ground crew will take great care of her. One of our crew members will deliver your final animal travel documents to you at your seats on the plane. Enjoy your flight."

We had miraculously squeezed our oversize carry-on bags through the X-ray machines without any protest from the security staff, and we were off.

The only hiccup on the flight was the continuous raised eyebrow response of "Are you sure?" from flight attendant each time I asked for another glass of wine.

- Chapter Two -

Pembridge Crescent Road or Bust

✦

Six large, loud metal bangs announced the arrival of our luggage as it crashed down the luggage chute and onto the conveyor belt to begin its journey around the carousel to where we were standing. We collected all the bags and pilled them onto two large trolleys. The weight of all the overstuffed bags just about crippled the sturdy metal frames as we pushed them to the car rental depot to pick up a car to drive to our temporary home in central London. With a small hit to our savings and a so-far-so-good attitude, we were not quite ready to breathe a sigh of relief just yet; we still had to find Sydney.

I stood guard over our heap of bags while Sarah ran off into the sea of rental cars to pick ours up. After a few moments, Sarah pulled up to the curb in the car. There was only one thing that seemed appropriate to say at the time—"What the hell is this?"—as I sized up the miniature car and the mountain of luggage that seemed to tower over it.

"No, no, no! Go back and tell them we need the biggest, baddest, most environment-destroying SUV they have."

"Well, you could at least ask me nicely," Sarah shot back as she turned the car around, driving back on the wrong side of the road, causing chaos and an uproar from the confused, oncoming businessmen who were trying to exit the car rental lot as fast as they could. The next car she pulled up in was a minivan—a skinny, size zero, runway model of a minivan. All the bags did fit, but we still needed to fit Sydney's large crate into the car. We shut the doors, and Sarah slipped into what she thought was the driver's side. Being half asleep still, she had quickly forgotten which side of the car the driver's wheel was on.

"Looks like I'm driving," I said, as Sarah noticed her mistake.

Four roundabouts, three stops to read the map, and two close calls from oncoming traffic later, we finally arrived at the Animal Reception Center at Heathrow Airport to pick up Sydney. Like two worried parents, we anxiously waited for word that Sydney had made it through the flight just fine. The woman at the reception desk asked us which animal we were there to pick up; we told her; and she asked us to have a seat in the waiting room while she checked to see when Sydney would be released.

After what seemed like an eternity—or just long enough to look through six old magazines—the woman finally appeared with a fluffy, oatmeal-colored, tail-wagging, overly excited dog, our Sydney. She greeted us with her usual face-licking, back foot-hopping, unmistakable "Wheaten greeting" that soft-coated Wheaten Terriers are famous for. She pulled on the leash toward the door. We opened the door where she found some lush, green grass, and squatted down for a long, wow,-does-this-feel–great!, satisfying pee.

Sydney continued to sniff the ground and air while I tried my best to cram the large plastic crate into the van without breaking any of the windows. After I successfully squeezed the dog crate in, Sydney hopped into the car and assumed her usual sleeping position on the floor. Her tail continued to bang back and forth with excitement. We waved good-bye to the nice people at the Animal Reception Center and drove off down the road, again on the wrong side, almost causing a small accident and eliciting a chorus of honking from annoyed drivers.

The relief that came from collecting all the bags, picking up the rental car, and finding that Sydney did not hold a grudge against us for sticking her on a plane did not last long. Sarah and I had always been able to communicate and work through difficult times, but we were heading into the dangerous couple's argument zone. Anyone who has watched the mental breakdowns that happen to every team competing on the television show *The Amazing Race*, where teams of couples race around the world, can easily picture the type of argument we had as we tried to navigate the roads to our new temporary home.

My vocabulary was quickly changing from "Yes, sweetie," into "I know, *sweetie*," and progressing to "Think *you* can do *better, sweetie*?" and finally to the "*Fine, we will stop and ask for directions. Are you happy now?*" of the full mental breakdown of being completely lost, starving, and feeling like it was three in the morning with my brain and body demanding to know whose idea this had been. With a little luck and an apology to each other for "losing it," we eventually found our new, temporary home on Pembridge Crescent Road in Notting Hill.

Finding a new home is much easier with the invention of the Internet, or so we had thought. From thousands of miles away, we had been able to quickly and easily look at places available for short- and long-term rent

"I thought you said London was really expensive?" Sarah had asked one day while looking at places to rent in London on a rental Web site.

"London is very expensive, if not the most expensive city in the world," I answered back while checking the TV remote to see if there were batteries in it or if Sarah had taken them out again to use in one of her cooking appliances.

"Listen to this: 'Situated in the heart of a sought-after London residential location, close to a wide selection of local amenities, this truly stunning two-bedroom flat offers exceptionally spacious and stylish accommodation throughout.' The rent is only 750 pounds." (Around $1,400 at the time.)

"That sounds great," I said, "but we will not be able to leave this truly stunning, sought-after, two-bedroom flat, and we will not be able to afford to eat or even feed Sydney."

"What are you talking about?" Sarah asked with a what's-the-catch look.

"The price listed in the ad is the cost per week," I said. "Rental prices in London are almost always listed on a per week basis."

"Oh," she said, followed by a louder "Oh," as she quickly did the math in her head and finally ended with a "Oh, no, this is not good!"

We decided to find a short-term lease, which would give us time to search for a permanent flat to rent in London, and found one in Notting Hill.

Our new, temporary home on Pembridge Crescent Road in Notting Hill was a first-floor flat in a three-story, light yellow, stucco building that had white brick trim, large sun-filled windows, and four architecturally detailed white columns supporting a small porch entranceway. The building looked like all the other buildings on the street; the only distinguishing features were the color of paint on the front of the building and the color of the front door. The pictures of the flat that the landlord had sent to us had looked great, and the rent was not too high. Because it was a three-week rental, the rent per week was higher than we wanted to pay, but I had felt that we might be able to convince the landlord to lower it closer to our price range after we lived in it for a couple of weeks. Sarah had heard of the Notting Hill area, which had helped her feel more confident picturing where we were moving.

We pulled up to the curb of our new home, relieved that we had found it and happy to be one step closer to some serious sleep.

Oliver, our new landlord, greeted us at the door. He was tall with sandy brown hair, and he dressed like a starving, bohemian artist. Every time we saw him after that, he always seemed to be wearing the same pair of jeans and a worn, dark brown blazer with patches on the elbows. His hair always looked like he had just woken up, and rarely did we ever see him without a lit cigarette hanging from the corner of his mouth.

He greeted us with a soft-spoken voice that had just the slightest hint of an English accent. He opened the large, black front doors and led us down the hallway to the interior door of our new home. Sydney followed him, exploring all the interesting odors she was discovering on his pant legs.

"Before I show you the place, I must apologize," he said. "I have not had time to clean it up yet, and the water is not quite working at the moment." Sarah and I gave each other quick trouble-on-the-horizon looks.

As we entered the flat, we were hit by the smell of first sawdust, then cigarettes, and finally stale wine. Unfortunately, that was just the beginning of the problems. We stepped inside and assessed the situation. There were no closets, the bathroom would require me to duck down two feet to enter, and the bedroom had somehow disappeared. You could walk through the entire place in three seconds, because there was only a kitchen, a living room, and a bathroom.

We discussed the problem of the lack of cleanliness of the place with Oliver and agreed that Sarah, Sydney, and I would walk over to the park for an hour while he cleaned the place up. By then, we needed some fresh air. Sydney was no longer sniffing Oliver's leg, because she had found three rooms full of new and fascinating odors to explore.

We walked Sydney down Pembridge Crescent Road, turned left onto Notting Hill Gate Road, crossed the street, and entered Kensington Gardens. During the ten-minute walk, Sydney discovered something new in the world to fear: the iconic, red, double-decker bus for which London is famous. She had to crank her neck as high as it could go to get a good look at each bus as it passed us by in the street.

"It's just a bus, Sydney," I said in an encouraging voice as I pulled her leash, trying to release her from the frozen state of shock she seemed to be in.

We entered Kensington Gardens, commonly referred to as the former residence of Princess Di, and sat down on one of the hunter green wooden benches throughout the park. Sydney ran off to explore what would soon become her favorite place in London. All the puddles of mud and endless bounty of wet, green grass were quickly turning her into a wet, muddy dog. I walked over to a small food stand next to the Diana, Princess of Wales children's playground and purchased two slices of heat-lamped pizza and two drinks for us. We sat in silence, eating the pizza and trying to ignore the exhaustion that we felt. After an hour of sitting mostly in silence at the park we took Sydney, who was now completely covered in mud, back to officially move into our new apartment, which had no closet, no bedroom, and no water to clean up a muddy dog.

As we walked back, Sarah and I concluded that Oliver must have placed all the furniture in the living room and taken a picture, then placed all the same furniture in the kitchen and taken another picture from an angle that did not show it was the kitchen, and then taken two final pictures of just the bed in the living room with no furniture and one of just the kitchen cabinets. Then he had e-mailed us the pictures, creating the appearance of, as well as inappropriately calling it, a one-bedroom flat. We passed our rented minivan on the way back—it now had an parking ticket on it for not having a residential parking permit—and proceeded into our new home to find that Oliver had decided that, since there was no water, he could not clean the place. He had left us a note saying that he would be back in the morning to take us to his fitness gym so we could shower at it. We brought our remaining bags in from the car and started to unpack, trying to make the place feel like home.

Sarah and I had been together for almost forty-eight hours straight, and since the pizza was more of snack than a meal, I suggested that I return the rental car and bring us back our first dinner in London. I also thought that some time apart to cry, scream, or punch the air would make us both feel better.

Notting Hill is filled with many great places to eat, but unfortunately, the only place that offered takeout service and was still open was the local Kentucky Fried Chicken (KFC) on Notting Hill Gate Road. Surprisingly, KFC had locations all over London and was incredibly popular. KFC actually beat McDonald's to London by about ten years.

I could tell Sarah was not pleased with my selection for dinner, but because she was too tired to fight anymore, we sat in silence and ate our bucket of fried chicken. Our first two meals in London had been cold pizza and KFC. I was not doing a great job of hunting and gathering food for my beautiful wife.

We placed the sheets on the bed, closed the living room curtains, and finally crawled into the bed, which we had decided worked best in the living room. We fell into a deep sleep almost immediately. I slept in complete peace until Sydney, her sense of time being just as off as ours, woke me up by nudging her wet nose against my arm a couple of times, indicating that she needed to go outside. It was about three o'clock in the morning, but even with just a few hours of good sleep, I was already feeling much better. I put on my jacket and shoes and took Sydney out to do her business.

It was a crisp, cold January night in London, but it was still much warmer than Chicago in January. It was quiet, but I could hear an electronic humming noise slowly getting louder. I looked to my left and saw a large, almost golf cart-style truck as it pulled up. Out stepped the milkman.

"You all right?"—an English phrase for "How's it going?"—the man said as he walked past me and up the stairs to drop off real glass bottles of cold milk on the front porch.

I walked farther down the sidewalk until Sydney stopped abruptly and sniffed the air. A small animal a short distance directly in front of us stared right back at us. It was a small fox, and after a quick staring match with Sydney, the fox crossed the street and ran down the road, disappearing from sight. I walked back to the flat, and for the first time in almost two days, I genuinely smiled.

Sarah and I slept until noon that first morning. Either Oliver forgot to come get us to take us to the gym to shower or his morning did not start until the early afternoon. I don't know if I was more surprised that he did not show up or that he belonged to a fitness gym. Either way, we decided to get up and walk around the neighborhood to start our new adventure.

We purchased some coffee and walked down Portobello Road towards the antique market. Notting Hill was filled with many celebrities, enjoying the area or living in the many beautiful homes. Spotting a celebrity like Kate Moss, Sienna Miller, Sean Connery, or Keira Knightley was routine to many of the business owners and residents along Westbourne Grove Street. House prices were ridiculous; a two-car garage was recently sold to be demolished for $500,000.

Sarah and I walked toward the main market road known as "The Lane," holding hands in silence, reflecting on what might lie ahead for us in the upcoming year as we soaked in the atmosphere of the Georgian, Edwardian, and Victorian architecture of the surrounding buildings and homes. We stepped into the Books for Cooks bookshop, a warm and welcoming place filled with all kinds of cookbooks and, fittingly, even has a small restaurant in the back of the store that hosted cooking demonstrations and had a delightful just-out-of-the-oven smell coming from it. While Sarah quickly lost herself in a sea of cookbooks, I crossed the street to visit The Travel Bookshop, called The Travel Book Co. in the movie *Notting Hill*, and immersed myself in a colossal selection of travel memoirs, guidebooks, and maps. We ended our afternoon by purchasing some cleaning supplies and heading back to try to make our new flat feel a little more like home.

The apartment had been painted two shades of purple, with white decorative ceiling trim in the living room and light yellow and white decorative ceiling trim in the kitchen. Each room had a small but beautifully ornate fireplace that, at one time, had burned coal to heat each room. The amazing, large, antique wooden plank floors in each room badly needed some attention. The place really had great potential, but even after a cleaning and a small makeover, the potential it truly had was still far from what we would be able to achieve.

We finished unpacking our bags, got rid of the food Oliver had left in the refrigerator, and even managed to get a little bit of water to work in the bathroom to flush the toilet and take a quick shower.

The day was trouble free, until the scream of "Oh, no!" came from the far corner of the living room. I quickly ran into the room, not knowing what to expect. Sarah was kneeling on the floor, holding a radio that we had brought. She had wanted to turn some music on and had plugged it into the electrical socket using an electrical adapter. A small cloud of smoke had risen from the back of the radio and floated up into the air, as if the radio's soul was floating to the heavens upon its apparent death. She looked up at me, smiled, and proceeded to slowly move her favorite and irreplaceable hair blow-dryer away from the electrical outlet.

"I don't think I'll be trying that in there."

- Chapter Three -

A Place We'll Call Home

✦

Unfortunately, our year in London was not a one-year vacation from the realities of life. Sarah would be working in the London office of the large consulting company she worked for, and I would be attending a one-year, intensive MBA program.

Even with all the problems we had encountered during our first week in London, our first few days had been memorable and exciting, but it was time to get back to reality. Sarah insisted that I did not need to, but I wanted to go with her to help her find her new office on her first day of work in London. We walked a couple of streets and down the stairs of the Notting Hill Gate underground train station—more often referred to as the Tube, because of the cylindrical shape of the tunnels that have been dug deep in the ground through which some of the train lines travel.

The London Tube is the world's oldest underground system and has a long and incredible history, both tragic and triumphant. The Tube's bull's-eye or target logo is instantly recognized around the world as a cultural icon. The deep underground tunnels served as bomb shelters during the war to save lives; unfortunately, the tunnels are also a common choice of a means for those looking to end their lives. Suicides happen quite often and are usually noted with the grim announcement of "Delays due to persons on the track." The peak hour for suicides is eleven o'clock in the morning. We arrived at the St. Paul's Tube station and heeded the "Mind the gap" announcement as we exited the train, carefully stepping over the small gap between the train and the platform.

I pulled out another London icon, the bible (
London A to Z, and navigated us through the narrow s.
area of London until we came upon Sarah's new office.

"Quick, hurry up. You're *really* embarrassing me!" Sarah s.
the camera out of my pocket and took a picture of her in front
office. I watched as Sarah entered the building for her first day in the London
workforce, like a child going to school for the first time.

"Don't let any of the kids pick on you!" I yelled. She walked into the
building without turning back. With Sarah safely at work for her first day, I
walked back to the Tube station and journeyed home to figure out what to
do about our living situation.

After arriving home and a period of procrastinating, I finally built up the
courage and called Oliver on my new cell phone, one of the two that Sarah
and I had picked up over the weekend. The cheap plastic cell phones were
our first piece of a London identity—phones with a real, working phone
number. It seemed so strange and foreign to look at my new, eleven-digit
phone number.

I was happy when Oliver did not answer his phone, and I left him a
message voicing my concerns about the water not really working, the place
being a mess, and having to pay a small fortune in rent each week.

In our relationship, Sarah and I had found a successful formula in working
through confrontations and disagreements with others. I usually played the
role of good cop, and Sarah was the bad cop. I was often too trusting and
willing to give people the benefit of doubt. If a telemarketer called, I would
talk to them and make up a bad lie to explain why I had to get off the phone.
Sarah, on the other hand, just hung up on them. When dealing with any kind
of salesperson, I usually paid close to full price, while Sarah offered "half price
or the highway" to the salesperson who had just sized me up for a sucker.

Oliver returned my phone call, and I let it go to voice mail. In his message,
he apologized and said that he was working on the water situation and wanted
to know if we had decided on renting the place for the entire year. I called
him back and was once again relieved that the call went to his voice mail.

Were we both anti-confrontational and this was our way of dealing with
the problem through leaving each other pleasant voice mail messages? I left
Oliver a message saying that we really appreciated everything he had done for
us (Sarah would have kicked me if she had heard me say that), but we were
going to pass on renting the place for the year.

I was barely able to place the phone back into my pocket before the front
door buzzer rang. I opened the door to find a group of estate agents with
clients in tow asking to come in and see the place. Word must travel fast in
the city when a place becomes available to rent. I let the small procession of

ate agents and new home seekers into the flat, and Sydney greeted them one by one. I stood in amusement as the estate agents looked over their papers, walked into the kitchen, looked again at their papers, walked into the living room with the bed in it, ducked down and entered the bathroom while looking at their papers, before they worked up the courage to ask me, "Where is the bedroom?"

"You know, I have been wondering that as well," I said, trying not to laugh. That scenario repeated all afternoon as estate agent after estate agent brought prospective clients to see the place.

Oliver called again in the evening, after the last set of estate agents had stopped by. Of course, I let the call go to voice mail. Oliver said that he was having a problem finding new renters and would need us to stay for the full three weeks. He would lower the rent £25 for the three weeks, which we laughed at, because it would hardly even cover the water bill for that time. When Sarah arrived home from work, I gave her the news, and we decided it was time to find a new place to live ASAP.

We picked an estate agency in London that is famous for zipping their clients around town in little, green, MINI Cooper automobiles with the company logo splashed all over the vehicle. We met Jamie, our newly hired estate agent, at his office, and with a time-is-money attitude, he pushed us into his little green MINI Cooper, and we were off to find a new home. Jaime was short, well dressed, and had what I imagined an Oxford-educated, English accent sounded like. He looked very stereotypically upper class British and was only missing the bowler hat and umbrella to complete the picture.

The first place he showed us was close to a college that I had attended as a study abroad student many years before; it was an area that I was very familiar with. The unit was a garden unit, meaning it was below the street level and required us to walk down a set of stairs to reach the front door. The unit was part of a garden or private park that only the homes in the immediate area had access to. Most rental places did come furnished, and the place was furnished like my great-grandmother's house. It had a beautiful, working fireplace, but I gave the bathroom the shower and flush test and found that the shower had no water pressure and the toilet was a low-flow toilet.

"My American clients always check the water pressure and toilet. Why is that?" Jamie asked.

Even though I was all for saving the environment, I needed a shower that could just about peel a layer of your skin off and a toilet that needs extra bolts to hold it to the floor, so when you flushed it, the toilet would not blast through the ceiling.

The next place Jamie showed us was in a similar central London area and was also a garden unit. The place had great light for a garden unit and a small patio area with fifteen foot-high French doors and windows leading out to it. The water pressure was amazing, and the toilet easily passed the flush test. The only problem was that the place was the next best thing to an actual IKEA showroom. Every piece of furniture, the pictures, the shelves, the kitchen cabinets, the bathroom sink, the mirrors, the tables, the dishes, the spoons, the pots, the towels, the mattress, and the bed linens were all from IKEA. Even the small plant was from IKEA. That was not good news because my courtship with Sarah before our marriage had almost ended many times inside an IKEA store because of the IKEA shopping experience of traffic, no parking spots, out-of-stock items, and missing pieces when putting the flat-pack furniture together at home. Our courtship survived only because of a vow to never go to IKEA together again. The place also had a private garden for the residents, and Jamie confirmed that dogs were allowed in it.

Like a good estate agent, Jamie sensed a kill was close and took us to a third place that was way too expensive for us and then asked, "So, what do you think? Which place do you like?" We decided to make an offer on the IKEA showroom. Jamie said that he would call the landlord to inquire about the dog and that he was confident that he could even convince the landlord to lower the rent slightly.

We spent the rest of the day running errands, anxiously awaiting his call. Jamie finally called and informed us that he had great news: that the landlord had said yes on the dog and he was even able to get us a discount on the rent. I guess he had forgotten the price he had told us he could negotiate, because somehow he had managed to get the rent increased and the security deposit doubled, requiring just about the rest of our budgeted savings for the year.

We decided to take it. The best part was that we could move in right away. We signed the year lease, and with the keys to our new place in hand, we had the freedom to move in anytime. It was getting late in the evening, so we took the Tube back home to get some sleep and figure out when and how to tell Oliver, our current landlord, that we would be moving out early.

Upon walking into our temporary home and taking in the sight of all our bags scattered on the floor and furniture because of the lack of closet space, remembering that the water still did not work properly all the time, we decided right then and there it was time to move out immediately. Why spend another night in our Notting Hill disaster home and not in our new IKEA showroom? We stuffed our bags like bank robbers and decided to execute our getaway plan by taking as many bags as we could fit into a taxi, dropping them off at the new place, returning to get Sydney's crate and the last remaining bags, and never looking back.

With our tower of bags piled high on the sidewalk, we flagged down another London icon: the black cab.

The design of the black cab is like no other vehicle found in the world. The cab had a turning radius of only twenty-five feet, allowing it to turn around in the smallest and narrowest of London streets. Just like the red double-decker bus, the London black cab was a unique and hard-to-miss sight on the street. Earning the right to drive a London black cab took a long and intense journey, requiring by far the toughest training for taxicab drivers in the world.

Becoming a taxi driver usually required an average of thirty-four months of preparation and twelve attempts at the final test called "The Knowledge" before passing. Successful drivers had to be able to navigate twenty-five thousand different streets within a six-mile radius of central London without looking at a map or navigational device and had to be able to calculate the quickest and most sensible route quickly.

We piled the bags into the cab, told the driver the address, and were off on our great getaway. Our driver weaved in and out of the smallest alleys and streets of central London, avoiding some of the more congested roads. Within a few minutes, he had us sitting in front of our new home. We paid the driver—no tip was expected—and delivered the first set of bags. We took the Tube back, left a note for Oliver saying, "Gone traveling," and left a couple more days' worth of rent money and the keys.

Sarah and I had always thought of ourselves as honest people, but we felt that we were being cheated. With a combination of bad cop and good cop strategy, we shut the door behind us and never looked back. A couple of weeks later, I walked by the place and saw that there was still a "For Rent" sign in the window. Six months later, the "For Rent" sign was gone, and through the large front windows, I could see that the walls had been painted a nice, antique white, and a wall with built-in bookshelves had been built in the center of the large room, dividing the one room into two. It appeared that the missing bedroom had returned home. The place had finally received the attention it had needed.

In our new place, Sarah and I unpacked all our bags like a newlywed couple opening wedding presents and deciding where to put everything. The place was small, but it did have a separate bedroom, lots of closets, and a large refrigerator—by European standards. I went around collecting all the little IKEA wrenches from each drawer and dropped them in a small jar in the kitchen. We divided up the Hemnes eight-drawer chest, fought over where the red Arild two-seat sofa and chair should be placed, and rearranged the glasses and plates in the Faktum/Askome kitchen where the Kavalkad frying pan just barely fit into the cabinet. I do have to give credit to IKEA for sticking with the crazy Swedish names on products sold outside of Sweden.

After the dust had settled, we climbed into our IKEA bed and enjoyed the fabulous feeling of finally being in a nice, warm, clean bed without a suitcase in sight. Sydney was already fast asleep in her own bed when we turned off the lights. It is estimated that ten percent of European babies are conceived on IKEA mattresses. We were way too exhausted to even think of going there.

- Chapter Four -

Meridith

✦

Since I was not eligible for a work permit in the United Kingdom and being a full-time tourist for a year did not win Sarah's approval, I decided to use our time in London to satisfy my strong desire to earn a master's degree. The thought of attending graduate classes in a classroom where, for once in my life, I would be in the minority appealed greatly to me. In a place and time in which everyone seems to be in the wake of globalization, I could not think of a better location to complete my graduate degree than in London. In my application essay, I wrote that I had promised to bring "an open mind that is willing to learn and grow," and that was what I intended to do.

I had applied and been admitted to a small private school located in the Bloomsbury area of central London, an area rich with public and private universities. The school overlooks the second largest square in London, Russell Square, and is literally a stone's throw away from the British Museum and the large, looming building of the University of London's Senate House Library. The Senate House Library was thought of as London's first skyscraper when it was completed in 1937, and Hitler had supposedly wanted to use the modern-looking building for his London office if he had been able to successfully invade the country.

The student body of the university was composed of students from over sixty countries, giving it the feel that I imagine you would experience walking the halls of the United Nations' headquarters. The school lacks a long and distinguished reputation of intellectual superiority but makes up for that in its diversity and uniqueness. During the first day of orientation, I met Paul, a twenty-five-year-old from Boston, Massachusetts, and Amir, a thirty-one-year-old from Tehran, Iran. Paul was the type of guy that I typically would have sought out as a friend back at home. Amir was not, but attending school with diverse individuals like him was the reason I wanted to be there.

The next day was the start of the semester and my first official day. It was never easy being the new guy, and wearing a sweater-vest on the first day of class did not help either, as my friends would later tease me. Was I really that out of it in the fashion world? I had wanted to attend Huron to meet new and interesting people from all over the world, but on my first day of class, I met Meridith instead.

"Hi, I'm Garrett," I said, wearing my blue sweater-vest.

"Hi, I'm Meridith," she said, checking out my sweater-vest. Was it really that bad?

After a couple minutes of silence as we waited for the other students to walk in and find their seats so class could begin, I asked Meridith where she was from. A simple question, followed up with additional questions, ultimately unraveled an amazing coincidence that we were both originally from the same small hometown in the suburbs of Detroit, Michigan. The only difference was that she was a couple of years younger and had attended the rival high school in our hometown of Grosse Pointe, Michigan.

After telling Sarah about the incredible coincidence, she provided me with some additional questions to ask Meridith to find out if this was possibly a Meridith that she knew from her childhood. From Meridith's instant reaction to my first asking Sarah's only-the-Meridith-that-I-knew-would-be-able-to-answer-this question, the complete picture began to come into focus. Meridith and Sarah had been good friends growing up and had first met in a dance class when they were just ten years old.

Sarah and I had traveled nearly four thousand miles to a place where we thought we did not know anyone, only for Sarah to find a good friend that she had lost in the complexities of life as they both got older and moved in different directions with their lives. It provided Sarah with a feeling of surprise and disbelief; she could only shake her head and smile at the news that fate had decided it was time to bring the two of them together as good friends again.

During that first week of school, I also met Andy, a fellow American from New York, as well as Max, Felix, and Denis, who were all from Germany. Meridith, Andy, Max, Denis, Felix, and I would all become close friends over the year. I like to think it was destiny that we all became good friends, but I think it was all due to timing—or the time we arrived at class each day.

The Dirt in the Garden

Our new home was located in the central London borough that was called The Royal Borough of Kensington and Chelsea. That borough, along with two other London boroughs, received the legal right to the title of "Royal Borough" during the reign of Queen Victoria, who had wanted to honor areas that held a special meaning to her family. The Royal Borough of Kensington and Chelsea was given the Royal Borough honor by Queen Victoria in honor of her birthplace. Additionally, our little slice of London consisted of three affluent areas of London: Chelsea, South Kensington, and Knightsbridge. Even though the area was home to a large number of wealthy Londoners, small pockets of affordable housing, hostels, bed-and-breakfasts, and tourist hotels could also be found.

Not even the ultrarich residents of London had homes with a parking spot or a garage, so much of the area resembled an exotic used car lot. While walking around the area, it was common to hear numerous foreign languages spoken. We didn't even mind the late-night screaming matches of young lovers drunk on the street outside at three o'clock in the morning, because they were often screaming at each other in one of the romantic languages of French, Spanish, or Italian. They could be threatening to kill each other, but to us, it sounded romantically charming and right out of a movie.

On top of the weekly rent payment, we were also required to pay a monthly property tax of sorts called the council tax. It was standard for renters, not the home owner, to pay the tax when renting a flat. A small portion of the monthly tax also paid for the professional, full-time gardener who maintained the beautiful, private garden that our square block of buildings circled and that could only be entered using a key given to each household upon paying the tax. We wanted a key to the garden, so we paid our first monthly council tax early to the shock of the woman at the council payment office. There's something slightly more honorable and fulfilling, if not downright fun—if you can call paying taxes fun—about making out a tax check to "The Royal Borough" instead of the plain old, boring IRS.

Since we were then official property taxpayers, we were allowed to participate in our local community association meetings and gatherings. The year's first general garden meeting was scheduled for that Wednesday evening. I thought the meeting had been scheduled to discuss the garden dirt and that I would have the opportunity to argue my case for letting Sydney use the park. Upon receiving our key to the exclusive club for the block, we discovered the long list of garden rules. Just after the rule that declared "No fun shall be had in the garden," the rule stating "No dogs allowed in the garden" literally made my knees buckle. But at the meeting, I quickly discovered that the dirt that would be discussed was much more interesting than the dirt in the garden.

A woman with a very American accent hosted the meeting. She was in her mid-forties and lived in a top floor unit with her husband, two kids, and a full-time nanny. The home had a beautiful view, overlooking the entire private neighborhood garden park. The entry foyer seemed larger than our entire apartment. From what I could tell, the home had a library, living room, four bedrooms—possibly more—and a dining room that was attached to a fabulous kitchen with more stainless steel than a morgue and numerous copper pots hanging from the ceiling over a black granite-covered island in the center of the kitchen. *If only Sarah could see this kitchen,* I thought to myself.

We were each poured large glasses of wine, before we took our seats for the start of the meeting. Feeling slightly shy and finding myself in a room full of people I did not know, I picked a seat on a small couch at the back of the room. The meeting agenda that was passed out included a local crime report, a discussion about installing closed-circuit television (CCTV) around the garden, and finally a discussion about the neighborhood whore problem. I felt that the last topic on the agenda would have every male in the neighborhood wanting to attend the meeting. I had to reread the agenda three times before I decided that, yes, I had read the agenda correctly. I felt like an audience member watching a small play as the drama unfolded before me.

PC Smith of the London Metropolitan Police was the first to speak. He recited the crime statistics for the area during the past year. The numbers were not bad and actually slightly better than those for the area around our home back in Chicago. An older gentleman sitting next to his wife balanced himself against his wooden cane as he started to stand up to speak, but his slightly younger wife beat him to it.

In an angry I-want-action-now tone, she interrupted PC Smith and asked in a voice that was louder than necessary, "What about all the whores that will be living in our neighborhood shortly? What are you planning to do about them?"

"We will get to that topic in due time," the host said, trying to keep the meeting moving along the lines of the agenda.

The next question concerned the installation of CCTV around the streets bordering the garden park. At the time, it was estimated that the average British citizen was caught on CCTV over three hundred times every day. If you looked closely while walking the streets of London, you could see that there are small, usually black, cameras everywhere. Those cameras provide a great tool to help protect businesses and solve crimes for the police. On average, there was one camera for every fifteen citizens in the country. My entire journey from the end of our street to the reception area at school was caught on CCTV each day.

"Installing CCTV is a difficult decision that requires not only a large initial investment in the equipment, but also someone to monitor all the cameras and store and maintain the tapes," PC Smith said, hoping that would end further discussion on the topic.

As if written in the script, another elderly man, who had been part of the police force in his younger years, stood up and said, "We have discussed the proposal, and dividing the initial cost and maintenance between the hundreds of people who live in the square is just a small amount. As for monitoring the tapes, I am willing to take on that responsibility."

I looked for any indication that his eyesight was starting to fail, because I was envisioning that elderly gentleman sitting in front of all the video monitors late at night, observing me break the rules while I snuck Sydney into the garden for a quick, late-night pee and play session before going to bed.

I was sitting next to a woman whom I had recognized as a fellow dog owner. Claire had recently purchased a new puppy only to also discover the rule that banned dogs from the private neighborhood garden. I could see that she too was checking out how good the elderly man's eyesight was and most likely had the same vision in her mind.

I whispered to her that I was going to ask for permission to use the garden with the dog.

"No use in asking," she whispered back a little too loudly; those sitting around us listened in with curiosity. "I arrived early and asked if I could please bring my puppy into the garden, and apparently the garden committee is more interested in the welfare of the foxes living in the garden than allowing dogs," she lowered her voice so those around us who were now increasing the audio level on their hearing aids to listen in on us, could not hear us.

I almost said out loud, "I thought fox hunting was considered the national pastime in England," but I held back the temptation.

"It's because of the 'granny window watchers' who make other people's business their business," Claire said.

After a long debate of the pros and cons of CCTV, the subject was put to a vote and passed by a large majority.

An awkward silence filled the room as we all waited for the final topic to officially be opened for discussion. I was on my third glass of wine, and I was ready for the dramatic ending of the meeting. I was ready for the naming of names, the accusations, the airing of rumors and dirty laundry. The same elderly woman who had so aggressively inquired about the whore problem finally broke the long silence, as no one knew how to start the discussion.

"So, get on with it. What have you got to say about keeping this filth out of our neighborhood?"

The filth that she was referring to was the subject of a controversial proposal to amend the local prostitution rules. A little-known fact that is not usually advertised in travel guidebooks because of the muddy confusion of the true legality of the subject is that, technically, prostitution is legal in England. Brothels and streetwalking are illegal, but there are no prohibitions against a girl working alone from her home. A girl could even advertise, provided that she worked alone. Many of the ads were placed inside the red telephone boxes found throughout London, giving first-time visitors quite the shock when stepping inside for the first time while a friend snaps a picture. More than one girl in a flat had been considered a brothel before, but the government was considering changing the law to allow up to three women to work as prostitutes from a single premise. The change was being considered to make life safer for women by increasing the number of women together so they could look out for each other and get off the street, but my fellow residents viewed it as the possibility of an invasion of prostitutes moving into the area.

PC Smith thought long and hard before responding, because the possible change in law really was out of his hands.

"Madam, your concern is a very serious and quite controversial government change in policy. However, I don't think these unfortunate women who have decided to take up such a profession can possibly afford to live in your neighborhood. I don't think you have anything to worry about."

Surprisingly, that answer was just what she wanted to hear, and that was the end of it—no fireworks, nothing.

Some grumblings and side discussion between a few small groups gave our host the perfect opportunity to jump in and relieve herself from the fidgeting I had observed her doing in the corner for the past ten minutes.

"Thanks again to everyone for coming. If you have any additional questions or comments, feel free to e-mail me." She turned and mouthed to another woman across the room, while tapping her watch, "*Desperate Housewives* starts in five minutes."

- Chapter Five -

Swedish American

✦

After reconnecting with her childhood friend Meridith over the phone, Sarah planned a night out for her and I to meet Meridith and her husband Petter (pronounced Pet-her). We met them at a restaurant in the touristy Covent Garden area and tried to talk over the loud music as we ate our dinner. Sarah and Meridith chatted away like they were ten years old once again while Petter and I drank our beers and got to know each other. We started with the usual questions—Where do you work? Where did you go to school?—hoping to stumble upon a common interest. The icebreaker we quickly hit was the sport of ice hockey. Over a large plate of chicken wings and with the cold English beer flowing and a huge mutual interest in ice hockey, Petter and I became friends.

I found Petter incredibly interesting because of all the places he had lived and the life experiences that he shared as we drank our beers and laughed together as friends. Petter's family had moved to the United States from a small town thirty miles outside of Stockholm, Sweden. At the time of the move, Petter was seventeen and had technically passed the Swedish requirements for an American high school-level education. It had been recommended that Petter's family enroll him in the local high school as a senior. Petter elaborated in great detail about his initial culture shock on his first day at an American high school, which sounded more like the script of an American sitcom in which the foreign kid is the butt of most jokes.

"The students did not know anything about Sweden," he told us. The first question most of the male students asked him was if he was friends with any of the girls on the "Swedish Bikini Team." The students had been referring to a group of female, American models that was featured in a beer advertisement that played off the American stereotype that Scandinavian women all have blond hair and large breasts. Petter had never heard of such a team. He said, "I thought the bikini team sounded like a great idea, though!"

Petter told us how he had been shocked, when he had first arrived in America, by the attitudes that American teenagers had toward consuming alcohol and how attitudes were dramatically different in Sweden, where he felt he had a greater degree of freedom at his age and was treated more as an adult instead of a child who actually had to ask for a hall pass to use the bathroom during class hours. Moving to a new school as a senior is never easy, but doing it as a foreigner who knows nothing of how an American teenager should act, outside of what he had seen in American movies, had been a difficult and amazing experience for Petter. He did manage to find a date to the prom, albeit with his mother's help.

Petter attended college upon graduation and chose the University of South Carolina, where he even joined a fraternity. Over the next couple of years, Petter became more Americanized and even completed the United States citizenship process after marrying Meridith.

Petter's American friends have never accepted him as being truly American, while his Swedish friends feel the amount of time he has spent living outside of Sweden has made him less Swedish, leaving him stuck somewhere in the middle, hearing phrases like, "You don't really understand because you're really not a real American," while also hearing the chorus of, "You have lived outside of Sweden for so long, you're not Swedish. You just don't understand anymore."

We paid the dinner bill and headed to a club in London that Meridith had heard was a popular place to go. We arrived at the club to find a long line to get in. While waiting in line, a drug deal went on behind us. We all laughed, and once the awkwardness of the moment wore off, I finally found the courage to suggest, with a tone that said "Yeah, we are still cool if we do not go here," that we go someplace else. Everyone agreed, and we spent the rest of the night talking at a local bar that stayed open late.

We finally said good-bye, after many drinks and a long debriefing by Petter on how to navigate the London night bus system. Since the Tube shuts down at midnight, Sarah and I had to find our way home starting from the nearest bus stop.

Without a doubt, the best seat on a red, double-decker bus is in the front row on the top deck of the bus. The view is amazing, and you feel as if you are actually driving the bus. The night bus system in London is extensive and requires knowledge, experience, and a sense of adventure to find your way home successfully. By far, most of the passengers on a night bus have spent most of their money drinking and need an inexpensive ride home; but they don't want the partying to end, which gives the bus ride a booze cruise party almost every night of the week.

The bus ride went as planned as we navigated the streets of London with a confidence that we were heading in the correct direction, until the bus turned left when we needed to go right. By the time we made it down the stairs of the bus and got off at the next stop, we were in a part of London we did not know. After getting on another bus to head back in the right direction only to find ourselves worse off than before, we gave up and got a taxi.

Not So Super Sunday

We woke up late the next morning and tried to shake off the cobwebs from being out so late the night before, swearing that we were too old to stay out that late anymore. Even though my head was still in a cloud of haze from the night before, something about the day just did not feel right. Something was missing.

Sarah and I walked to one of my new favorite places to visit in London— the grocery store. A great way to learn about a new country is to visit a local grocery store. I loved walking the store aisles, feeling no tug of brand loyalty whatsoever (we had never heard of the majority of the brands). We used a combination of exploring, guessing, and trial and error to figure out which foods and brands we liked best. Cookies were called digestives; chips were called crisps; sliced bread only lasted five days; eggs were sold on a shelf that was not refrigerated; and we had to bag our own groceries. On that day's visit, it took another five minutes of walking the aisles for it to hit me as we turned down the crisps aisle—it was Super Bowl Sunday!

Back at home, cash registers were ringing, and the grocery stores were being emptied of beer, chips, and snacks in preparation for the big game. On this unofficial American holiday, we Americans gathered in front of our televisions with friends and family and enjoyed a true American tradition of watching the big game while eating and drinking as much as we could, with a large majority of us really not caring which teams were playing or even who won. As Americans, we were told that "the world is watching"—or more precisely a global audience in over 232 countries with an estimated audience of one billion people. During the weeks and days leading up to the Super Bowl, we never heard anything about the game while in England. All the sporting enthusiasts in the country had been watching and talking about the Six Nations Rugby Tournament, and the buzz on the street was all about Scotland's big upset victory over France, the tournament favorite.

Sarah decided to cook up a great Super Bowl feast for the two of us to enjoy during the game, which did not start until eleven fifteen at night in London and aired pretty much commercial free. We stayed up as late as we could, enjoying our Super Bowl spread. The British television guide described the game as "not much in terms of entertainment value, but the Rolling Stones are playing during intermission."

The next afternoon was a different story, as news of the game was featured on the front page of many of the afternoon papers, but for a different reason than I had expected. The headlines shouted, "Rolling Stones Censored in America!" Two of the three songs that the Rolling Stones had performed during their halftime performance had been censored—the sound had been cut from front man Mick Jagger's microphone. Most of the articles discussed the songs and lyrics that were censored and blamed it on Janet Jackson's 2004 "wardrobe malfunction" halftime performance, in which she exposed her right breast to the American viewing audience. Other papers also described how people over forty-five had initially not been invited to take the field and dance during the performance, as the task was considered too physically demanding, but the articles reported that the decision was later reversed. The papers were quick to point out that the youngest member of the Rolling Stones was fifty-eight, and the band had a combined age of 246. None of the stories mentioned who had played and what the final score was. Other than a few Americans studying or living abroad or the American military personnel, no one outside of the United States and Canada really watched the Super Bowl.

- Chapter Six -

The World Is Indeed Flat

✦

It was one o'clock in the morning when I stumbled out of bed, still half asleep but mentally awake enough to not make the mistake of stepping on Sydney, who was sleeping next to the bed. The phone was on its fourth ring by the time I gave a groggy "Hello?"

"Good evening. Is Mr. or Mrs. Ryan home, please?"

"Yes, this is Mr. Ryan."

"Good evening, Mr. Ryan. This is the Chicago Fire Department calling. How are you tonight?"

"I'm fine," I said. My heart stopped for a second as the frightful thought crossed my mind that our home back in Chicago might have just burned down and that this was the call to tell us so. But why no urgency and a genuine niceness to the introduction to the call?

"I'm calling this evening to see if you would be interested in making a donation to a special cause."

"I'm so sorry," I said with a small laugh of relief because our home had not burned down and because I could tell a whopper of a story without lying. "I don't mean to interrupt you, but you are calling me in London, England, and it is one o'clock in the morning here at the moment." From the long silence that followed, I figured the man on the line had never heard that excuse before. "Thanks for calling," I continued. "Have a nice night." I hung up the phone and climbed back into bed.

"Who was that?" Sarah murmured.

"The Chicago Fire Department."

"Did our house burn down?" she asked.

"No, just calling to say hello," I said.

Before we had left for our year in London, Sarah had set up a wonderful convenience that was also the cause of many nights of slumber being interrupted by phone calls. Sarah had signed us up for a phone service that worked through the Internet and forwarded all the phone calls to our Chicago number to our London home, without requiring the caller to pay any long-distance charges. Our friends and family just dialed the number as they always did to call us in Chicago, and just as if we were there, we could pick up the phone and talk to them in London. Not only did this make it easy for our friends and family to call us, but it also meant that we continued to receive calls from telemarketers, wrong number calls, and all the other annoying calls we had routinely received back at home during the day and early evening, but in London, the calls came in the middle of the night. We did not like to turn off the ringer on the phone, because we usually forgot to turn it back on, and messages would pile up before we noticed it was off.

At first, it was fun to tell callers, "Sorry, but you are calling us in London, England," which always required that we describe the technical specifications that allowed them to call us in the middle of the night. One caller did not believe me, and I actually went as far as turning on the television and holding the phone up to it so the caller could hear the English accents being spoken.

One particular call I answered was from our credit card company, asking if we wanted some sort of credit protection service. I could tell from the woman's voice that English was not her native language. She told me she was calling from Bangalore, India. I told her she was calling me in London, England, and explained how she had come to call me in London. I asked her what time it was where she was. She replied that it was six thirty in the morning. She asked me what time it was in London, and I told her it was one o'clock in the morning. She apologized with a laugh, and we both said good-bye. Thomas Friedman is correct: the world is indeed flat.

Teaching an Old Dog New Tricks

During our year in London, I decided to use the opportunity to run three of the great European marathons. I decided I would run the Paris, Stockholm, and London marathons while they were conveniently just a short train ride or flight away. To complete the endeavor, I would have to run all three races within a seven-week period. A suicidal mission for sure, but I had the attitude of "Hey, I'm not trying to win any of the races."

The first marathon was the Paris marathon, and it was quickly approaching. I desperately needed to start doing some long training runs, and since it was a sunny day in London, I grabbed my running shoes and Sydney's leash.

I have attempted many times to train Sydney to run next to me while I jog, but each attempt has resulted in failure, when Sydney usually found some incredibly fascinating scent in the city that she insisted spending five minutes sniffing. But today I was determined to give it another chance. I thought that Sydney could at least join me for the first half of the run.

Since the weather was slightly cooler, I put Sydney's brown winter coat on her. The jacket fit her perfectly and gave her a warm look. My goal for the day was a three-hour run, with the first part through Kensington Gardens and Hyde Park with Sydney. I thought it was best to show Sydney that I was in charge, so instead of letting her go through the routine, I picked her up and carried her a hundred yards down the street and around the first two corners. Sydney has a wonderful sense of direction, and with only a few trips, she could easily navigate, on her own, the mile distance through all the many small streets and over twenty-five turns that were required to arrive safely at Kensington Gardens and then repeat the exact same route when returning back home.

We entered the southwest corner of Kensington Gardens, with Kensington Palace straight in front of us. I let Sydney off her leash, as dogs are not required to be on a leash in the park, and we began to run. Sydney always runs great in the beginning, as she is excited to be in the vast openness of the park and far away from the red, double-decker buses passing by on the nearby Kensington Road. Wheaten terriers had originally been bred in Ireland to be working farm dogs, with the responsibilities of herding and guarding livestock. When Sydney is around other dogs, she prefers to chase them as if she is trying to herd them. Throwing a tennis ball for her to fetch and bring back usually results in nothing more than a look of disinterest from her.

I started running west toward the Albert Memorial along the hard-packed sand path. Sydney, still thinking it was a game, was more than happy to keep on running next to me. A minute later, she realized that she did not like the game she thought we were playing, and she made a sharp, left-hand turn, headed toward a pack of five small dogs chasing each other. The temptation to herd five small dogs was too great for her, and I was forced to jog through the tall, wet, green grass, soaking my feet as I tried to catch up to her. By the time I reached her, she had successfully herded the five small dogs back to their owners, who were standing together observing what had just happened.

"Come on, Sydney, let's go," I said, as I picked up a stick, trying to distract her simply with what I had in my hand.

"Is this your dog?" one of the five sweet-looking, grey-haired, grandmotherly ladies asked as she noticed me holding the stick in my hand.

"Yes," I said.

"Well, isn't she just the smartest dog!" the woman said, as the others nodded their heads in agreement.

I could not tell if she was referring to how Sydney looked in her brown jacket or if she was referring to her intelligence for successfully bringing the five small dogs back to the feet of their owners. English people truly believe in the art form of minding their own business, and if it were not for long queues or dogs, the English would never speak to each other without being formally introduced first.

"What kind of dog is she?" she asked.

"She is a Wheaten Terrier," I said.

"Oh, a wheat-ten terrier," the five women all said in unison, placing strong emphasis on the "ten" in Wheaten, but pronouncing it as "tin."

"How is the dog's temperament?"

"Is she good with children?" the group asked.

"She is an excellent family dog, and she does not shed, so she does not make a mess in the house," I said. My reply brought an instant look of confusion over the group of women, almost as if I had somehow insulted them.

"She doesn't? That is quite odd," they said, as they vigorously nodded in unison.

"It's great that she does not shed. She does not make a mess on the couch, on the bed, or even in the car, so you don't have to keep washing it off your pants," I said, not really understanding why I was now on the receiving end of such a strange reaction from the group of women.

"Not even in the garden?" asked the one woman who had yet to say anything.

I wondered to myself, *Why that would be a problem if a dog shed its hair outside in the garden?*

"No," I said, with a tone of "where are you going with this question?"

"Fascinating," was the consensus and delayed response from the group.

Sydney had lost interest in the group of five small dogs and was ready to move on.

"Enjoy your day," I said with a wave and jogged back toward the path. It took me a full minute to process the strange conversation that I had just had with the group of sweet-looking grandmothers, but when I finally figured it out, I had to stop running, because I could not stop laughing. The group had interpreted my pronunciation of the word "shed," with my American accent, as the word "shit." The group of women had thought I was saying, "Sydney does not shit. She does not shit in the house, in the car, on the bed, or even outside or in the garden. And since Sydney does not shit, it does not get on my pants." This only added to the confusion because the English use the word "pants" to refer to underwear. I was tempted to run back and tell the group of sweet, old ladies that I had meant to say that Sydney was a non-moulting dog. "Moulting" is the word used by the English to describe shedding of dog hair.

I decided that the best way to get Sydney to follow me as I jogged was to keep running and ignore her. Sydney would lie down in the lush, green grass and try to figure what I was doing. As soon as I was far enough for her to lose sight of me, out of a fear of losing me, she would sprint as fast as she could to catch up with me, sit back down in the cold, wet grass, rest, and complete the same process over and over. The technique worked well and allowed me to jog around the park without fearing that Sydney would get lost.

We ran through the tunnel under West Carriage Drive that connected Kensington Gardens and Hyde Park and ran along the edge of the Serpentine, or the recreational lake built in 1730. We quickly came to one of the newest additions to the park, the Diana, Princess of Wales Memorial. Kathryn Gustafson, an American landscape artist, had designed the oval-shaped fountain in an attempt to express Diana's spirit and love of children. The fountain was not your typical water fountain; it's a ten-foot-wide, granite streambed built into slightly sloping ground. Water cascaded down opposite sides, representing different parts, both good and bad of Diana's life. The water flowed downward and finally collected at the bottom.

The memorial was supposed to be a place for reflection, but ever since it had opened in July 2004, the fountain had been labeled a "white elephant." The shallow streambed of the memorial had been designed to reflect Diana being an accessible princess to the people, allowing people to wade through the water and interact with the fountain. Unfortunately, the granite selected was slippery to walk on and often caused injury to the children and adults enjoying it. The chemicals that were used to prevent algae from growing in the fountain also killed the surrounding grass as water leaked out of the fountain, turning the surrounding area into mud and making the sloping hill a slippery mess. Shortly after it opened—after multiple people had been hospitalized from slipping—the fountain was closed and alterations were made to fix the problems. The fountain had since reopened, but it required constant supervision and maintenance, making the simple-looking fountain a heavy financial burden on the royal parks budget for years to come.

The memorial was most likely doomed from the beginning, due to the impossible task of building a memorial to honor a woman who had been considered a living saint at the time of her unexpected death. The fountain, while beautiful in appearance, had never really been accepted as a place of honoring or mourning the princess. Kensington Palace still had that honor as evident in the number of flowers and notes still left there along the black ornate gates in front of the building.

We ran along the water's edge of the Serpentine, and Sydney quietly slipped past the geese and white swans sunbathing along the edge of the water. Off in the distance, I could hear the Corps of Drums marching down the Mall to Buckingham Palace for the Changing of the Guards Ceremony, which continues even when the Queen is not staying at Buckingham Palace. We continued around the end of the Serpentine and headed back to Kensington Gardens.

We crossed back over through the north side tunnel and followed the path until we passed the Italian Fountains by Lancaster Gate, where we took a sharp left and headed toward another of the most-beloved sites in Kensington Gardens, the bronze Peter Pan statue. The statue had been chosen by the author, J. M. Barrie, who had created the popular character. He had had the statue placed in the park during the middle of the night, so that the children would stumble across it the next day and believe that it had magically appeared. The following announcement was placed in the *Times* newspaper to tip off those who did not regularly cross through the park each day:

"There is a surprise in store for the children who go to Kensington Gardens to feed the ducks in the Serpentine this morning. Down by the little bay on the southwestern side of the tail of the Serpentine, they will find a May Day gift from Mr. J. M. Barrie—a figure of Peter Pan blowing his pipe on the stump of a tree, with fairies and mice and squirrels all around. It is the work of Sir George Frampton, and the bronze figure of the boy who would never grow up is delightfully conceived."

Shortly after the statue had been placed in the park, a debate arose in the House of Commons as to whether the park should be used to promote J. M. Barrie, perhaps because Barrie was Scottish.

Sydney and I wove our way past the tourists, who were trying to take pictures of the statue, and stopped by the water's edge for a minute so that Sydney could join the other dogs who had ignored the "No dogs allowed in the water" sign and were cooling off in the shallow water. After Sydney's quick dip, we made our way home, where Sydney was happy to climb into her bed for a long afternoon nap; she was exhausted. Since a marathon is twenty-six miles long, and I had only run about six, I headed back out the door for two more hours of running.

There is no other city in the world better suited for running, where you can completely immerse yourself in the incredible historical significance found around literally each corner, and with the flat elevation and cooler, running-friendly weather, I looked forward to each long run. I headed down toward one of my favorite streets in London; King's Road was a long, mostly straight road that had reinvented itself many times over and was currently one of the wealthiest streets in London. It was full of unique shops and sights. Yet, it was nearly impossible to walk down either side of the street for more than a few minutes before you ran into a Starbucks, adding to the criticism that Kings Road, along with many other notable "High Streets," or designated shopping areas of the local area, were all starting to look alike with the same stores and coffee shops.

The Chelsea area had become one of London's most expensive areas to live in and was often criticized for all the "Chelsea Tractors" or large SUVs that lined the streets. Some of the most beautiful women in the world could be seen pushing prams or baby strollers down the street, always walking on the side of the street where the sun is shining. I suspected most of those women were not the real mothers but the nannies, usually from Russia and looking like they were on their ways to fabulous parties.

Another delight of the street was encountering the Chelsea pensioners, or elderly and retired British soldiers, who lived in the nearby Royal Hospital, which was a retirement home where British soldiers to spent their last few years of life. Walking down the street, the men cut striking figures on Kings Road in their old military uniforms of bright red, scarlet coats and tricorne hats. They often stopped to tip their hats at beautiful women passing by on the street.

A favorite place to study of mine was at the public library on Kings Road. I always found it amusing when the Chelsea Pensioners would stop by the library during their morning and afternoon walks to kick out the homeless people who would grab newspapers and sit in chairs, pretending to read the papers while catching afternoon naps. The Pensioners would smack the sides of the chairs with their wooden canes—they were always dressed in their military uniforms—startling the homeless people and awakening them with the standard phrase of "not in my library" to get the offenders up and on their ways out the door.

I turned right off Kings Road and headed down Oakley Street until I reached the Albert Bridge, where I turned left and kept heading east along the river. I found it interesting that the Albert Bridge had a sign on it from 1873 that stated that troops marching in columns across the bridge must break step. The thought, as well as urban legend, was that the vibrations of the soldiers' synchronized footsteps would shake the bridge violently and cause it to sway until it would ultimately collapse into the River Thames below.

Feeling like I too had been marching all across London and satisfied that I had adequately tortured my leg muscles enough for one day, I turned around and made my way home.

- Chapter Seven -

I Say Soccer, You Say Football

✦

"Hurry up! We're going to be late," Sarah said, letting me know she was annoyed by what I was doing.

"Hi. You've reached Garrett and Sarah. Sorry, but we are not home at the moment. Please leave a message, and we'll call you back when we can. Cheers!" I was trying to record the message on our answering machine using the universal English word "cheers." The difficulty was that I hated how I sounded like an American tourist the way I said it. I was on the fifteenth attempt, and it still wasn't close to being right.

"Is that what I really sound like?" I asked Sarah as I played back the last attempted recording. "Like I have a stuffed-up nose?"

"Yup. The truth hurts, doesn't it?" she said, smirking.

I decided to work on recording the message later. We grabbed our jackets, gave Sydney a good-bye treat, told her she was in charge while we were gone, and walked out the front door.

It was a cool night, and you could just about see your breath in the air. We walked down to the corner of our street, turned left onto Earl's Court Road, and made our way down to Fulham Road, where, within ten minutes, we became part of a growing crowd that was walking in the middle of the street, making its way to Stamford Bridge, home of the Chelsea Football Club. We were meeting Andy and Petter, and it was an exciting and special night; Sarah was about to experience her first English football match.

It is safe to say that football is the religion of choice in England, and it plays an important part in everyday life. It is nearly impossible to get through a day without hearing about or experiencing firsthand the national sport of England. Large sections of newspapers are dedicated to the sport, and it is not uncommon to hear people on the Tube or in a pub discussing the various healing techniques for an injury to a star player. In some parts of the United Kingdom, more gravestones have references to the departed's favorite football team than to God, Jesus, or Mary. Referring to football as soccer can get you punched in the nose in the wrong crowds. Football in Europe crosses every national border throughout Europe and draws tens of millions of fans each weekend to their local stadiums.

I had become a Chelsea Football Club fan over a decade before, when I had attended my first match. Back then, the tickets had been much easier to get than a ticket for one of the other London Premiership clubs, because the team had lost more games than they had won. In the mid- to late 1990s, the team had experienced limited success and had rarely made headlines outside of England. Everything had changed in 2003, when the team had been purchased by Roman Abramovich, a Russian oil tycoon and one of the richest people living in the United Kingdom.

Upon purchasing the team, he had done something that dedicated fans of teams loved to see: he had gone on a spending spree that disregarded any fiscal responsibility and would have made George Steinbrenner, owner of the New York Yankees, jealous with envy. Abramovich quickly purchased some of the most talented and promising players in the world, causing outrage from many of the smaller, far less wealthy teams in Europe. Adding to the intimidation of the new Chelsea Football Club was the rumor that the owner, Roman Abramovich, has had many of his business rivals back in Russia literally eliminated. Now, if that is not intimidation, I don't know what would be. The new Russian ownership of the club has earned the team the nickname "Chelski." There is no better time in the history of the club to be a Chelsea fan, and I was proud to say that I was no bandwagon fan, who only followed a club because of its tremendous success and prospects of future continued success.

We met Andy and Petter at our designated meeting spot and made our way into the forty-two thousand-seat outdoor stadium to find our seats. The stadium has been located on the same grounds since 1877, and at one time, it had had a capacity of one hundred thousand spectators, though the majority of them had to stand. The facility had undergone many refurbishments and additions and had become a modern-looking stadium. Sarah, Andy, Petter, and I stood in silence as we caught our first glimpse of the perfectly manicured, green grass, referred to by the English as the "pitch" rather than as the "field." Our seats were close to the pitch and within a rock's throw of the visiting fans—a dangerous place to sit in many stadiums outside of England.

One of the most interesting and energetic aspects of attending a European football match, adding to the brawling atmosphere was the large section of the stadium specifically reserved for the visiting team fans to attend each away game. Almost a quarter of the stadium was filled with the visiting team's fans, and they were doing their best to be heard. Many fans of the football clubs throughout Europe were so dedicated to their teams that they would travel hundreds of miles to show support, even when their team was considered a heavy favorite to lose the match. A line of about a hundred police officers in bright yellow jackets stand as a human barricade between the home crowd and the visiting crowd, preventing them from giving each other "the business." Each stadium also has an entrance specifically dedicated to the visiting crowd, and an army of policemen on horses were usually present on-site to keep the peace outside the stadium before and after each match. Men with their sons standing next to them made obscene gestures toward the visiting fans and sang chants with swear words in unison, but it was all in good fun.

Over the previous twenty years, the sport had dramatically changed from a working-class-attended sport to an event that commanded exorbitant ticket prices, so that the majority of the hooligans or troublemakers had been priced out of being able to cheer for their favorite football club in person. Many of the men around us were still dressed in suits and ties from work.

The teams took to the pitch, and with the joy that every man felt while explaining the details of his favorite sports team to his girl, I started to recite the names of the Chelsea players to Sarah.

"What team are we cheering for again?" she asked vaguely.

"The team in blue," I said, slightly annoyed because I felt she had not been listening to me.

"You mean the Samsung team?"

"Yes," I said.

"I thought they were called the Blues?"

"They are. Samsung is just the sponsor of the team," I said. That was something that I had always had a difficult time accepting—the selling of the chest portion of the jersey, referred to as a "kit" by the English, to a sponsor with deep pockets. That "selling out" of the front of the uniform turned all the club's fans into walking billboards when they showed support for their favorite team by wearing the official uniform shirt at school or at the park. Some of the teams were even sponsored by gambling Web sites. Surprisingly, gambling was a big part of the sporting experience. Sarah could not believe that there was a booth located inside the stadium dedicated to accepting official betting wagers up until the start of the match.

As the game began, we sat down and watched the action on the pitch.

"I read somewhere that there was no reason women should not love English football—all the players look like male models," Sarah leaned over and told me in a flirtatious but observant tone. Even in the cold, bitter air, all the players wore shorts, showing off their perfect legs and buttocks and toned bodies, unlike most American football players.

Similar to hockey in the United States, English football is difficult to watch on television, as the action and atmosphere in the stadium or arena does not translate well onto the television sets in our homes. Attending a live match changes your entire perspective of the sport. The game does not produce nearly the amount of scoring that Americans love and come to expect, but the nonstop energy of the crowd was why I had fallen in love with the sport again.

In the United States, there was an incredible amount of competition to attract and retain fans, who had all the professional, minor league, and collegiate teams to choose from. Professional American sports leagues were constantly changing rules and retooling different aspects of their games to keep fans and attract new fans to the sport. Not enough scoring in basketball? Move the three-point line, or change the defensive rules. Not enough home runs in baseball? Make the strike zone bigger, or change the dimensions of the outfield wall. Not enough touchdowns in football? Change the defensive rules to favor the wide receivers and quarterbacks.

American sports even make it easier for fans to enjoy the game by creating artificial crowd noise and generating loud rock music to help do the cheering for them. Through the oversize jumbotrons, they are instructed when to cheer. Cheerleaders told them what to cheer. The arena announcer would order them to "Make some more noise!" while rock music blasted at a deafening level.

American sports have to be television-friendly to truly succeed. All of the major American sports have dedicated time-outs and television time-outs as part of the experience. The last two minutes of a close basketball game can be extended to a half hour, to the delight of the television network executives, given the prices they can charge for airing commercials during an important game. Each American football game requires almost four dedicated hours of our television viewing attention. With two forty-five-minute, nonstop halves, European football has no designated stopping of play to air television commercials.

In American sports, it is even acceptable—if not beneficial—to lose, because the teams with the most losses are rewarded with the opportunity to select the best young players in the following season's new player draft, all but taking away any incentive to try to win at the end of a losing season. In European football, the bottom two teams in the standings are severely punished and dropped down to a lower league, costing huge losses in revenue. The teams are replaced by the top two teams in the lower league, which rewards those teams for their successes by elevating them to the next level for the next year. Some of the most entertaining matches are between the struggling teams at the end of the season, as they battle it out and attempt to avoid being dropped to a lower level of play the following season. That would be equivalent to my beloved Chicago Cubs being dropped down to the minor leagues for their past habits of finishing last in the league, to be replaced by a minor league team that had finished in first place.

Fan etiquette in England is much different than in most American sports, in that it is considered incredibly rude to get up and leave your seat while the game is going on. There are no concessionaires walking the aisles selling beer, food, or souvenirs. The long gaps between scoring or scoring attempts are filled with standing on your feet and listening to, responding to, or singing along to the chants and songs that are thrown back and forth by the home and visiting fans like a game of catch—an essential ingredient to the overall experience.

At first, it was tough to decipher the chants and singing because of the strong accent. But if we listened closely and asked the people sitting next to us, we found that the history, meaning, and source of inspiration of each chant or song was fascinating. The chants are intended to amuse the crowd, inspire the home team, honor a star player, insult the visiting team and their fans, or show displeasure at the referee. We all stood and sang along with the home crowd:

> *Come to the Shed and we'll welcome you*
> *Wear your blue and see us through*
> *Sing loud and clear until the game is done*
> *Sing Chelsea, everyone*

The match ended with an easy 5–1 Chelsea victory, but not before a naked streaker made his way onto the field, scampering around and eluding the policemen. He finally dashed back into the stands and, from our standpoint, appeared to run out of the stadium.

You would never have guessed that such a lopsided defeat had just occurred from the continuous chanting of the visiting fans, who were still standing and cheering with pride even after the game had ended—their smaller, less wealthy team had scored a goal against the mighty Chelsea Football Club.

In the United States, European football highlights usually do not make the local news unless a riot or a severe tragedy has occurred. The biggest tragedy in English football history that dramatically changed the atmosphere inside of stadiums was the Hillsborough Disaster on April 15, 1989, during which 180 people were injured and close to one hundred spectators were killed. Fans were crushed to death because of the massive overcrowding conditions.

Pictures of children with their faces crushed up against the metal fencing were seen all over the world. As a result of the tragedy, English stadiums removed the metal fencing, and all stadiums were converted to sitting room only. Unfortunate events like the Hillsborough Disaster prove that the saying "football is more important than life" is simply untrue.

One of the largest rivalries was between two Glaswegian football clubs, the Rangers and the Celtics. The hatred between the fans of the two clubs centered around religion (Catholic and Protestant) and the history of Northern Ireland politics and sectarian violence. That hatred has resulted in multiple deaths of fans of both clubs outside and around the stadiums. The rivalry between the two clubs earned it the nickname of "The Old Firm," primarily because the clubs made so much money by hating each other.

Soccer may have an uphill battle in competing for fans' attention in the United States, but that has not prevented Americans from recently purchasing of some of the biggest and most globally recognized teams around the world, the biggest being the holy grail of football clubs, the Manchester United Football Club. In the 1990s, the Manchester United Football Club became a publicly owned team when it was floated on the stock market. The high stock valuation of the club made it unthinkable that a hostile takeover could be possible. However, an American—Malcolm Glazer, owner of the Tampa Bay Buccaneers of the National Football League—successfully took over the club. To purchase the club, Glazer had to take on substantial debt. His first order of business was to raise ticket prices. A public relations disaster ensued, primarily because of how secretively the Glazer family had acted during the transaction and the first thing the new owners had done was raise ticket prices. The Glazer family seemed to go to great lengths to avoid addressing the public and fans, giving the impression that they did not respect the long historical tradition of the club. When Glazer suffered a series of small strokes, the news created a buzz among fans that Glazer would die soon. They hoped that if he did die, an American might no longer own the most well-known team in the world.

- Chapter Eight -

Garmisch-Party-Kirchen

✦

"Have you decided to give up and return home to America?" Denis jokingly asked, as he watched me struggle up the winding spiral staircase at school with my backpack and suitcase and into the classroom for the last class of the week.

"I don't know about you, Denis, but I am in no mood for a three-and-a-half-hour lecture on queuing theory," I said. Denis smiled and agreed. I took my regular seat in class next to Felix and in front of Denis, Max, and Andy.

"So, you're off to Germany for the weekend?" Denis asked.

"Yes. I'm pretty excited about it," I said. "I'm flying to Munich tonight and then taking a train to meet Sarah and her friend Jill."

Sarah's good friend had invited us to join her for a skiing trip to Garmisch-Partenkirchen in Germany. Jill had flown in to London for a day of sightseeing and then on to Germany with Sarah. The plan was for me to fly to Munich and take a train to Garmisch-Partenkirchen, arriving late at night at the hotel where we would be staying.

"Hey, Denis, I should have asked you this earlier, but how do I get from the airport to the train station to catch a train to Garmisch-Partenkirchen?" I asked as I got out a pen and paper to write down the directions. I could tell Denis was happy that I had asked him. He was also happy that I was heading to his home country of Germany for a weekend trip. Denis pulled out his computer and started pulling up maps to show me where to go.

"What time do you land?" he asked.

I pulled out my ticket.

"Ten twenty-two p.m."

"OK, you need to make your way to—" Denis started to explain.

41

"No, Denis, you should have him take this train," Felix interrupted. His curiosity had gotten the better of him as he had looked over his shoulder.

Denis and Felix begun to argue in English, but they quickly moved the conversation into German. This was very unusual because upon arriving in London, Denis, Felix, and Max had agreed to always speak English in front of their British and American friends—not because they thought it was rude to speak German in front of them, but because they felt it was the best way to master the language. I could not tell if they were arguing or truly figuring out the best route for me.

"Are you checking any bags?" Felix asked.

"Nope," I said.

"Skis?"

"Nope. Just a smile," I said, but they did not get my lame joke.

"And you say you have been training for marathons?" Felix asked.

"Something like that," I said, not really sure what the point of the question was.

"I don't know, Garrett," Denis said, with a look of concern.

By then, Max had joined the argument, and I was beginning to wish I had never asked.

Andy could not resist the temptation and shouted over our shoulders, "What do Germans know about running a train system?"

"Oh, Andy, you almost had me," Felix said, once he understood Andy's joke about the German stereotype of efficiency.

"Um, Garrett, I'm very sorry, but even if you run as fast as you can, you will miss the last train of the day that can take you to Garmisch-Partenkirchen by twenty-two minutes," Denis said, with a tone that suggested disappointment that my trip to his country would not start out as great at he had wanted it to.

"Yes, it's true," Felix said. "Who made your travel plans?" Since Sarah was not around, I placed the blame on her.

"I will have to have a talk with her before she plans future trips to Germany," Felix said.

I laughed out loud, not really understanding if Felix was joking or not.

Class ended. I was running late, so I had to make a mad dash to the Tube station to catch a train to the airport. The Tube was running on time without any major delays. I exited the train as it pulled into the station at the airport and rushed to the turnstiles to exit the Tube station and enter the airport terminal, but the machine rejected my travel card, instantly locking the turnstile and knocking the wind out of me as I tried to pass through it.

"Oh, crap," I said out loud as the station attendant descended on me to see what the problem was. My travel card was only valid for travel in zones one and two, and since the airport was in zone five, I was required to pay an incremental amount of money for my Tube ride to the airport. Any further delay and I would surely miss my flight. The station attendant explained the problem.

I hesitated for a moment as I thought about how to address the situation, when a little white lie just came out: "I'm terribly sorry, but I am a tourist and I did not know any better. I promise I will never let it happen again."

The station attendant looked at me for a moment before swiping his security card, unlocking the gate for me to pass through.

"Thank you so much! Cheers!" I said, trying my best to say "cheers" like an American tourist.

I made it through the airport terminal and onto the plane as the flight crew was preparing to close the doors. I quickly sat down in my seat, relieved that I had not missed my flight. But a feeling of panic was quickly setting in as I thought, *Oh, my god, I think I am going to throw up.*

On her flight from San Francisco, Jill had been kind enough to bring a bag full of American peanut butter, mac and cheese, Doritos, ranch dressing, brownie mix, and a whole bunch of delightful, American, fat-filled goodies. I could not resist the temptation, so earlier for lunch, I had eaten about half of everything she had brought us, and I was starting to regret it.

The flight took off, and I shut my eyes, trying to think happy thoughts in hopes of my stomach settling and forgiving me for what I had put into it.

An hour into the flight, I woke up to find myself sitting amongst five American college girls, who must have convinced the other passengers seated around me to switch seats during my nap so they could all sit together. If it had been ten years earlier, I would have been thanking the god of airplane flight seating for my incredible luck. Each of the girls had a copy of the unofficial student travel bible, *Let's Go Europe.* They flipped through the pages while they talked to each other. I could not help but listen in on their linguistically challenged conversation, as I was sitting right in the middle of it.

"I went to KFC the other day, and it was, like, terrible. It was nothing like KFC at home, you know," said the girl seated to my left, who was leaning forward to talk around me. The girls went on to describe how the food was nothing like it was at home and how even Starbucks tasted different.

"And what's with having no Taco Bells anyplace. I mean, come on!" said the girl sitting to my right in the next row over.

I tried to ignore the girls, but their conversation had turned into a game of trying to name who was American and who was British. Their list had so far included Kate Moss, Gwyneth Paltrow, Gwen Stefani, Keira Knightley, and Madonna. They had correctly identified the nationality of three of the five women. I wondered why their list did not include any guys. Did they not know any British male actors or singers? For fifteen minutes, they argued back and forth, all giving examples and various miscellaneous information to back their claims about who was British and who was American. I was about to reach my wit's end, and even though I had not been invited to participate in the argument, I was starting to think about the impression these five college girls were making on the European passengers seated around us.

"You are all wrong," I finally said out loud. The girls looked surprised; they must have thought I was still sleeping. "Kate Moss and Keira Knightley are both British born. Gwyneth Paltrow, Gwen Stefani, and Madonna are all American born. So there, you're all wrong. Please talk about something else now," I pleaded.

"Dude, Keira Knightley may be British, but you are so wrong about Madonna. There is no way she is American," said the girl seated to my left.

"Madonna was born in Bay City, Michigan," I said. I was using my hand to represent a map, as people from Michigan often do, to show the girl where Bay City, Michigan, was located. "Look it up when you get home, and you'll see that I am right."

"Whatever," said the girl sitting to my right.

It was obvious that the girls didn't want me to be a part of their conversation because they chose to be quiet the rest of the flight and instead immersed themselves in their travel books. Hearing the American words "dude," "like," and "whatever," as well as hearing sentences ended with the phrase "you know" was a nice and pleasant reminder of the everyday, generational American language I no longer heard each day.

The plane landed, and I made my way off and started my sprint to reach the train station, hoping that the train had been delayed and I could still make it. I decided that I could run faster if I stopped and used the bathroom. I walked into the bathroom with slight hesitation, until I confirmed that I had walked into the men's bathroom and not the women's, as I was not sure if I had correctly deciphered the gender indication on the door. Etched into the porcelain urinal was a picture of the common fly; it caused me to focus on the image while relieving myself, avoiding splashing on the floor—a perfect example of process control. *Wow, these Germans think of everything,* I thought to myself.

I continued on my way to the central train station and ran up to the ticket counter. To my disappointment, the last train of the night had not been delayed and had left twenty-three minutes before. Denis and Felix had been right, and incredibly, they were off by just one minute. I guessed that they had forgotten to factor in one bathroom stop. I purchased a ticket for the first train the next day at six o'clock in the morning and left the train station to find a cheap hotel for the night and to call Sarah and tell her the news that I would not be arriving that night.

I checked into a hotel across the street from the train station, made my way up the stairs to my shoebox-size room that was not as cheap as I had hoped it would be, and collapsed onto the bed. I called Sarah, and she was disappointed that I would not arrive that night, but she understood. We said goodnight, and I turned on the television. I chose between watching the American show *Family Guy* and full-frontal naked women being shown on government-run television and went to bed.

The train ride the next morning was beautiful as I left the city behind and slowly made my way to the picturesque, mountain town of Garmisch-Partenkirchen, which was close to the Austrian border. Garmisch-Partenkirchen was once officially two separate towns: Garmisch and Partenkirchen. Adolf Hitler had forced the two cities to combine in preparation for hosting the 1936 Winter Olympics. The train was mostly empty, and only a few people exited the train at each stop along the way. Once I arrived at my destination, I took a moment to breathe the fresh mountain air and admire the many beautiful, snow-covered peaks that surround the city.

Garmisch-Partenkirchen is a place that most American tourists skip when visiting Germany, and we did not expect to see many, if any, Americans during the weekend trip. I waited in the taxi line, and then got into a Mercedes-Benz that had been converted to a taxi—common in many parts of Europe—and handed the driver the address of where I wanted to go. Off we went over the cobblestone streets and a covered bridge to meet Sarah. The taxi pulled up to a large, Bavarian-looking house that was being used to operate a bed-and-breakfast for tourists. The large, four-story structure looked like a gingerbread house directly out of the German fairy tale *Hansel and Gretel.*

Jill had exchanged a large number of her frequent flyer miles to fly from San Francisco to London and then on to Germany for a long weekend of skiing with her brother Steve, his blond-haired, blue-eyed, Swedish wife Eva, and their six-month-old baby Mikaela. They all flew in from Sweden along with Eva's two brothers, Magnus and Mats for the long weekend. Jill's brother was a smart, likable guy, and he and I quickly became friends as he shared with me all his experiences of living and working in Sweden and in Europe. He had met his wife Eva while she had been working in the United States. Upon marrying, they had moved from the United States to Linköping, Sweden. Being of Korean ethnicity, Steve joked that if he ever committed a crime in Linköping, he would easily be identified as the culprit because of his obvious non-Swedish, Korean appearance, which made him stick out slightly wherever he went in the town.

We spent our first day together enjoying the sun, cold beer, and snowy slopes. Eva's brother Mats, a farmer back in Sweden, was a tall and large guy with some of the largest and strongest hands I had ever seen. He did not speak much English, but he was willing to try whenever he could. Magnus, Eva's younger brother, was a student with a trendy artist look to him that reminded me of one of my own brothers. Magnus spoke very good English and spent much of the trip interpreting my questions and jokes.

We completed our day of skiing with a late afternoon enjoyment of après-ski, or socializing with your ski boots still on. We watched the other skiers dancing and socializing in their ski boots at a makeshift outdoor bar at the bottom of the mountain. We all drank beer and *Glühwein* (hot, spiced, mulled wine) and enjoyed the experience of being together.

We spent the evening enjoying a nice dinner at an eclectic, German restaurant where I ordered *schweinsbraten*, which was sliced, pot-roasted pork that had a crunchy crust, and Sarah asked for *schweinshaxe*, whish was braised pork leg served with flavorful gravy. We took turns trying each other's meals and washed it all down with a local German *Weißbier* or wheat beer before heading to a nearby nightclub for a few more drinks and fun.

Even though Magnus's English was not perfect and Mats could not speak very much English, we spent the night entertaining ourselves by playing a series of spontaneous drinking games and telling jokes using hand gestures and quick translations. We toasted our friendship over a shot of the bitter-tasting Jägermeister, a worldwide well-known drink invented in Wolfenbüttel, Germany, with a name that translates to "master hunter." We sang along together to the mostly American songs that blared at an ear-splitting decibel; we sang right along with the club goers, whose heavy accents imparted a unique and charming sound to the words. Sarah and I smiled at each other as we continued to sing along to the music, enjoying the moment and laughing together at the novel and almost comical sound of the crowd singing together in English.

The night was great, and we paid dearly for it the next morning. We had successfully joined the other European tourists in turning Garmisch-Partenkirchen into Garmisch-Party-Kirchen, and it was taking us all a little longer to get out of bed and make it back onto the slopes for another day of skiing. Unable to repeat the previous night's performance, we decided on an early meal and a good night's sleep.

We woke up Sunday morning before the sun had started to rise so we could catch the first train heading back to Munich to make our flight back home. Sarah rested her head on my shoulder and tried to get a little more sleep on the train as it hummed along on the rails, slowly making its way out of the mountains and back into the big city.

"Dude, what a great weekend this has been," I said to Sarah.

"Whatever" she said with a smile.

- Chapter Nine -

A License to Watch TV

✦

It was Thursday, the 23rd of February, exactly forty-six days since we had arrived in London, before Sarah and I felt like we were no longer on an extended vacation. The honeymoon period had officially ended.

The day started out with my morning routine of walking to Starbucks to get a cup of coffee and the three newspapers that I liked to read each day. Walking out of the front door of our building, there were four different directions you could take. Within a five-minute walk in each of the four directions, you passed a Starbucks. My morning did not officially start without my sugar-infused, milkshake-calorie-count drink, the caramel macchiato.

In 1986, *The Economist* introduced the "Big Mac Index" as a humorous way of measuring the purchasing power between two currencies. The Big Mac had been chosen because it was available in an exact specification in most countries around the world. Since Starbucks was then made available in the exact same specifications in many countries, *The Economist* often used a tall latte from Starbucks, or the "Tall Latte Index," as another judge of purchasing power. With the American dollar now well into its nosedive against the British pound, my $4 morning coffee at home cost me $7.50. After my stop at the corner newspaper stand to purchase my three daily newspapers at a cost of $3.50, I was spending $11 each morning. Throw in a muffin from Starbucks, as I did many mornings, and I was spending the equivalent of $15 a day, adding up to around $100 per week and close to $400 per month on my simple morning routine. With the American dollar quickly losing value, our purchasing power in the United Kingdom was getting weaker by the day. Thank goodness I did not smoke, or my morning routine could have gotten really expensive. I returned home, and after greeting Sydney, I picked up the ringing telephone connected to our London phone number. I was thrilled that we were getting a call on our London phone, because we never received any calls on it.

"Hello?" I said with an over-caffeinated voice.

"Is Mr. or Mrs. Ryan available?" the voice asked in an extremely Scottish-sounding accent that was so strong I could barely understand the pronunciation of the name Ryan.

"Our records indicate that you have not paid your television license," the caller said.

I did not know what a television license was, so my silent response was giving an impression that it was true; I was guilty of not paying it.

"Please hold on for one minute while I check my records," I finally said, quickly grabbing my computer and performed a Google search for "British television license." The search results stated that a television license was required for every TV in the house, at a cost of about £12 or around $25 per month per color television—you got a slight discount if your television was a black and white set. I picked up the phone again, confident that the caller was not running a scam.

"I'm sorry. You are correct. We have not paid the license, because our television is not working." I was not lying. Since we had moved in, we had not been able to figure out how to get the television to work properly. We could turn it on, but we could not receive a clear picture. The caller told me that once the TV was working, we would have to pay the television license required to operate a broadcast television receiver or we would have to pay a penalty.

"Thanks for calling. Cheers!" I said and hung up the phone, proud that my use of the word "cheers" was starting to sound genuinely English.

Great. Our first call on our London phone number and it is someone demanding money, I thought.

After a quick shower, I was out the front door again and on my way to the Tube station to go to class. The train arrived at the platform and was empty, so I had my choice of seats and I carefully picked a seat that had no gum and had no drink spilled on it. Usually the train was extremely packed in the morning, and a seat was never an option on the heavily traveled Piccadilly line, which carried tourists hauling large suitcases into the city from Heathrow Airport. Tourists also used the line to go to Harrods or Covent Garden. Often, they would cram their ways onto the train, just to get off at the next station, irritating me to the point where I wanted to say to them, "You know, you could actually try to read one of the six maps you have in your hands and walk the three blocks to the next tourist site on your itinerary."

As I sat down, I noticed an advertisement along the top side of the train, a "Big Brother is watching you" message that said that if you did not pay your television licensing fee, "the computer will find you" and pretty much make your life miserable. So, that was what all those radio ads, billboard signs, transit advertising, and general harassment were all about. Another glorious "aha" moment that meant we would have to add another item to our list of monthly expenses.

After class, I ran into Amir.

"Hey, dude. How's it going?" he said in his standard greeting to me, which I think he might have learned from an American movie. Amir's English was quickly getting better, and I enjoyed talking to him and getting to know him better. As we exited the university together and crossed through the park, I told him about my television not working and how I had received a call asking if I had paid my television licensing fee. Amir laughed so loud at me and my television problems that we had to stop walking so he could catch his breath.

"Don't you have a television cable?" he asked.

"No, I don't have a television cable," I said, trying to mimic his English with an Iranian accent.

"Then I will show you what you need, my American friend who does not know what a television cable is," he said, mimicking the way I had answered him. We made an abrupt U-turn and walked in the direction of Tottenham Court Road, which was a road close to the university with a large selection of small electronic shops selling cameras and computer accessories.

"Here we are," Amir said, as he gave me a slight push on my arm to signal that I should enter the store we were about to pass.

Amir told the Middle Eastern-looking man behind the counter what we were looking for, and within seconds, the man returned with a small, three-foot, white cable. I pulled out my credit card to pay, but before I could hand the man the card, he pointed to a sign that said "Cash Only." I did not have any cash, so I told the man I would come back the next day to get it.

Amir overheard this and offered to pay the man in cash, saying I could pay him later. The man told Amir the price of the cord, and before I could make sense of what was happening, Amir grabbed my arm and started pulling me toward the door. Just as we were about to leave the small store, Amir stopped and responded to something the man was shouting at us. The shop owner and Amir were speaking in a different language, nearly screaming, with hands flailing through the air as if trying to reinforce their points. Amir turned around and began walking back toward me, once again grabbing my arm to leave. He did this two more times before he finally pulled out his money, handed it to the man, shook his hand, and picked up the white cord. We walked out together, this time without Amir grabbing my arm and pulling me out the shop door.

"What was that all about, Amir?" I finally had the confidence to ask, as we got halfway down the block.

"That man back there was trying to charge you an excessive price for the cord. He should know better. You are not a tourist," Amir said.

I was not sure if I should tell Amir that I did not think many tourists purchased television cable cords there, but I decided against it since I was not a hundred percent sure he would understand the joke.

"So, how much did he want us to pay him?" I finally asked, still in shock at the events that had just happened.

"Ten pounds," he said.

"Oh. How much did we pay him?"

"Nine pounds," he said, as he handed me the cord.

"Thanks, Amir!" I said. I smiled and looked at the strange round ends of the white television cord. I had an expensive coffee addiction, so I felt I should be thankful for the savings that Amir had fought so hard for on my behalf. I never would have had the courage to bargain with the shop owner the way Amir had. Somehow, the excursion was a real bonding experience for the two of us. There we were—an Iranian showing an American how to use a television. I thanked Amir again and told him that I would pay him the next day at class. Then I hurried home, because later that night, Denis and his fiancée Jenny would be coming over for dinner.

"Bierleichen" (German for "beer corpses")

I rode the train home and stopped by the small grocery store close to the Earl's Court Tube station to pick up the food and drinks Sarah had asked me to get for dinner. As I looked over the alcoholic beverage choices, I deliberated over what we should serve them to drink—not an easy decision.

Two weeks before, Sarah and I had invited Denis, Max, Felix, and Andy over for dinner. The four of them had shown up with Budweiser beer. Andy, the lone American had smirked at me and shaken his head in embarrassment as I had accepted the American beer from each of them and placed it in the refrigerator next to the German Beck's beer that I had purchased to serve them. Beck's beer was sold in the United States with the advertising tagline "Beck's, German for beer," and I had always thought it was good beer. I had tried to purchase St. Pauli Girl beer, the German beer with the label of the busty girl wearing the traditional Bavarian outfit from the 1800s, only to learn later that it was sold only in the United States, where it is marketed as a prestigious and expensive German beer. The entire night, the Germans drank the Beck's beer and the Americans drank the Budweiser, with everyone enjoying being together, but secretly wishing that they were drinking a different type of beer and too polite to say anything.

I decided that since Sarah and I were just getting to know Denis's fiancée Jenny, it would be better to avoid the chance of making any statements with the drinks we served them, so I stayed away from any European or United States beer and wine choices and purchased some wine from South Africa. On my way home, I passed Starbucks. The twin-tailed mermaid siren in the Starbucks logo called my name, and I could not resist, so I stopped in for a venti caramel macchiato—my second of the day.

Denis and Jenny arrived and greeted Sarah with a kiss on each cheek as I took their jackets. I was starting to suspect that Sarah enjoyed spending time with our friends so she could greet them and say good-bye to them with a kiss on each cheek. I thought I too was getting really good at that two-cheek kiss greeting, which had somehow found its way into how Sarah and I greeted each other or parted ways when the other left or came home from school or work each day.

Jenny had blond hair and blue eyes, with a distinctive European look and style of dress. She always seemed to be smiling. Jenny's English was still improving, and we had to speak very slowly for her to understand us, though she would often nod her head in acknowledgement that she had understood just to be polite. I told her that even though she could barely speak English, her English was much better than my German. I could tell she had not understood the joke when she nodded and smiled politely. Jenny had just recently moved to London to join Denis while he finished up his graduate degree. She planned on spending her time in London taking English lessons and working hard on learning the language. Over the year, it was amazing to see how quickly her English was improving.

Sarah is such an amazing cook, and even though she would never admit it, she loves cooking for dinner parties so she can show off her talent. Sarah had made a fabulous fish entrée and served it with green beans and garlic-roasted potatoes.

While we enjoyed the dinner, Denis and Jenny explained how they had met and first started dating. Denis explained that they had both attended the same college in Germany. He had planned to work during the summer, but he still wanted to take a class. He attended the first lecture with the sole purpose of finding someone who would take notes for him and keep him updated on the progress of the class. Denis would return at the end of the summer, and with Jenny's notes, he would try to get a passing grade on the final and pass the class.

"Jenny was an easy choice. Not only was she beautiful, but she always sat in the front row," Denis said.

"Jenny, how did you agree to this?" Sarah asked, somewhat knowing the answer that was forthcoming.

"He was … how do you say … "—a phrase Jenny often inserted halfway in a sentence as she took a minute to think before she spoke in English—"too good-looking to say no to." We all laughed at her reply.

Halfway through the dinner, I remembered the delicious American condiment that could turn a perfectly healthy meal into a fat-filled party that Jill had brought us, and I quickly ran over to the refrigerator to find it.

"Denis, you have to try this. It's great on potatoes," I said, as I covered my potatoes with a tidal wave of the rich, creamy sauce. Denis and Jenny both tried the Hidden Valley Ranch Dressing and claimed they really liked it. I explained to them the popularity of ranch dressing in America and how it can now be found in every American home, along with ketchup and mustard.

"Is there a German word for ranch dressing?" I asked.

"No, we do not have ranch dressing in Germany," he said, trying really hard not to laugh at my stupid question.

We finished our dinner and talked for an hour, while I cleaned the dishes. It was so nice having friends to sit and talk with. The time passed quickly, and before I could offer our guests another glass of wine, Denis stood up and said, "We leave now." It made for a comical moment because Sarah and I understood what Denis wanted to communicate, but his English was not good enough yet for a more typical, sugar-coated English phrase that would normally be used to indicate that it was time for them to leave, such as, "It is getting late and we don't want to keep you up much longer."

With a kiss on each cheek, Sarah sent them off, and we walked them out the door.

After our guests had left, I went to find my backpack and told Sarah I had a surprise for her. While she closed her eyes and waited in anticipation, I plugged the white television cable into the back of the television, searched the wall for the circular shaped outlet that Amir had described, and plugged the cord into it. I pushed the power button, and within a few seconds, our little, nineteen-inch television had a glowing and perfectly clear picture.

"Surprise! I figured out why the television was not working. Now I just have to figure out how to pay that silly television-watching tax."

- Chapter Ten -

Turn on the Telly Please

✦

British television quickly opened up a whole new world for us to explore. News programming, documentaries, game shows, and even teenage soaps—we watched them all. Having a working television gave us the opportunity to participate in "watercooler talk" and gave us another perspective on the politics, people, and pop culture of Europeans. At home in the United States, we had had access to almost two hundred TV channels, and by picking up the phone and placing a call to our cable company, we could probably have easily doubled that number. In our small London apartment with the small kitchen, small bathroom, small living room, small bedroom, small patio area, and small television, we received one channel for every room in our apartment—five channels in total.

"We receive five channels? Five channels? *Five* channels?" Sarah said, each time saying the word "five" louder and louder. I inspected our glorious new white television cable and the television to see if I had installed it wrong somehow.

"Yup. Five channels, I guess," I said, while I flipped through them.

We received BBC 1, BBC 2, ITV—Independent Television, Channel 4, which is branded as Channel 4, and finally Five, which had previously been branded as Channel 5 but had changed its name to just Five.

I have never complained about the huge number of programming choices available twenty-four hours a day, seven days a week (British television does not air programs twenty-four hours a day) that we received at home on our television that was the size of most people's kitchen tables, but the vast number of channels seems to create a paradox of choice—I could never find anything to watch. We quickly learned that less was more with our five television channel choices.

The main source of funding for the BBC was the television licensing fee that we were being hunted down like criminals for not paying. Some of our friends told us that they hid their televisions when they were not watching them so they would not get caught if someone stopped by their house to see if they had a television when they claimed they didn't. We had friends who claimed they actually did receive a visit from an "agent" wanting to inspect their homes to see if they were hiding a television. We were not sure if they were being honest or just passing on urban myths that a "friend of a friend" had experienced it.

Because the BBC is primarily funded by the collection of essentially a TV tax, the shows produced to be aired have very small production budgets that are probably on par with what the production companies in the United States spend on food catering for most television shows. As a result, a large majority of shows had a reality show foundation to them, such as documentaries, lifestyle insights, singing or dancing contests, talk shows, game shows, or cooking shows.

In a country that has been deeply stereotyped as a nation of terrible food, primarily as a result of food shortages and rationing during wartime efforts, there was almost always one type of cooking or food show on one of the five channels during every hour of the broadcasting day, with a wide range of shows that star a specific cook, such as Gordon Ramsey or Jamie Oliver, to game show-style programs with chefs competing against each other.

Sarah and I often enjoyed watching Gordon Ramsey's show *The F-Word*, in which he actually used "the F-word" in almost every sentence, and it is not beeped out. It took a little while to get used to hearing him constantly swear on the show, something that he did to belittle or praise someone. Some of our other favorite shows included the reality show *Big Brother: A Place in the Sun*, and the game show *Deal or No Deal*.

I was surprised to learn that Britain was the largest exporter of television formats; many shows that succeed in Europe were purchased and "Americanized" for the American television-viewing audience, mostly because the shows had proven to be successful and drawn the attention of television executives. Even my parents' favorite show, at the time, was a British export, a show they loved so much they had been known to leave a dinner party early to get home before it began or even ignore a ringing telephone so they did not miss a minute of *Dancing with the Stars*. *Strictly Come Dancing*, as it was called in the United Kingdom, was one of the most-watched shows in Britain, and like *Big Brother*, it had earned watercooler status. The show had been exported to over twenty-five countries under the name *Dancing with the Stars* and was especially popular in Eastern Europe and Scandinavia.

The British must be pleased when they visit the United States and see the large numbers of British citizens hosting, judging, or starring on American television shows. Hugh Laurie played the protagonist on the show *House*. Nigel Lythgoe and Simon Cowell threw the dirt as judges on the shows *So You Think You Can Dance* and the megahit *American Idol*, respectively. Chef Gordon Ramsey's show had been exported to the United States as *Hell's Kitchen*, minus the on-air swearing, and Jo Frost was teaching Americans how to raise proper kids in the show *Supernanny*.

British actors had often been cast as the villain in Hollywood movies, but it seemed American television producers had found success casting British actors with their sharp accents and painful put-downs of others. Sarcasm and irony is something the British seem to be born with and excel at. Americans do not like to be told what to do by others, but we seem to really enjoy watching other people on the receiving end of criticism and direction, especially if it comes from a sharp-tongued Brit.

Sarah and I settled on watching a show called *How Clean Is Your House*, described in the television listings as an hour of bossy women offering lifestyle advice. I can hardly wait to see it on American television someday.

Halfway through the surprisingly interesting show, Sarah walked over to the kitchen and threw away some trash.

"I see you went to Starbucks twice today," she said, noticing the two venti Starbucks cups in the trash can. "You know, I really don't appreciate you spending my money on your Starbucks habit."

"Excuse me?" I answered her back in a defensive tone.

"I said I really don't think you should be spending so much money on things like Starbucks each day," she said. "Every now and then is fine, but not every day. Small things like Starbucks really add up quickly. It is too expensive to be going to Starbucks every day." Any financial planner could quickly point out how much money you can save by avoiding Starbucks each day, and I could not agree more, but the two words that had caught my attention were "my money." Maybe if I had not been so tired or maybe if I hadn't been doing an activity that I hated so much—cleaning dishes—I would have ignored the comment or not reacted in the aggressive those-are-fighting-words manner that I was demonstrating.

"Your money? So, when did it all become your money?" I asked with a bite.

"Well, you're not working right now, so technically we are spending my money," she said. I could see by the expression on her face that she probably regretted saying "my money," and I wish I had ended it there, but I was really hurt and felt the best defense was to go on the offensive. A shouting match began.

It is estimated that a major factor in nine out of ten marriages ending in divorce is money issues or money stress. Money is a topic that many couples feel is almost too personal to talk about, honestly.

Sarah and I have never had a problem talking about money; we just had a problem talking about money without turning it into a fight. In our marriage, I had always played the role of the spender and the avoider, meaning I spent money freely and avoided talking about it with Sarah, while Sarah was a saver and a worrier, preferring to save and worry about money. I have also felt that Sarah might enjoy life a little more if she started living for today instead of saving for tomorrow, while Sarah would prefer that I save a little more today to be able to live tomorrow. We were the classic example of a saver marrying a spender and then arguing over money, because we were often out of financial sync. My most common answer during our financial discussions was, "Don't worry about it so much. We'll figure it out later."

Sarah and I had always found it interesting to talk with other couples about how they merged their finances. Did they have joint checking accounts, joint credit card accounts? Did they each keep a personal credit card? Sarah and I had never really thought about it. We had just combined our financial accounts and did not really keep any personal credit cards, except for the cards given to us as corporate credit cards for work expenses. My financial assets and liabilities had become Sarah's, and hers had become mine. Sarah would always be the logical voice of reason when it came to money, while I would always be the optimistic voice of "Don't worry; we'll figure it out later" in the relationship. A saver and a spender marrying each other in most cases was a recipe for disaster, but in our case, we had succeeded because of patience and understanding. We were still learning to talk about money honestly, and in the middle of that argument, I was wishing that I had never elevated Sarah's remark into the full-blown fight it had turned into.

We had saved up a nice amount of our hard-earned money, and we were surprised by how quickly the money had disappeared. Paying for Sydney's flight cost, the large security deposit on our new London apartment, having only one salary instead of two, and living in one of the most expensive cities in the world were adding a huge amount of stress to both of us. If we wanted to be able to travel and "live life a little," we would need a well-balanced commitment and dedication from Sarah the saver and worrier as well as me the spender and avoider.

We decided that I would be in charge of watching the amount of money we spent and making sure that the bills were paid. I promised Sarah that I would try to cut back on the small things, such as coffee each day, and Sarah promised to relax a little bit and accept that most likely we would return home with a little unpaid balance on the credit card, but that it was debt caused by experiences that would enrich our lives. We also promised—or at least I did—to make our regular financial meetings more constructive, take them more seriously, and not blow them off, by being honest and open. We promised to not turn our meetings to review our finances into opportunities to start a fight. We ended the night by following the number one rule in a marriage: Don't go to bed angry.

"I no longer feel like we are on vacation," Sarah said to me, as she rolled over and kissed me.

"Me, neither," I said. "It was a great vacation, though. I will show you the pictures sometime."

- Chapter Eleven -

Have Passport, Will Travel

✦

The month of March and, with it, a week-long semester break from class had arrived.

"We British do not go on vacation, but we do take a holiday or go on holiday," my professor explained to me, when he asked how I would be spending my week off. Sarah was also "taking a holiday" from work, and we had decided to spend the week skiing and exploring in Switzerland.

Since our arrival, we had only left Sydney alone at home for a long weekend when we traveled, and since all our friends were also "taking a holiday" and leaving town for the week, we were left with no friends to ask to watch Sydney and experience for themselves the "Sydney Routine." We looked into local dog kennels and boarders and found the prices absolutely shocking, with day rates anywhere from £45 ($90) a day for a steel cage, a bowl of water, and very little one-on-one attention, to £80 ($160) a day for three walks a day in the park and a nice, warm bed each night. Since we would be gone for eight days, the cheaper of the two options would still cost us around $720 for the week.

We thought long and hard about what we should do. The solution we came up with was pure genius. We were able to find a round-trip flight from Los Angeles for an incredibly low fare of just $350. I called my cousin who lived in Los Angeles and asked him if he would be interested in a free flight over to London, with the only catch being that he had to stay in our place and watch our four-legged friend Sydney for us.

"A free flight to London, a free place to stay in central London, and all I have to do is watch Sydney?" was his response to the question.

"So, you'll do it?" I asked, not sure from the tone of his reply who he thought was getting the better deal, given that he was aware of the "Sydney Routine."

"I'll stay a month if you need me to!" he said.

Sarah and I were happy, because we would have someone we knew watch Sydney in our own home for half the amount of money it would cost to place Sydney in a local dog kennel while we were gone.

Sarah and I anxiously awaited my cousin's arrival from the airport. We sat in our bedroom playing a geography game in which we tried to stump each other with difficult geography questions.

Upon moving into our apartment in London, I had purchased a sprawling wall map of the world and taped it to the large wall next to our bed. I had made a real effort to sharpen my geography skills and learn the exact location of each country as well as the capitals and names of the current government leaders of each European country. We Americans were criticized for having below-average geography skills and had to endure the joke that we were unable to locate a country on a map until we started bombing it. Thankfully, along with Canadians, the British also ranked low on the geographic knowledge scale and did not know that Guinea and New Guinea were thousands of miles apart.

It was Sarah's turn, and she was asking me what I thought was an easy one.

"Name all the countries that border Switzerland." I thought the question was pretty easy, but I was a little worried about the way Sarah had emphasized the word "all," giving me the suspicion that I was walking into a trap.

"There's Germany, France, Austria, Italy, and … "

Sarah said nothing and kept smiling, tipping her cards to indicate that, yes, I had walked into a trap. I was stumped. What was I missing?

"Do you give up?" asked Sarah with a smug, satisfied grin on her face, knowing she had won that round.

"Yes, I give up. What did I miss?"

"Liechtenstein!" she said with a loud laugh, throwing her arms up into the air and dancing in an apparent sign of victory.

"Liechtenstein? Liechtenstein! I've never heard of the place." I got up from the bed to look at the map and see for myself that Sarah was telling the truth. Sure enough, there it was; the size of my fingernail and bordering Switzerland to the west was Liechtenstein.

Upon Andrew's arrival, we gave him a crash course in how to keep Sydney happy for the next eight days. We told him that the place was his and to enjoy the fridge full of food that we were leaving him. Then we headed to the airport. I spent the flight reading about the tiny, German-speaking, rich, banking country of Liechtenstein, one of the few odd countries that had more registered companies than citizens and a place where most people went just to say they had been there and collect the souvenir stamp in their passports to prove it.

The plan for the week was to fly to Geneva and spend the first night there, get up early the next morning and take a train from Geneva to St. Moritz, spend three days in St. Moritz, and take the world's slowest express train (the Glacier Express) to Zermatt for three days, before returning to Geneva and flying back to London.

The plane landed, and we made our way through the airport terminal to pick up our bags and catch a train into the city. Switzerland had not transitioned to the Euro and still used the Swiss Franc, which meant that we had to stop at the money machine and take out Swiss Francs for the week. We boarded the train and rode it into the city center of Geneva, to the Gare de Cornavin station. I had purposely booked a hotel room close to the train station, because we needed to be back at the train station by seven thirty the next morning to catch the train to St. Moritz. As we rode the train in, I tried to find out where the hotel was located, but I just could not spot it on the map. Since we could not locate the hotel, we decided to just catch a taxi from the train station to the hotel, figuring that if the taxi driver became angry because he had to drive us just one or two blocks, we would just apologize and give him a nice tip.

We quickly found a taxi, and I handed the driver a printout with the hotel address on it. The driver nodded in acknowledgment and did not make a fuss about what we thought might be a short distance. We drove away from the curb of the station, turned right, made another right turn, and then a left-hand turn, after which the driver quickly accelerated down the Rue du Mont-Blanc and crossed over the Pont du Mont-Blanc bridge, giving us our first view of Lake Geneva.

Sarah looked over at me and whispered, "Do you think he is taking us for a ride? I thought the hotel was close to the train station."

"I don't know. I hope not. He is driving a Mercedes-Benz," I whispered back. It was difficult to call the taxi driver a crook when he was driving us in a Mercedes-Benz and was dressed much nicer than we were.

"Well, say something to him, then," Sarah said, nudging my arm.

"OK, I'll ask him. Sir, how much farther to the hotel?" I asked the taxi driver.

"Not much further. Five, maybe ten, minutes. There is little traffic, so we should arrive soon," he answered.

"Where did you book us a hotel? France?" Sarah said jokingly.

She continued to laugh at her own joke for a few seconds, until it became apparent that it was no longer a joke, but a reality, as the driver waved at a couple of policemen standing by a checkpoint. The policemen waved us through and into France! The driver continued down the road for another minute or two before pulling in front of our hotel, two blocks from a small train station and next to a small Chinese restaurant.

Somehow I had booked us a hotel that was close to a train station, but it was the wrong train station. We had never planned to go to France, even though Geneva is a very short distance from the border with France, but I did not let the moment for a bad joke pass me by.

"Surprise, I thought I would also take you to France!" I said as I paid the driver and exited the taxi to get our bags out of the trunk of the car. The hotel was inexpensive and only a ten-minute drive from the train station, so the mistake was not too bad.

We were both getting tired, and we just wanted to take a shower and get a good night's sleep. We tried to enter through the front doors of the building, which looked more like an apartment building than a hotel, but the doors were locked. We saw another couple sitting in two chairs in the lobby, smoking and arguing while talking on their phones. The couple noticed us and came over and opened the door for us. I walked up to the front desk, only to find a large, wooden board had been pulled down over the front of it. A metal sign on the desk displayed the hours: "7:00 AM–9:00 PM." I looked at my watch, which read eight forty-five in the evening.

"It is only eight forty-five. How are they closed? And how does a hotel close its front desk?" I said to Sarah.

Sarah looked at her cell phone and said, "It's nine forty-five. Geneva is an hour ahead of London."

"Shit, shit, shit, shit, shit, *shit*!" was all I could say. The couple arguing in Italian heard me say this, looked over at us, and laughed. It appeared they were experiencing the same problem that we had just walked into.

"Well, what should we do?" I asked Sarah in a tone that I hoped she would interpret as "Sorry, I screwed up."

"I don't know. I really don't know," she said. "This is not good. I'm tired and I just want to get some rest, so you'd better figure this out quickly."

The hotel was in a residential area, and the only other sign of life was the small Chinese restaurant next door.

"I'm going to go next door and see if they can call a taxi for us. I think we should just go back to Geneva and try to find a hotel room by the train station," I said.

I walked into the small Chinese restaurant that was mostly empty and appeared to be closing up for the night. The smell of the restaurant was incredible, and my stomach sprang to life. I walked up to the front counter, and to my surprise, the first words that came out of my mouth were not "Can you please call me a taxicab?" but "Sweet and sour chicken with fried rice, please."

The woman smiled at me and walked back into the kitchen to tell the cooks to stop cleaning up and turn the stove back on again. I paid the woman with my credit card, since Sarah had the Swiss Francs that we had taken out of the ATM at the airport. I walked back to find Sarah while the food was being cooked.

"Are they calling us a taxi?" asked Sarah.

"Uh, yes, it is on its way," I said, flat-out lying.

The incredible smell of the Chinese restaurant had distracted me to the point that I had completely forgotten about my original purpose for walking into the restaurant. While I was gone, Sarah had called just about every hotel listed in our guidebook to find that every place was completely booked or so far out of our price range that sleeping on a bus bench was justified.

"It does not look good," she said. "I have called every hotel I can find in Geneva, and they are all booked for the night."

Little did I know that this was just her setup for what she was about to tell me. "I did find one place that has room," she said.

"Great, let's go there," I said hopefully.

"It is a hostel, though," she said.

"A hostel? A youth hostel? No, I am not staying at a youth hostel," I said.

I was now picturing in my mind the bunk bed-style dormitory atmosphere that I swore I would never stay at again. "I'm over thirty! Only dirty, old men over the age of thirty sleep in youth hostels. No way."

"Then you find a place for us to stay," Sarah said.

Luckily, I was looking up, and at the last second, I was able to avoid the small but dense travel guidebook that quickly approached my head, just missing me and producing a loud bang as it smacked the wall behind me, causing the Italian couple to look over at us once again and laugh.

"Fine, I will just suck it up and spend the night at a youth hostel. I'm going next door to see how much longer until the taxi will be here," I said as I stormed out the door, shaking my head and mumbling under my breath, "Stupid youth hostel."

I could feel the Italian couple following me with their eyes as I walked straight into the glass doors, forgetting to push the security unlock button first.

"*Shit!*"

I entered the restaurant and asked the kind woman if she could please call a taxi for us. She called the taxi, and within a minute, the taxi was out in front. Sarah waved at me to tell me that the taxi was here, as she struggled to carry all the bags. I just stood there and looked at her. I couldn't do anything; the food was not ready yet. The driver helped Sarah put the bags in the trunk, and she was sitting in the backseat.

I could only imagine what she was thinking, sitting in the back of the taxicab looking out at me, wondering why I was still standing in the Chinese restaurant. *I really hope she does not tell the driver to drive away and leave me standing here,* I thought.

The food came, and I thanked the woman again for her help and ran out the door.

"You're getting food as I am sitting in here waiting for you. And let me take the time to remind you that I am doing all the work in finding us a place to sleep for the night. How is it that you are still hungry, and why would you want Chinese food in France, the land of the culinary experience?" Sarah said.

"Well, you know me. I can always eat," I said.

Sarah and I sat in silence as we passed through the checkpoint that was by then completely deserted and drove back into Geneva. The taxi driver had the radio on and was softly singing all the words to a popular English rock song. I was impressed that he could sing all the words to the song perfectly. The taxi driver pulled up in front of the youth hostel and kept singing and tapping the steering wheel while pointing to the meter.

I handed him some Swiss Francs and waited for him to give us back the difference. He looked at the money, looked back at me, and said, "My English is no good," pointing to the meter and then to the Swiss Francs while he kept on saying "no."

"What is he trying to say?" Sarah asked as she looked at me.

"I don't know," I said.

The driver was now using his hands to try to communicate, but it was only adding to the confusion. His voice and tone were starting to get louder, and the only thing I thought to do was to give him more money; maybe we had not given him enough. I handed him another Swiss Franc note, but he just handed it right back. The game of charades continued, and we were not getting anywhere. How was it that he could sing all the words to a song in perfect English but spoke no English himself?

The driver appeared to be getting angrier, and I was starting to think that it was going to turn into a real fight. He picked up his radio and spoke French into it very quickly. A few seconds later, a voice spoke in English.

"The driver is more than happy to accept your Swiss Francs but does not have the small change owed to you."

The problem was almost comical and a big relief. We had originally been driven to the hotel, just over the border by a Swiss taxi driver who had no problem giving us change in Swiss Francs, but a French taxi driver had driven us back into Switzerland. Since France used the Euro, he had no Swiss Francs to give us as change. He wanted to give us what amounted to fifty cents in change, because taxi drivers in Europe never expected a tip.

"Keep it, please," I said to the driver.

He smiled and said, "Merci!"

We entered the youth hostel, and Sarah went to check us into our room as I found a small table and dove into the Chinese food. Sarah appeared to be arguing with the youth hostel clerk. We were not doing a very good job of making friends on this trip. Sarah finally walked over with the key in her hand.

"This is the best Chinese food I have ever had," I said.

"That's wonderful. I'm so happy for you," she said sweetly. Her unexpected reply and over-the-top and completely unnecessary niceness meant something was up. "There is a small problem with the room."

Sarah went on to explain that the only room they had available was on an all-girls floor. However, there was only one girl in the room, and we could go up and ask her if she would mind if I also stayed in the room. We went up to the room, but the girl was not there. We went down to the front desk and were told that she probably stepped out for a little bit and would be back soon. We waited for an hour, but the girl had still not returned. We decided to get into bed and try to rest while we waited. If the girl returned to her room and said no to me staying there, we would have to leave and find another place to stay, no matter what time she returned home.

I took the top bunk and sat in the darkness, wondering how I had somehow ended up at a youth hostel.

"Good night, Sarah, my little bunkmate. I love you," I said.

"Maybe you should just hide under the covers when the girl comes in, and I will do all the talking," she said.

Just as I was about to fall into a deep sleep, all the lights came on. I hid under the covers and looked at my watch. It was two o'clock in the morning.

Sarah greeted the woman, who smelled like she had just completed a marathon of drinking. She was a young American student with an obviously drunken slur to her words. She said she had no problem with me being in the room.

"Suuuurrrreeee, nooooo problem."

Upon hearing this, I poked my head out from under the covers like a groundhog. "Thanks, I really appreciate it."

The girl spent the next hour packing her bags, with a quick trip to the bathroom to throw up. She finally turned off the lights at three o'clock in the morning. We were awakened at five o'clock in the morning by the sound of her alarm, as she woke up and went through the same process she had completed only two hours before—packing and throwing up in the bathroom.

I just love youth hostels, I thought, as I stuck my head out to check on my bunkmate below. The girl walked out the door and closed it behind her with a loud bang.

By seven o'clock, we were comfortably sitting in our seats, waiting for the train to leave the station. Our eyes were red from lack of sleep. We would be spending just about the entire day on the train traveling from one side of the country to the other. We had to take a train from Geneva to Chur and then transfer to another train that would take us the rest of the way to St. Moritz. The train finally pulled out of the station, and we made our way out of the city center. For the first half hour of the trip, the train traveled along the edge of Lake Geneva, occasionally giving us beautiful views of the lake.

Switzerland was a landlocked, alpine country overflowing with beautiful scenery both in the winter and summer months. When I thought of Switzerland, the first picture that came to mind was not one of a sailing-crazed country, but Switzerland was then the holder of the most prestigious and historical sailing trophy, the America's Cup, and was the first landlocked country to win the cup. The Swiss-owned boat *Alinghi* took advantage of the removal of the nationality rule, which required that all crew members be nationals of the challenging syndicate, and hired some of the best sailors in the world—a bunch of New Zealanders—and in what many consider an act of disloyalty to their own country, the Swiss boat *Alinghi* soundly defeated Team New Zealand in 2003 to win the cup. Since Lake Geneva was too small to host the race, Switzerland chose to defend its title in waters along the coast of Spain. In 2007, Switzerland was successfully able to defend its title, defeating Team New Zealand again.

The rhythmic sound of the train was putting us to sleep. Just as I was about to drift off, the train came to a stop. I woke Sarah up and pointed out the window. Not far away was the unmistakable, large, blue and yellow industrial warehouse building of IKEA. We seemed to be in the middle of nowhere, and the only thing in sight was the obnoxious-looking IKEA building. A few people boarded the train with large flat pack, IKEA boxes and bags. The train kept going, and all the IKEA passengers got off at the next stop.

Switzerland's neighboring countries heavily influence the culture of Switzerland. German is spoken by the majority of the country, followed by

French, Italian, and Romansch. Traveling around Switzerland is very easy, because many people also speak very good English, especially anyone who works in the transportation or tourism industry. We were never sure whether we should be saying *danke, merci, grazie,* or even thank you. As the train made its way from Geneva to Chur all the way on the other side of the country, the announcements made at each stop were made first in French, then in German, then in English, and finally in Italian. As we got closer to the Austrian side of the country, the train announcements changed to German first, and then English, followed by Italian and French.

St. Moritz is known as a pricey, glitzy, fashionable place to see and be seen and as an outdoor playground for jet-setting, Chanel-toting Europeans. It was a place where polo was played on the snow-covered, frozen Lake St. Moritz during the winter while the sun shone over three hundred days a year. The sun was shining, and I was starting to get anxious while the workers at the ski rental place seemed to be moving at a snail's pace, mostly due to being hungover from the night before, it seemed. Since there are mountains within an hour's journey of just about every town and city in Switzerland, the Swiss don't have any excuse for not all being world-class skiers.

"Can't they go any quicker? It is a perfect day. We need to get out there!" I said.

"Settle down. No need to be the ugly American," Sarah said.

We finally completed the ski rental process, and with skis in hand, we made our way up to the chairlift, enjoying the beautiful panoramic mountain scenery. We laughed at the matching blue jackets and black snow pants that we were wearing.

"Oh, no. We are that couple!" Sarah said with a laugh.

The thin, bitterly cold, mountain air whipped across our faces as we made our first descent down the steep mountain slope. It felt great to be flying down the mountain through the light white powder while the sun baked our cheeks, giving them a healthy glow. I made it down to the bottom first and looked up to see where Sarah was. It took a full minute before I spotted the small speck of her blue jacket way up on the mountain; she appeared to be trying to put her skis on after a fall. She finally made it down to the bottom.

"Wow, that was amazing! The snow is really deep, and that run was really steep. I fell three times. Let's do it again!" Sarah said, as she brushed the snow from her jacket.

Sarah was a great skier, and I enjoyed skiing with her. In the beginning, I would follow her down the mountain so I could help her up in case she fell. She had hated that I did that, and we had worked out a system: she would follow me, and I would have to trust her that she could make it down on her own. There were not many ski runs that Sarah would not ski down, so we had always been able to enjoy skiing together on the tougher, more advanced ski runs. As a couple, we enjoyed skiing and exercising together, and it seemed to form a bond that drew us together. Just before we had gotten married, Sarah and I had run a half marathon together, and we had enjoyed the training runs each morning in anticipation for the big race. It was an emotional moment when we had crossed the finish line together.

It was a marvelous day of skiing, and we were exhausted by the afternoon. We spent the evening having a stereotypical fondue dinner at a restaurant. We were still in our ski boots, and the restaurant owner's large family sat next to us at a large table enjoying dinner together. After dinner we walked through the heart of St. Moritz, passing luxury hotels, art galleries, and high-end boutiques, while dodging the occasional Ferrari whose driver was brave enough to try to navigate through the icy, snow-packed streets—or maybe he was just drunk. We passed many people in the streets, who were dressed from head to toe in fur coats, hats, and boots; most of them spoke Russian. Our hotel was on the other side of town in an area called St Moritz Bad. We found the name funny, because it was a far less glamorous and industrial area where the locals lived.

The next morning, we were sore from the prior day's skiing and decided that because we would have many other days of skiing during the week, we would take the day off. We spent the day exploring and riding the small mountain trams and trains around the area. At night, we dined at a pizza place that allowed patrons to bring their dogs with them.

"Too bad we don't have Sydney with us," Sarah said, as she secretly dropped another piece of pepperoni on the floor for the large Burmese mountain dog sitting under the table of the couple next to us.

"We should hurry up—I don't want to be late," I said to Sarah, as I gave the waiter the universal sign for "check, please." I was excited because it was my turn to choose the night's activity, and I knew exactly what I wanted to do.

Just down the street and on the edge of the lake sat the St. Moritz hockey rink. I had never seen an ice rink like it, because it was an outdoor hockey rink. Even though it was freezing cold outside, Sarah had agreed to attend and "be a good sport about it." We brought a blanket with us from our hotel and stood in the stands huddled together.

My two brothers and I had been raised at a hockey rink. Every winter, our father had built us an ice rink out of the snow in the backyard, where we would spend long winter nights playing, arguing, and fighting while we tried not to break any of our neighbors' windows with a flying hockey puck.

The stands were packed with all the St. Moritz locals who were not working that night, as their local professional hockey team was playing a team from the next train stop away. It was a wonderful atmosphere there with the locals, who held banners and shook cowbells as we cheered for the home team under the bright stars above the snow-capped mountains, which completed my vision of heaven on earth.

We joined the locals during intermission in drinking warm glug wine and warming up our frozen bodies before heading back out for the next period. During stoppage of play, loud American music blared from the loudspeakers, and the crowd danced along to the music to stay warm, and also because many were getting drunk from all the warm wine. The game ended with a St. Moritz victory, and we headed back to the hotel for a dip in the hotel hot tub and sauna.

Our bodies were tired and sore from skiing the day before, and we looked forward to spending an hour soaking in the warm water of the hot tub. The water was relaxing, and we occasionally jumped into the pool to cool down and then got back into the hot tub. I was in a state of pure relaxation with my eyes closed as the water jets massaged my aching back.

I felt Sarah kick my legs under the water, and I opened my eyes to see her motioning to the other side of the pool. There right in front of us and in front of all the other people at the pool a woman who had just exited the pool had proceeded to take her bathing suit completely off, and was standing at the pool's edge, drying herself while completely naked. Sarah and I both gave a small giggle and shook our heads. We seemed to be the only people to notice what this woman was doing.

We decided to end our spa experience with a few minutes in the sauna. We could not see who or how many people were in the sauna, but when we opened the door, the steam quickly escaped out the door that I held open with a deer-in-headlights look on my face, as Sarah nudged me forward and into the sauna. The sauna was not very big and could only hold about eight people. We sat down, and I immediately focused my eyes on the floor. We had joined a group of three middle-aged men, who were completely naked, facing three teenage girls in bathing suits. We sat down in the middle.

I thought to myself, *It is considered a crime to completely expose yourself to a group of teenage girls in the United States, and it could get you put on the sex offenders list.* Once again, Sarah and I seemed to be the only ones noticing the awkwardness of the situation. After about a minute of sitting in silence with my eyes completely focused on my feet, I got up the courage to say to Sarah, "It's hot in here. I think I have had enough." I got up from the wooden bench and walked out the door.

The night's spa experience was very awkward, and I could not stop thinking about it. *Why was it such a big deal? Why do we Americans blush at the mention of the word sex? Why do we Americans immediately associate nudity with sex?* The sight of the naked body means sex to Americans and is a big reason why guys feel they sometimes have to gay bash in the locker room, because they want all the other men standing around, also naked, to know that they are not thinking about sex.

Even a guy wearing a Speedo bathing suit in America is viewed as gay or European. I would be a hypocrite if I did not admit that I did not wear a Speedo bathing suit for that reason. Denis and I enjoyed starting some of our mornings by swimming a few laps at a local pool before class, and I was usually the only one not wearing a Speedo at the pool.

One day, Denis jokingly said to me, "You know, people here laugh at you for wearing that American bathing suit." He said it jokingly, but I could tell there was some truth to it. When Denis left his bathing suit at a hotel, I had offered him one of mine that was brand new and still had the tags on it. I did not like the bathing suit; I had never worn it; and I was planning on getting rid of it. Denis had thanked me but said no, and we had stopped at a store so he could buy a new Speedo on our way to the pool that day.

Who doesn't like to be naked? Americans, I guessed. If I ever had to travel to Finland for work, I would have to remember to pack a bathing suit, because it was perfectly normal to discuss business in the sauna in accordance with the regional custom—nude.

After our week of skiing, it was time to make our way back to Geneva for the flight to London. Sarah and I slept in a little bit longer than planned and missed the train we had wanted to take back to Geneva by seconds, so we were left waiting on the platform for an hour until the next train came. At first, the platforms were empty. Over the next half hour, the platform directly on the other side of the train tracks filled up with what looked like military soldiers.

I was surprised to learn that along with Austria, Denmark, Finland, Sweden, Germany, Greece, and Norway, Switzerland requires every able-bodied man between the ages of twenty and thirty-six to complete 260 days of basic military training. According to our travel guidebook, Switzerland had the largest militia army in the world. I had thought that the only military Switzerland had is the Vatican Swiss Guard. Many European countries required military service, but individuals could opt out of it and instead complete 390 days of community service.

The young men looked more like a fraternity traveling to a bachelor party. Just about all of the men were smoking cigarettes and holding either a case of beer or a couple bottles of wine in one hand and a duffel bag in the other, with large assault rifles slung over their shoulders. The train the soldiers appeared to be waiting for finally pulled into the station, and once they had all boarded the train, it departed. Seconds later, a dozen or so men in uniform came sprinting down the platform also carrying beer and wine, just missing the train. They did not seem too concerned as they sat down and lit cigarettes, appearing to be happy to sit there and wait for the next train.

"So, that is what that wine bottle opener is for on the Swiss Army knife. And why do the Swiss need an army? An evil tyrant would never invade Switzerland. Without Switzerland, he would have no place to hide his money," I said.

In March of 2007, the Swiss army accidentally invaded Liechtenstein. Two hundred soldiers accidentally wandered a mile over the unmarked border and into Liechtenstein. I really hoped it was not our friends from the train station.

- Chapter Twelve -

Partner Up

✦

It wasn't just an ordinary Friday, but one of the best Fridays most males wish for. It was Friday, March 17—one of those rare treats when St. Patrick's Day falls on a Friday. Back in Chicago, the river would be filled with green vegetable oil, making it a vibrant green color in celebration of the holiday.

The computer lab at school was completely empty—a rare sight, even for a Friday. Just about all the undergraduate American students had found cheap flights to Dublin so they could celebrate the holiday with the Irish. Most of them did not have a place to stay for the weekend and would end up sleeping in a park or a train station. That sounds awful at age thirty, but at twenty, it sounds like the time of your life.

I returned home to get Sydney and start celebrating the holiday myself. Sydney stretched her legs as she started her standard routine of looking both ways down the street before stepping down from the front steps. She gave a small bark of acknowledgment as I turned around to see who had opened the front door of the building.

"Hello, Garrett. Hello, Sydney. You all right?"

"Hello, Gareth," I said. It was the building porter and our next-door neighbor. The name Garrett is unheard of in the United Kingdom, but Gareth is a common name.

"Happy St. Patrick's Day!" I said as Sydney sniffed Gareth's legs. Gareth was a great cook, and some of the most amazing-smelling food came from his apartment, filling the hallways, driving Sydney crazy, and requiring a stop by his door so Sydney could get a good sniff of whatever meat he was cooking that week. In true English tradition, Gareth "minded his own business" and never asked us a lot of personal questions, even though I could tell he was incredibly curious about the young American couple and their dog living right next door to him. Most of our daily conversations had something to do with the weather. We were slowly feeding him answers about us—not too quickly, so we would not somehow appear to be bragging by telling him everything about us, but just enough so he did not think we were drug dealers. Just the week before, I had finally told him that I was a graduate student, satisfying his desire to know why Sarah left the home dressed in her professional work clothes while I seemed to spend most of my days in jeans and T-shirts.

"Are you and your partner celebrating today?" Gareth asked.

"Yes, she is still at work, but Sydney and I are off to the pub to get a start on the weekend," I said. Sydney had decided it was safe to proceed off the front steps, and down the street we went.

Upon arriving in London, Sarah and I had quickly discovered that many pubs allow dogs to join their owners inside—even pubs that served food. Often when we asked the bartender at a pub if they allowed dogs, the answer was delivered in a tone that suggested we were stupid for asking the question: "Yeah, we allow dogs, but there is a two-drink minimum for them!" Being allowed to take man's best friend to the pub was one of the greatest experiences in the world. If you couldn't find a drinking partner, you could bring your four-legged friend. The girls loved to stroke Sydney's soft coat, and who was going to start a fight with a guy who had a dog with him? If I drank too much and could not remember how to get home, Sydney knew the way.

As Sydney and I made our way to the pub, I thought about Gareth referring to Sarah as "my partner." That was not the first time someone had referred to Sarah as "my partner"; it was a common occurrence. Upon arriving in England, it was difficult to get used to having people refer to Sarah as "my partner" rather than as my wife. For Americans, the phrase has been reserved to refer to a same-sex couple. Many Europeans choose not to get married and instead live together as a traditional married couple would.

At school, I was often asked about "my partner," and I made a fool of myself by telling a school office administrator, "No, I do not have a partner. I don't know where you heard that, but I will have to tell my wife about it," when first asked.

Many Europeans view marriage as a religious commitment, and since many Europeans have lost interest in religion, they do not see the need to walk down the aisle. Since everyone in the United Kingdom receives health insurance and other benefits provided by the government, there is not really much of a financial incentive, other than sharing everyday living expenses under one roof together. If Sarah and I were not legally married, I would not have been eligible to be covered under her health insurance, and I would have had no health insurance at the time. Over the year, Sarah and I met many people who had children with their partners but were not married and didn't think it was necessary. Even people who had had a partner for ten years and had children with that partner and were with a new partner and having more children with the new partner.

Because of the use of the term "partner," Americans view Europeans as being more gay-friendly. Gays and lesbians are not in the streets of Europe protesting for some of the rights they are excluded from in the United States because they are not legally or technically married. During slow news weeks, some of the European papers filled space with stories about anti-cohabitation laws in a few select states in the United States, such as Michigan and North Dakota, where cohabitation is considered a sex crime. Some states have those laws to prevent fraud but never enforce them, but from the perspective of an outsider looking in who believes that all laws are strictly enforced in the United States, they conjure up an interesting picture of American culture.

Dog Days at the Pub

From the direction we were walking, Sydney figured out that we were heading to one of our favorite pubs. She made all the correct turns and walked us straight into the front door. It was late afternoon, and most people were still at work, so the pub was not too crowded.

Any travel guidebook will tell you that the pub is an important part of the English life and culture, and without a doubt, it is true. It is impossible to truly understand what it means to be British without spending some serious time in a pub. Seventy-five percent of the adult population visited the pubs, and a good proportion of those were considered regulars. The pub was considered a second home to many residents and was frequented by people of all ages, education levels, incomes, occupations, and social classes. I was surprised to see older men and women socializing with friends late into the night on Sunday nights, enjoying one another's company and conversation.

The pub was one of the few places in England where you could purchase something without having to wait in a queue, leaving it up to the bartender to keep the invisible queue in his head. Tipping was absolutely not required or expected, so leaving a tip would not move you up in the invisible queue. There was usually no waiter service at the pub, so you had to make a trip up to the bar to purchase a drink. It was interesting to watch foreigners come in and sit at a table for a considerable amount of time, waiting for a waiter to take their drink order, before walking up to the bar in frustration. The pub was also one of the few places where it was considered socially acceptable to start a conversation with a complete stranger.

The pub was a place where I had had many fascinating and sometimes heated conversations with friends and complete strangers. The pub was also one of the places that I had heard many anti-American remarks. Surprisingly, the comments usually come from the mouths of fellow Americans. It seemed like we Americans felt that the quickest way to make friends was to walk into an English pub and sprinkle our conversations with complete strangers with negative comments about America and put-downs about George Bush or other government officials. A good majority of the comments seem to come from American students backpacking through Europe or studying abroad. Feeling insecure about traveling far from home and wanting to make friends with the locals quickly, this tactic seemed to be very successful and almost always found a willing listener.

I never heard any Europeans openly say negative things about their countries' people or governments. Throughout Europe in cafés, bars, and restaurants, we often heard Americans saying to Europeans, "We're Americans, but blue state Americans." Europe is probably the biggest blue state, and sharing this personal voting preference somehow made it acceptable to be in Europe, since those who claimed it felt they were not responsible for any negative feelings Europeans may have had about Americans or America. We Americans liked to think of Europeans as being sophisticated, cosmopolitan, and international-minded, and Europeans liked to hear this from us and liked to see themselves that way. But anyone who had spent a considerable time living in Europe would know that it was not entirely true.

I sat down at an empty table while Sydney sniffed the floor and enjoyed the attention she was receiving from those sitting near the table. Next to me, a group of young adults were telling stories about their "gap year" experience. It was a common ritual for young adults to take a year off from school before going to college and spend the year traveling abroad, usually completing some sort of community service. The experience was meant to help transition students into being more mature and reliable adults before they moved out of their parents' homes and into college dorms.

That life-learning experience was something I wished would catch on in the United States. It would probably lower the number of freshman students dropping out of school because they could not handle the transition to being on their own once their parents dropped them off at college and pulled away from the curb.

Prince William had spent his gap year volunteering in Chile and teaching English, as well as visiting African countries where he had worked on a dairy farm, getting up before dawn each morning to milk the cows.

While I enjoyed my first pint of Guinness in celebration of St. Patrick's Day, I opened the newspaper that had been left on the table. Earlier in the week, Britain had passed a milestone anniversary—the tenth anniversary of a tragic and violent day in the country's history. On March 13, 1996, a misfit named Thomas Hamilton had walked into the school gym of Dunblane Primary School just after nine thirty in the morning with four handguns and proceeded to kill or wound everyone in the gym. He had continued his shooting spree outside on the playground before returning to the gym and killing himself. Sixteen schoolchildren and one teacher were killed. Within days of the massacre, 750,000 people signed a petition to ban handguns in Britain. Britain had already banned assault weapons after a previous school shooting. There is a low murder rate per capita, and many police officers do not carry guns—it is true.

Many people in the United Kingdom do not understand why guns have not been banned in the United States, and I was often asked about our American gun culture. "Did I own a gun? Had I ever shot a gun? Is it true you can walk into a bank and get a gun for doing business with them?"— the last question arose from Europeans seeing Michael Moore's 2002 movie *Bowling for Columbine*. No, yes, and no were my replies. Michael Moore was hugely popular in Europe, but while American critics have done a good and fair job of demonstrating his misrepresentations, Europeans seem to believe everything they see and hear in his movies as unquestionable fact.

Numerous articles about the United States gun culture could be found in newspapers across Europe. Much of the reporting focused on "stand your ground laws" and "take guns to work laws." These self-defense laws in the United States have mostly come out of states like Florida. "Isn't George Bush's brother the president of Florida?" was commonly asked of me during discussions of those law proposals. Articles with creative illustrations showed the large disparity in the number of guns that the United States exports each year to around the world.

The news covered various American groups floating the idea of cutting down school shootings by allowing all students to carry guns on college campuses. If someone started shooting, another student could just pause his iPod for a minute, pull out a gun from his bag, and shoot the troublemaker himself. Problem solved. The argument of solving gun violence with more guns was a tough one to find any kind of ground to defend.

I was asked, "How many times do school shootings need to happen before you Americans finally get it?" My response to such questions was that unfortunately the Second Amendment to the United States Constitution is one of the most misinterpreted sections of that document, and as a result, it made gun control very difficult because of the deep-pocketed pro-gun lobby groups in the United States. It was very difficult to change laws and nearly impossible to disarm American citizens, who loved their guns more than their neighbors. Hearing that the interpretation of the Second Amendment had divided Americans for decades and that there were a large number of citizens who favored stricter gun laws, if not a ban on guns altogether, seemed to provide a side of the argument that they had never heard, because the Europeans had assumed that all Americans felt the same way.

Europeans love to debate issues, especially politics. If you are an American who is fortunate enough to walk into a pub in England someday, please don't feel like you have to bad-mouth America just to break the ice and make some new friends. Just walk in with an open mind and start a conversation with someone standing at the bar.

If you feel like you need to tell an anti-American joke to win them over, tell them you have discovered where the Iraqi weapons of mass destruction have been hidden all this time. Tell them they have been found in the Budweiser factory back in America and are being used to make some of the most boring but well-advertised beer in the world. They love the joke. I know because they used it on me many times.

- Chapter Thirteen -

A Fool in April

✦

It was Saturday, the first day of April, and it was imperative that Sarah and I be mentally sharp and question everything with severe suspicion. A BBC program had announced that David Beckham would not be playing for England in the World Cup later in the year, because it had been discovered that his parents were Scottish. One of the largest English newspapers ran a story claiming that the famous front door at Number 10 Downing Street that had been traditionally painted black for 270 years, had been painted red by Tony Blair's orders—shocking revelations, but all in good fun because it was April Fools' Day.

Suddenly, there was a knock at the front door.

"Make sure you see who it is," I said to Sarah, "and question everything they say with suspicion. We don't want these Brits pulling the wool over our eyes today."

We slowly opened the door just enough for Sydney to stick her nose out to sniff the air. Her tail started to wag vigorously, banging against the wall as it swooped back and forth, signaling that it was a friend and not a foe. We opened the door, and there standing in the hall was my older brother Eric.

"Hello! You found us!" I said as I extended an arm to give him a welcome hug. It was funny to see Eric with his fashionable, bed head-style haircut, trendy square-rimmed glasses, and black shirt with a large spit-up stain just below the shoulder.

Eric and his wife Ingrid, along with their five-month-old daughter Anya, had flown over from San Francisco for a couple of days in London before heading to Norway to spend Easter with Ingrid's family. They had rented a nice two-bedroom place a street over from us that backed up to a large, private garden twice the size of our neighborhood garden and nearly the size of two football fields.

We spent the day with them, strolling through Kensington Gardens and Hyde Park and enjoying the warm spring sunshine. Eric and Ingrid had brought their ultrahip, Bugaboo stroller that was on the must-have list for most of the residents in Central London, because it was the only baby stroller—or pram as the English call it—to be seen with while cruising the streets of the upscale area. A dream of Sarah's and mine was to someday stroll through Kensington Gardens and Hyde Park with Sydney and a baby of our own in a stroller. Fulfillment of the dream was still in the future, but we didn't let the chance go by to cruise the park with their blue Bugaboo stroller passing by the red, yellow, maroon, and green Bugaboo strollers.

Even though Eric and Ingrid had both been to London many times, they still loved the experience of a nice morning walk through the bustling Portobello Road Market with a large cup of warm coffee in hand. So, the next morning we took Anya on her first ride on the Tube and joined the large mass of people traveling to the market.

After a nice, late morning breakfast in Notting Hill with Eric, Ingrid, and Anya, Sarah and I said good-bye and headed to the Tube station to make our way to the first and most significant event in London's social calendar—a national treasure event that attracted a quarter of a million attendees and was seen by hundreds of millions on television around the world and simply goes by the name The Boat Race.

Row, Row, Row Your Boat

The social season in London officially began in spring and lasted late into summer. Historically, the social season was a time for the socially and politically elite of society to hold dinner parties, charity events, debutante balls, and weddings. When we were there, the social season featured large corporate-sponsored events that include sports, art, music, and culture, such as the Chelsea Flower Show, The Proms performances, the Royal Ascot Horse Races, the Edinburgh Fringe Festival, the royal celebration of Trooping the Colour, Wimbledon, the Lord's Cricket Test Match, and as the first event of the new year, The Boat Race.

The race brings together two all-world, academic goliaths, Oxford and Cambridge, to battle it out for the rights to be called "the fastest at going backward." The Boat Race is a time-honored event in England in which the two schools field teams of eight rowers—not just any rowers but some of the best in the world, many of them Olympic gold-medalist rowers. Each selected participant must be a student at the university for which he or she races. For many months prior to the event, the teams wake up hours before the sun rises to train. The rowers are not always English-born citizens; they are also from other countries such as France, Canada, and even the United States. A quarter of a million people line the banks of the Thames in London and millions more in England and around the world watch the event live on television, making it the most-watched amateur sporting event in the world.

The first race was held in 1829, when two friends who were attending the two colleges challenged each other to a race on the river. A large crowd watched the race; the race was repeated the following year; and the tradition of the year's previous loser challenging the winner to a rematch was started. Being selected to participate in the race was an enormous and intense honor that carried high pressure. The Boat Race had been held 151 times, with Cambridge holding a slight overall series lead, with 78 wins to 72. Surprisingly, there had even been a tie.

Oxford had been victorious the previous year, so it was the defending champion coming into the race. The members of each team traditionally rowed in blue uniforms, with Oxford in dark blue and Cambridge in light blue. Men had always dominated the event as the source of the muscle in the boats, but in 1981, Sue Brown had become the first woman to participate; she was Oxford's coxswain, or the person who steers the boat and screams out instructions to the rowers, keeping them rowing in unison.

Sarah and I exited the train at the Putney Bridge Tube station and followed the crowds toward the river, since we did not know where to go. The pubs were packed, and it seemed as though we were the only ones walking down the street without a case of beer or wine under one arm. As we approached the river, we made our way through the crowds, which had the appearance of a large group of Ralph Lauren-dressed, Ivy League college students tailgating in preparation for the event. The atmosphere of the large crowd was exciting and reminded me of being at a large college football event—the air was filled with the smell of beer, hot dogs, and burgers cooking on grills. We squeezed ourselves into one of the many small pubs that lined the river and situated ourselves on a large patio looking out along the shore of the river.

The two boats race upstream, with the official start time of an hour before the day's official high-water level of the incoming flood tide. The morning sunshine had given way to overcast, grey skies, and a steady stream of rain began to pour. A strong wind had also kicked up, making the conditions miserable. The soft rain quickly turned into a downpour, and the people who had arrived hours earlier to stake out spots on the patio gave up their precious positions and pushed their ways into the overcrowded pub. Seizing the opportunity, a few brave individuals opened their umbrellas and grabbed spots in the front of the patio. Sarah and I looked at each other, knowing what the other was thinking.

"Let's do it," she said, and we pushed our way back out onto the patio. With pints of beer in hand, we, too, grabbed a spot in the front of the patio and tried to stay dry, which required holding the umbrella sideways, as the rain hit us from a strange side angle.

Unfortunately, the start of the race was not for another hour. In between the time we claimed our highly desired real estate and the time we actually saw the boats pass by in front of us, we experienced all the best and the worst of English weather—even the English rain while the sun was still shining. The wind had turned the river to an ugly brown, mud color, with good-size waves crashing up against the shoreline. Normally, conditions like those would have resulted in any monumental international race being postponed, but The Boat Race would go on, no matter what the conditions.

It was hard to tell what exactly was going on with the race. Had the race started? Who was winning? When would the boats go by?

We had formed a bond with the other brave souls who had also stood in the rain for the front row view, and they made sure to include us when pushing their way back inside for another round of pints so we would not lose our space. Our new friends told us to watch all the helicopters in the distance hovering above the river; as the helicopters came closer, we would know the boats were approaching.

The rain stopped again, the sun shone down just long enough for us to see the two boats pass us by at an amazing speed, and the crowd let out a deafening roar, cheering them on. A large army of speedboats full of cameras, judges, and coaches followed shortly behind them in their wake. American Jake Wetzel, an Olympic silver medalist, stroked the water with his oar vigorously and in rhythm with the other rowers in his boat, who appeared to have a slight lead over Cambridge. Within twenty seconds of the boats finally coming into view, they both turned past a bend in the river and were out of sight.

"Now what?" I said to Sarah.

All of a sudden, our highly cherished and well-earned spot on the outside patio had become the worst spot; the rain began to pour down, and we were far away from all the televisions in the pub that everyone had rushed inside to watch as the race ended.

A few minutes later, a roar exploded from inside the pub as Oxford crossed the finish line first, five lengths ahead and winner of The 152nd Boat Race. Oxford had won, because the team had decided, during the race, to install a pump to remove the water that was collecting in the boat from the rain and waves—a move that was legal and brought up questions as to why Cambridge had not done the same.

Sarah and I were soaked, and the pints of beer were no longer keeping us warm. It felt like an incredible amount of standing around for just twenty seconds of excitement, and a warm shower was starting to sound really nice.

Voulez Diriger le Marathon de Paris

Eric's arrival in London also signaled the end, as it meant that I was out of time to train for the first of three marathons I was planning to run during the year. The next weekend, Eric traveled with me to Paris to cheer me on as I ran through the streets of Paris in the Paris Marathon.

We arrived early in the morning and laughed together as the locals cut in front of us and all the other tourists while we waited in line to buy tickets for the metro. It was obvious that the English tradition of orderly queuing in line had not caught on in France. The French had probably made line-cutting a part of everyday life just to be completely different from the English. It was also unusual to see French people buying tickets, because it seemed they preferred to ride for free under the theme of "public transportation is the right of the people"—often hopping over the unmanned turnstiles without paying, while tourists struggled to figure out which way to stick their fully paid tickets into the turnstile to gain entry to the train platforms.

The sound of French being spoken was marvelous and intoxicating, even when it is spoken by someone who was trying to sell you used train tickets that have no value, at a huge discount, as a man was trying to do to Eric and me. Every time, I traveled to Paris, that happened as soon as I arrived, so even though I appreciated the encounter, I declined the offer with a smile. *Why didn't I make more of an effort to learn French when I had the chance?* I thought.

By then, even the French people who had cut in line were starting to complain about the large number of people cutting in front of them, causing us all to move backward in line instead of forward. Since my first trip to France, I had developed a love-love-hate relationship with the French. For every two things that I loved and admired about France and the French people, I found something that made me just shake my head.

It was a beautiful morning to be in Paris. We decided to spend the day walking the streets of the city, enjoying the beautiful scenery of the extra wide boulevards that were lined with buildings of significant cultural importance and iconic status. We walked along the river Seine, stopping at the Eiffel Tower to take a quick picture of the two us to send to Mom and Dad before continuing along the river. We stopped for an occasional cup of coffee at one of the floating bars or cafés and watched the tourist boats pass by on the river.

It was really nice to have Eric there with me. We had both been to the must-see tourist stops many times, so instead of stepping inside of the Louvre or Notre Dame Cathedral to view the wonders, we simply appreciated the beautiful landmarks as a scenic backdrop for two brothers, who did not get to see each other very often, to spend some time catching up on each other's lives. Eric and I walked and walked and then walked some more, which we followed up with more walking.

"Hey, hold on, Eric, I'm the one running the marathon tomorrow, and my feet are starting to get a little tired," I finally said, motioning that it was time to do more people watching while sitting in a café rather than being the people that those sitting in cafés were watching.

We ended the day with a late dinner at an out-of-this-world, trendy restaurant that Eric knew about and was hidden down a small street. I had not given in to Eric's attempts to get me to have at least one glass of wine with him while in Paris, but it was getting tough. The wine he was drinking smelled so good and would have gone so well with the duck I was eating.

"Come on, don't be such a baby! I bet you more than half the field of French runners are sitting at home right now drinking wine. It's like Gatorade for them," Eric said, as he poured me a glass. The wine was delicious, and one small glass turned into two.

I knew I was in trouble the next morning when the alarm was going off and the last thing I felt like doing was getting out of bed and putting on my running shoes. My legs and feet were actually sore from all the walking we had done the day before, and the two glasses of wine did not help the cause either.

"I'm going to go with you and watch the beginning of the race, and then I'm going to head over to Starbucks to do some work. I will meet you at the finish line, and then we can walk around some more," Eric said in an tone that said "I'm glad I'm not you."

Starbucks had invaded the Parisian café scene and was succeeding, primarily because it was the only place in Paris where you could get a good cup of coffee to go in under twenty minutes, for less than seven dollars.

We took the metro to the start of the race and discussed which side of the course I would run down so he could see me and take some pictures. The weather was doing its part; it was a beautiful morning to run. One of the strangest sights at every marathon with a large number of participants was the volume of people openly going to the bathroom at the start of the race and along the first mile. Many waited in line to use the supplied portable bathrooms brought in for the race, but abandoned the idea when the race started and they were still stuck in the long line. You really would not want to live along the course of a marathon or your bushes would never be the same after the enormous herd of runners passed through, looking for any bush, entryway, or alley to use as a bathroom.

There was no better way to see a city than to run a marathon through it. Even though I was tired and sore from the day before, I was glad I was out there with all the other runners. The race started, and I made my way down the amazing Avenue des Champs-Élysées toward the Place de la Concorde. I located Eric early in the race and stopped for a minute so he could snap a couple pictures of me.

You could not find a more historically scenic and beautiful marathon course in the world, but one shortcoming was that no French people came to view the race—instead, they appeared to be annoyed that a race was going on. The second problem is that in the heavily residential areas of Paris, where Parisians love their dogs but strongly feel that God did not put them on earth to clean up after their dogs, there was dog poop everywhere. The first half of the marathon was strangely familiar, as we passed by the Louvre and the Place de la Bastille, and I thought, *Oh, yeah. I walked this entire distance twice yesterday,* cursing Eric, who was sitting in a Starbucks enjoying a cup of coffee.

Any chance of breaking a personal best marathon time was lost somewhere between the first and second glass of wine during dinner the night before. The course continued through beautiful parks and neighborhoods before looping back along the rivers edge and through a series of tunnels similar to the one in which Princess Di had been killed. The last few miles of the race provided a final glimpse of the Eiffel Tower, and even though the scenery was picture perfect, I was struggling and exhausted, and the last six miles of the race were turning into hell. I started to question why I was doing a marathon, thinking that my idea of running three great European marathons in thirty-some days was suicide. My pace had dropped dramatically to a slow jog, and it seemed, I had run out of fluid to sweat out of the pores in my skin as I desperately looked for a water station. I came upon a group of French people playing French music and dancing in the street while pouring glasses of wine into small cups for the runners passing by.

"Why do you keep running? Please stop and enjoy some French wine and cheese!" sang out one of the men to me in English, after determining from my blank response to him that I did not speak any French. I had been unable to say no the night before, and I could not say no then. I stopped and enjoyed a glass of red wine and aided in the effort to recruit other runners to stop to enjoy "the French way of life."

The origins of the distance of a marathon are based on a military victory near the ancient Greek town of Marathonas, which was "a good distance"—or approximately twenty-six miles—outside of Athens, Greece. The story went that to get out word of the victory, a soldier was sent to run the long distance to Athens, and upon his arrival, he had broadcasted the news and then collapsed and died of exhaustion. The first marathons varied in distance but were all around twenty-five or twenty-six miles. The 1908 Summer Olympics Marathon in London was originally set to be closer to twenty-five miles and to start on "The Long Walk," or the grand avenue leading up to Windsor Castle. The start of the race was moved to the east lawn of Windsor Castle so the Princess of Wales's children could watch the start. The change had added a mile to the race, but the changes didn't stop there. Queen Alexandra, being royalty, felt that she should have the best view of the finish, and 385 yards were added to the end of the race to push the finish line right under the Royal Box in the Great White City Stadium, pushing the total distance to 26.2 miles.

The extra .2 miles was exactly the distance that I had remaining before I would cross the finish line at the Arc de Triomphe, located on the western end of the Champs-Élysées. Another runner a short distance in front of me passed out in mid-stride with less than two hundred yards to go, falling hard on the pavement and smacking his head hard against a curb. I stopped to see what I could do, and medical help arrived promptly to aid the fallen runner. I said a small prayer that the man was okay as an ambulance pulled alongside the unconscious runner, and the medical staff yelled at the runners to keep moving and not block the street. Those were not the ideal conditions in which to finish a race, but I completed the short distance to the screams of encouragement of the spectators lining the end of the course, crossed the finish line, and raised my arms high into the air, enjoying the feeling of the pain momentarily being replaced by a strong emotional sense of accomplishment that made it all worth it.

I received my finisher's medal. Fortunately, I was not too far back in the pack of slow runners or I would have been going home without a medal. It would be a tragedy to complete a marathon and not get a nice new medal for it. I later found out that the event organizers were severely embarrassed because they had run out of finisher medals. A large group of the public, some two thousand people, pretended to be runners in the race and only ran the very end to collect a finisher medal upon crossing the finish line.

After a short search, I found Eric resting under a tree in the shade.

"Well, it's about time!" he said jokingly.

It was by far my worst performance in a marathon, but I did not care.

"We need to go find a café in the sun, and I need six huge glasses of water followed by three huge glasses of wine," I said.

"I thought we would go walk around some more today," he said with a smirk.

"Have I told you lately how much I hate you?" I said with a smile, as I limped down the street, making Eric carry my stuff.

- Chapter Fourteen -

Tak fur I Dog

✦

"How is this place ranked as the best country to live in?" I said to Sarah as I looked out the window of the plane as the wheels touched down safely on the snow-covered runway. A blizzard of swirling snow seemed to swallow the large plane. When I imagined the climate of the country that was ranked number one to live in, I certainly did not think of a country blanketed in snow in the month of April.

Sarah and I had just landed in Norway. According to the *Human Development Report* published by the United Nations, Norway tops the list, just as it had for the past five years. The United States ranks tenth in the same index.

It was Easter weekend, and Sarah and I had flown to Oslo, Norway, from London to meet Eric and Ingrid, who had invited us to join them and Ingrid's mom at their family cabin. Sarah and I shuffled out of the plane with all the other passengers and made our way into what looked more like a museum than a terminal.

The plan was for Sarah and me to take the train from the airport to Lillehammer, where Eric and Ingrid would pick us up and drive us the rest of the way to the family cottage. We made our way through customs, thrilled to have another new stamp in our passports. It was just after nine o'clock in the evening, and our time spent standing around admiring our new Norway passport stamp caused us to just miss the train leaving for Lillehammer.

We were hungry, and since we had an hour until the next train arrived, we went to find some dinner. Our only option was a small pizza place that smelled great. It was getting ready to close, but a woman said they could make us a quick pizza. We ordered a small pizza and two beers. The woman rang up our order at the cash register and told us what we owed. She waited patiently as, out of curiosity, I tried to convert the amount owed into United States dollars—a habit we had tried to stop, because it was so depressing. I concluded that we were paying close to forty dollars for two beers and a small pizza.

"Wow," I finally said as I completed the math and handed the woman the credit card. For close to a decade, Tokyo had held the most undesirable award as the world's most expensive city, but Oslo had slowly crept up to the top of the list, passing the more famous cities of London, Paris, New York, and Hong Kong. It was not polite to complain about how expensive the cost of living in Norway was—Norwegians already know how expensive their country is—but the woman gave me a nice and almost apologetic "Yes, I know" smile as she handed me back my credit card. I had the feeling that this woman was probably on the receiving end of a similar look of shock many times a day, since she worked at the airport and frequently had the first financial transaction with many first-time visitors to Oslo and Norway.

Sarah and I enjoyed the warm, freshly cooked pizza and washed it down with the two nice, cold, Norwegian beers. We thanked the woman again for staying open just a little bit longer and returned to the train platform. We purchased two tickets, boarded the almost empty train, and found two seats. We had only been in Norway an hour and hadn't even left the airport, and with the food and train tickets, we had already spent a small fortune.

Since it was dark out, Sarah and I did not engage in our usual argument over who got the window seat.

Most Americans only know Oslo as the home of the Nobel Peace Prize, and we were guilty of that as well. I had always heard how nice Oslo was, and I was slightly disappointed that we would not be seeing it on that trip. But to really experience a foreign country, you had to get out of the large cities, and we had a great opportunity to experience a Norway that was truly off the beaten path.

Norwegians live in a society that has the greatest affluence in the entire world, with its GDP ahead of Britain, the United States, and even Switzerland. Norway has no national debt and enjoys a huge tax surplus. Education is absolutely free all the way through college. Norwegians enjoy free health care and do not pay a dime for a hospital stay or doctor visits. And yes, the rumors are true: women receive an unheard-of forty-two weeks of paid maternity leave and are literally "hired" by the Norwegian government to stay home and take care of their newborn children.

The list of national amenities goes on and on, including one by which local artists are eligible to receive $30,000 a year in government grants to pursue their artistic passions, under no obligation to install, display, or sell any of their work. With a long life expectancy, low unemployment rate, low obesity rate, and with illiteracy unheard of throughout the country, Norwegians live with an incredible quality of life. How could that small country with a population of 4.5 million—half the population of Chicago and its surrounding suburbs—enjoy all the benefits of the Norwegian lifestyle that would make even the welfare-happy Danish jealous? One word: oil.

Norway discovered the vast amount of oil deep below Norwegian territory in 1969 and has used its good fortune to transform the country from one of the poorest countries in Europe to one of the richest. With the world's growing thirst for and addiction to oil and the price per barrel of oil skyrocketing in the past few years, Norwegians were reaping the benefits.

I had had no idea that Norway produced oil, and the first hint of that was seeing the many oil company advertisements displayed all over the airport terminal, showing large pictures of huge oil rigs in the icy waters of the North Sea. Norway was the third-largest oil exporter, behind only Saudi Arabia and Russia.

But where were all the fancy cars that should have been parked in every driveway? Norway had done an incredible job of avoiding what economists called the "Oil Curse," a label used to describe how the majority of oil-rich countries had greatly mishandled their oil fortunes and pumped the majority of money into the bank accounts of the royal family, corrupt authoritarian regimes, or dictatorships, resulting in many of their citizens suffering a decline in quality of life. In the same line of thought as the Scottish—just because whisky was made in Scotland didn't mean it should be free to the Scottish—gasoline was heavily taxed, and it was very expensive to fill your tank in Norway.

Just like Sarah and her theory of fiscal management, the Norwegians had wisely decided not to waste their fortune, and instead of going out and spending all the money, they had chosen to save it for the future and were putting the money into what was referred to as the Petroleum Fund or the Government Pension Fund. The fund had grown exponentially and had become one of the largest in the world. Norway's fiscal management of the oil was allowing Norwegians to live a high quality of life in a heavily socialistic society without many of the problems its southern European neighbors faced: rising unemployment rates, inflation, and burdening national debt. The Norwegian economy was heavily dependent on oil revenue, but had also diversified its economy to protect it from a severe drop in oil prices.

The highly educated Norwegians considered themselves internationalists and had a huge interest in global affairs.

Eric warned me ahead of time: "It is probably not wise to mention that you voted for George Bush."

"I voted for him twice, Eric. Will this earn me two punches in the nose if I mention it?" I said.

A fact that most likely irks Norwegians is that only one sitting United States president had visited Norway—Bill Clinton.

"I was amazed to discover that I am the first sitting president ever to visit Norway. I can't imagine what the others were thinking about," Clinton said during a news conference upon his arrival in 1999. Theodore Roosevelt won the Nobel Peace Prize in 1906 but did not travel to pick up his award until after he left the White House. President Woodrow Wilson had died before he could collect his Nobel Peace Prize, and Jimmy Carter had visited Norway several times since leaving office.

Norway had not joined the European Union; the last referendum had been narrowly defeated by a slight majority opposing membership into the European Union. The subject of European Union membership was a heavily debated topic within the society, and various political parties handled the issue with many different viewpoints.

Even the Royal Family lives a normal and modern Norwegian lifestyle; the Prince of Norway even spends a great deal of time with his family and considers himself a hands-on father in raising his kids. Prince Haakon even went as far as to break a thousand-year-old tradition when he married a commoner, who was also a single mother with a three-year-old son.

We enjoyed the train ride, as the train sped along the rails quietly and smoothly, and we caught a quick nap before arriving into Lillehammer, which was the host city of the 1994 Winter Olympics.

"Welcome to Norway!" Ingrid said as she greeted us with a hug.

I carried our bags over to the rental car that Eric and Ingrid had rented.

"How do you like our car?" Eric asked as he pointed to it.

Rental cars did not escape the high cost of Norway, and Eric and Ingrid had chosen a rental car that was slightly less expensive than others but came with a large advertisement in English on each side. In large green letters, it advertised the roomy interior space of the car: "Three in the front, three in the back, and still plenty of room for the bags."

We drove through twisting and winding snow-covered roads, and because it was nearing midnight, Sarah and I were having a difficult time staying awake. We finally made it to the cottage in Espedalen, near the city of Skaabu, after a long journey by plane, train, and automobile. It was dark and tough to see much as we quietly entered the small cabin. After a small tutorial on how to properly operate the toilet, we climbed into bed for a good night's sleep.

We awoke the next morning and were greeted with a big smile by Eric and Ingrid's five-month-old daughter, Anya. Ingrid's mother had prepared a traditional breakfast, and we all sat down together at the table to eat various breads, cold sliced meats, cheeses, cucumbers, tomatoes, hard-boiled eggs, fruit, and, of course, smoked salmon and pickled herring.

Since we had arrived in the middle of the night, we were getting our first good look at the cottage. It had one large room with lightly stained, wood plank floors, walls, and ceiling, with white-trimmed windows and doors. A small kitchen was connected to the main room and had a window over the sink that provided a panoramic view of the distant mountain peaks. There were two small bedrooms connected to the main room, one of which was filled with bunk beds. The main room contained a formal sitting area, a wooden table that matched the floors and walls, and a small, cast-iron, wood-burning furnace that heated the room and filled the air outside with the winter smell of burning wood.

A cabin was not a cabin unless it had something that differentiated it from a formal house, and the cottage prided itself with three items of uniqueness. First, the cottage did not have the luxury of formal plumbing, and the toilet resembled a luxury outhouse brought indoors, requiring the user to follow the proper bathroom etiquette of sprinkling a scented, tree bark-like substance into the removable toilet pit.

The second unique feature of the cabin was that, just like the toilet, the kitchen sink, bathroom sink, and shower were not connected to a main outside water source and required a bit of physical labor to enjoy water for a shower, brushing teeth, or cleaning dishes. A trip to a small outdoor pump to fill two large plastic containers and then return to the cottage to pour the water into the large water-holding tank inside the cottage was required. A sled in the winter or a wheelbarrow in the summer was the best way to transport the heavy containers of water down the path and street over the fifty yards from the pump. Five to seven cottages all shared the water pump, giving them a geographical reference as to where their cottage was located—subdivision water pump five.

There was something fulfilling about venturing out in the snow with the two large plastic containers and pumping the handle of the water pump vigorously until clean, clear, cold water came gushing out, while holding the containers in place to avoid spilling the cold water on my gloves. The hardest part was getting the heavy containers back to the cabin without spilling any water. This was not an easy task because the small, snow-covered, sloping hills demanded concentration and strength. I had to pull the heavy sled up each small incline and then guide the sled down without letting it pick up too much speed. Otherwise, it would crash into a snow bank and spill the water. Since acquiring clean, fresh water was such a physically taxing burden, showers were cut short and we did not leave the water running when brushing our teeth.

The third unique aspect of the cottage was that it had a grass-covered roof—truly a "green" roof. All the area cabins had grass-covered roofs, which helped keep the inside nice and warm in the winter and cool in the summer. There was electricity but no telephone.

A small television was placed against a wall, but it was not worth turning on other than to view a DVD movie, because only one television station barely came in. There was no Internet access, and cell phones were not entirely dependable. The absence of all these modern luxuries added to the romance, charm, and relaxation of spending time at the cottage, but with Eric's nonstop life, it gave him a severe case of ants-in-the-pants syndrome. He could not finish breakfast fast enough and wanted to get outside as quickly as possible to enjoy the Norwegian national pastime of cross-country skiing.

Cross-country skiing in the winter months was a form of Norwegian Prozac that helped the country get through the long, dark winters. Eric handed me a pair of cross-country boots, skis, and poles and showed me how to apply wax to the bottoms of the skinny, wimpy-looking skis.

"All right, here we go," he said, and he headed out the front door and immediately onto a small trail that connected the cabin with the wide, well-groomed, designated ski trails. Snowmobiles are not allowed in the area unless they are being used for work or emergencies.

"Try to keep up," Eric said in a competitive and joking manner as he sped off in front of me.

The sun was shining, and there was very little wind—perfect conditions for cross-country skiing. It took me a couple minutes to get the correct motion of left foot forward, right hand forward, push, and glide. Right foot forward, left hand forward, push, and glide. I was still slightly sore from the previous weekend's marathon, but it felt good to be outside doing physical exercise. The Norwegian Prozac was already working.

I followed Eric down the trail, admiring the beautiful scenery as we traveled up and down slight inclines on the trail. I could see the back of Eric's blue jacket as he rounded each bend on the trail in front of me. The trail curved around sharply and merged with a twisting and winding downward trail. I loved to downhill ski and considered myself to be an advanced downhill skier, so I enjoyed the sudden acceleration of the skis as they responded to the downhill slope. I started to go faster and faster, and it was becoming increasingly difficult to keep my skis in the two hard, snow-packed tracks that had been formed by all the skiers using the same trail. I picked up more and more speed, whipping around each turn faster and faster. I still caught an occasional glimpse of the back of Eric's jacket before he disappeared again around the next turn.

A concerned thought slowly crept into my mind: I was eventually going to have to find a way to stop. I adjusted my skis, bringing the front tips together to form a V shape, trying to slow down my momentum, but the skinny little skis did not respond like downhill skis, and I did not slow down.

I took my eyes off my skis and looked up just in time to see Eric completely stopped and standing on the side of the trail. I narrowly missed him and barely made out his shout of "STOP! There is a road ahead!" the hard pavement of the grey, snowless road was quickly approaching.

I thought it was over and felt death quickly approaching; I feared that I would either be run over by a car or that the road would instantly stop my momentum and throw me headfirst along the pavement as if I had flown over the handlebars of a motorcycle on the expressway. I closed my eyes and prepared for the worst.

It was over in less than a second. I was not run over by a passing car or truck, and I was not thrown to my death. Surprisingly, the skis continued right over the hard concrete surface, and I probably never would have noticed if not for the severe scraping noise of the skis on the road and the sparks flying from the metal edges.

I had cleared the road, but I was on a snow-covered trail that was noticeably steeper and narrower than the previous section of the trail. Large trees on either side of the trail slowly closed in on me. I decided that it was time to put an end to the run and that breaking a leg or arm would not be the end of the world, so I threw myself into the right snowbank alongside the trail. One, two, three! My body somersaulted again and again through the white snow, which was then entering every conceivable part of my long underwear through my jacket and pants. After the second somersault, I heard a loud crack. When I finally came to a stop, I looked up through the snow-covered pine trees, happy to be alive. I slowly moved my legs and then my arms before I felt confident enough to try to sit up. Other than the excruciating pain I was feeling, both mentally and physically, the only things that appeared to be broken were my sunglasses, which had snapped in half somewhere between the second and third somersault.

Eric slowly approached, with a look on his face that said, "I really want to laugh, but I guess I should make sure you're okay first."

"What the hell, Eric! I have only been on these stupid skis for five minutes, and you think I can handle skiing down the side of Mount Everest?" I said.

Eric had decided it was safe to burst out laughing. I picked up my skis and started walking back, stopping to put them back on when I was within sight of the cabin and the ground was as flat as a board.

I told Sarah about the trick that Eric had pulled, and instead of offering understanding and comfort, she, too, found humor in my brush with death.

Later in the day, Ingrid's brother Erik, his wife (who also goes by the Norwegian name Inger), and their two small boys, Daniel and Markus (ages four and two), came over for lunch. Erik and Inger had met in Norway when Erik was earning college credit by completing what is the equivalent of a fifth year of high school, known as *folkehogskole*. After college, he had moved there permanently, found success as a writer, and published many books in Norway. Erik looked, sounded, and, on the surface, appeared to be one hundred percent Norwegian. We would never have known he was an American, until he jokingly greeted us with, "What up, dude?" with a Midwestern American accent, as he often did when we saw him. Over the years, Sarah and I had gotten to know Erik and his family when they had visited his parents in the Milwaukee suburb of Mequon. We had really enjoyed spending time with them and their kids.

After extracting a promise to avoid the most difficult trails, I decided to join Erik, Inger, and my brother, on an afternoon cross-country ski trip. Erik brought along his youngest son Markus, whom he towed in a small, covered *pulk* or sled. Markus fell asleep as if he were in a car almost instantly as we started out on the trail. I had really found a new respect for the sport of cross-country skiing that morning, and what we were doing was not the boring activity of skiing on a flat surface that I had previously associated with cross-country skiing.

The weekend was filled with many activities that often included putting on cross-country skis as either a physical activity or a means of transportation to visit a hotel bar, which was a short distance away from the cabin; there, we drank beers outside in the warm sun and enjoyed the mountain scenery. Each night we were exhausted from the day's activities and sat around and drank warm, mulled wine and enjoyed being together.

The way Ingrid's mother had decorated the small red cabin that was tucked away in the Norwegian woods would have made Martha Stewart gush with envy. There was a Norwegian word to describe the way the cabin made us feel at night—*koselig*—which doesn't have a direct translation to English, because the feeling is uniquely Norwegian, but the meaning is best described as "cozy, warm atmosphere."

It was amazing and strange to see the sun not completely set until ten thirty at night with so much snow still covering the ground. Farther north from the cabin was a part of the country known as "the land of the midnight sun," due to its proximity to the Arctic Circle, where, for part of each summer, the sun did not set. In the winter months, most of the area remained dark for the vast majority of the day. Since it was already spring, the sun was beginning to fully set late into the evening hours. In a few months, the sun would only set for a couple of hours before rising and lighting up the sky again.

The *koselig* atmosphere inside the cabin was incredible, and we enjoyed it as we placed another log into the fireplace, poured another glass of warm wine, sank a little deeper into our chairs, and discussed whose turn it was next to go outside and get more water. I had heard so much about the Norwegian cabin and how special it was to the family. I had always wanted to see it and experience it. Finally being there was nice, but it wasn't complete, as someone special was missing.

Eric and Ingrid had met while I was also living in San Francisco, which had provided me with the opportunity to get to know Ingrid as a good friend before she became my sister-in-law, something I have always appreciated. The summer of 2003 had been a busy summer for my family, as my two brothers and I all got married within a four-month period—each in a different state. Each of the three weddings was distinctive and unique, and we even had a small group of friends and relatives who made it to all three, which was not an easy task because of the extensive long-distance travel.

During the years leading up to the weddings, we had all gotten to know one another's families quite well through endless family gatherings for engagement parties, wedding showers, and wedding preparations. We had gotten to know Ingrid's father, John, who would drive to Chicago from Milwaukee to have dinner with us and help us as our financial planner and with the purchase of our first home. Just shortly after the first of the three weddings, and with Eric's wedding next, we were all shocked by the news that Ingrid's father John had an aggressive brain tumor, and the outlook did not look good. John had lived a healthy and great life. He was fit, did not smoke, ate plenty of fish, and was an incredible family man, so the news just did not seem fair.

John had one goal left in life, and that was to live long enough to walk his only daughter, Ingrid, down the church aisle. A brain tumor usually affected its victims either mentally or physically. With John, it seemed to affect him more mentally, resulting in memory loss and not being able to completely articulate or communicate what he wanted to say, so physically walking down the aisle was a real possibility.

Eric and Ingrid had the opportunity to have their wedding plans and wedding day recorded for a special ABC program hosted by Diane Sawyer about various wedding stories. The two of them decided that they would not let the devastating twist of fate that had fallen on the family stand in the way and to continue, with the barrage of television cameras following them as they planned their wedding day.

There is an old Norwegian saying, *Tak fur I dog,* which in English means "Thanks for today," and that was how the family treated every day that John was with them as they continued to prepare for the wedding. The big day finally arrived, and even though John had just completed another round of radiation therapy days before, everyone felt confident that John would be able to do walk Ingrid down the aisle since he had done so well during the wedding rehearsal the day before. However, that day was a different story, and just before it was time to start, Ingrid's mother pulled her aside and told her that John would not be able to do it.

Ingrid looked at her mom and asked, "Mom, will you do this? Will you walk me down the aisle?"

The packed church was fully aware of the moment, and a wave of sadness crashed down on everyone in attendance as John was wheeled to the front of the church in a wheelchair. Ingrid and her mother put a brave smile on, and together they walked down the aisle of the church, while the entire church seemed to try, unsuccessfully, to hold back the tears.

The wedding reception was filled with many Norwegian traditions of speeches, toasts, poems, and songs. A few months later, we relived the moment on national television, as ABC aired the special telling of their wedding story. Diane Sawyer had interviewed Eric and Ingrid, and we had laughed at the small clip of my mother being interviewed and the other wedding guests shown enjoying the *Tak fur I dog* attitude that we had all tried to have leading up to and on the day of the wedding.

John had lived a few more months and even made it to Sarah's and my wedding. We felt blessed to have him there. John passed away at his home with his family by his side. The only consolation in dying young is that your memorial is usually heavily attended by family, friends, and coworkers, and John's was no exception; many people asked for the chance to get up at his memorial service and talk about how great John was, how much they loved him, how much the community would miss him, and what a great friend and colleague he had been.

Inside the simple, red cabin that John had spoken of so fondly was a small sign that read: "This cottage stands as a testament to John's love of his family's heritage and for a foreign country that felt like home to him." It was such an honor to be enjoying our time in Norway in the little red cabin in the woods, and though it was not the same without him there, the *koselig* atmosphere that filled the cottage made it feel like he was sitting there with us, thankful for the day.

- Chapter Fifteen -

A Queen for the Ages

✦

"Hello, Mom. Mom, is that you?" I said into my tiny, cheap, plastic cell phone, which was becoming increasingly unreliable.

The call was dropped, but I had recognized the number as my mother's cell phone number. My phone started ringing again. Of all the people who would visit us during the year, my mother's cell phone was the only cell phone that actually worked in Europe. After we told each visitor to count on their cell phones not working in London, they arrived to find it not working, even after calling their service provider to confirm that it would work. After much frustration, each visitor eventually figured out how to use the airport pay phone to call us and tell us that they had arrived.

I answered the phone, and this time, I could hear what sounded like the background noise of a train station.

"Mom, are you there?" I said.

"Garrett! Garrett! Can you hear me?" she said.

"Yes, I can hear you. Is everything okay, Mom?" I said.

Even though my mother's voice was frantic and sounded distressed, I was not too concerned. I knew from past experience that she was calling with good news, because when she did have unexpected and devastating news to share with my brothers and me, she had a unique approach. She usually started out by saying she had some bad news and then went on to list each person the news was not about, in order of importance to the family: "Your father and brothers are all okay, your grandmother is fine … " and the list went on and on, leaving me to guess along the way, until the list was complete. Then I had time to wonder which person she hadn't mentioned, because she always paused before saying the name. The last time I received a bad news call, she had told me that the family dog had died.

"You're not going to believe this," she said in the voice of an overly excited teenager who had just been handed the keys to the family car. "I touched the Queen!"

"What?" I said, even though I had heard perfectly well what she had said.

"I touched the Queen! We met the Queen," she said.

"The Queen? You touched the Queen of England?" I asked.

I was picturing my mom in a jail cell somewhere in London. Was that her one phone call she had been granted? Did England even have the one phone call upon arrest etiquette?

"The Queen walked right over to where we were standing, and as she reached over my shoulder to take a card from the person standing behind me, I reached out and lifted her elbow to help her grab the card. We met Prince Philip, too!" she said.

Poor Prince Philip. Always an afterthought.

"Sarah and I have been in London for four months, and we have not even seen the Queen. You and Dad have been here a couple of days, and you have already met her. This is so unfair," I said.

It was April 21, Queen Elizabeth II's eightieth birthday. My parents had flown over to London with some friends to visit us and spend some time in London and Paris. My mother had gotten everyone up at the crack of dawn and traveled out to Windsor Castle to stand outside the huge castle that had been founded by William the Conqueror for the possibility of a quick glimpse of the most famous woman in the world.

A minute or two after the clock struck noon, the large Henry VIII gate doors had slowly opened, and Queen Elizabeth II, wearing a cerise coat with a matching feathered hat, slowly walked out with her husband Prince Philip slightly behind her. A huge roar greeted the Queen as she made her way down the street for what the British referred to as a walkabout. She smiled and accepted bouquets of flowers and birthday cards. She passed by a group of schoolchildren, who were wearing blue school blazers and waving white flags with the red cross of St. George, the patron saint of England.

As television cameras and photographers snapped picture after picture to be seen around the world, the Queen walked over to where my parents and their friends had been standing for hours and accepted a birthday card from an elderly man standing next to them. My mother could have hugged the Queen if she'd wanted to, and I'm a little surprised she didn't try. Live television coverage of the event was being shown around the world and later in the day on newscasts in almost every country as the Queen walked down the street during her royal walkabout.

Millions of women around the world were saying to themselves, *I wish that was me standing there greeting the Queen of England.* My mother had always been one of those people, but that day she did not have to wish anymore. She was that person being shown in newspaper articles and news coverage on stations like CNN smiling in the background and greeting the Queen. I could not have been happier for her, and hearing her and my father tell the story made me so happy for the two of them. They had really deserved to experience the special moment in their lives.

Sarah and I had yet to meet the Queen or even get a glimpse of her as she passed by on the streets of London, but we were getting to experience life living under the reign of a queen and were loving every minute of it. The Royal Family had been hugely popular in the United States; many Americans had followed every glorious and heartbreaking event that the family had suffered. Living in London gave us the opportunity to actually live in the soap opera life that we could only read about or see on television back at home.

Prince William and Prince Harry had friends who lived in our area, and their favorite nightclub was a short walk away from our house. They were often seen leaving house parties at early hours of the morning just down the block from where we lived. We never knew they were there until we read about it in the papers the next morning.

It seemed that if the younger and far less constrained Prince Harry was visiting his favorite hangout with his friends, he more often than not seemed to find himself involved in a fistfight with other club patrons. Within hours, pictures of blood-stained individuals and a drunk-looking Harry or William seen leaving the club would be splashed across the pages of the day's newspapers or magazines. News like that really made me feel sorry for them and truly was an example of what had been said before—that the two boys were trying to live a modern life in an ancient institution.

Queen Elizabeth II had won the ultimate birth lottery when she was born on April 21, 1926, in London, England, but no one had known it at the time. When she was born, nobody had thought or expected her to one day become Queen of England. Her father, George, was not the king when she was born, and instead her father's brother, Edward, was the eldest son, making him next in line to become king. Upon the death of her grandfather, Edward ascended the throne as Edward VIII. As fate would have it, Edward fell in love with an American socialite. The problem was that his new love had been divorced twice, and, as a result, their marriage was opposed on religious, moral, political, and legal grounds. The King declared that he loved her and would marry her whether the government or the people approved of it or not. King Edward VIII kept true to his promise to marry his new love and abdicated his crown, paving the way for his brother George to ascend to the throne as King George VI.

At the age of seven, Queen Elizabeth II was photographed holding a Welsh Corgi in her arms and had been associated with the dogs ever since. At age fourteen, she made her first radio broadcast, speaking to evacuated children during the Blitz. She was also the only female member of the Royal Family to serve in the armed forces rather than accept an honorary rank. She had contributed to the war efforts when she had convinced her father to let her join the Women's Auxiliary Territorial Service. During Victory in Europe Day celebrations, she, along with her younger sister, dressed in ordinary clothes and slipped into the huge crowds to celebrate the victory as common people, allowing her to live for just a few short hours as an average person.

King George VI, died in his sleep when Elizabeth was just twenty-seven years old. At the time of her father's death, she was visiting Kenya at the Treetops Hotel, which was actually up in the trees, providing her official biographer the opportunity to write that she was "the only woman known to have gone up a tree a princess and come down a Queen." As the plane approached Heathrow Airport, the new Queen changed out of her summer clothes and into a plain black dress in preparation for arriving back in London. Winston Churchill was one of the first people to greet her at the airport that day. The year after her father's death, she was crowned in Westminster Abbey. The Queen's official title is: "Elizabeth the Second, by the Grace of God, of the United Kingdom of Great Britain and Northern Ireland and of Her other Realms and Territories Queen, Head of the Commonwealth, Defender of the Faith."

In her first televised Christmas address in 1957, she told her people, "It's inevitable that I should seem a rather remote figure to many of you—a successor to kings and queens of history; someone whose face may be familiar in newspapers and films but never who touches your personal lives. But now, at least for a few minutes, I welcome you to the peace of my home."

When Elizabeth became Queen, she inherited a country that was in the process of losing much of its wealth and power around the world, which had been a heavy burden on national pride. Parts of the empire were in the process of going or had already gone; India and Pakistan had become independent republics. Britain and the British Monarchy were losing their importance in the world, and the Queen's role had begun to transition into a more symbolic and ceremonial one. While Sarah and I lived in London, she was official Head of State for sixteen independent territories: Antigua and Barbuda, Australia, the Bahamas, Barbados, Belize, Canada, Grenada, Jamaica, New Zealand, Papua New Guinea, the Solomon Islands, St. Kitts-Nevis, St. Lucia,

St. Vincent and the Grenadines, Tuvalu, and the United Kingdom. Her official Head of State status for those sixteen independent territories provided her with a fantastic portfolio of vacation spots around the world, where I'm sure she had no problem getting the best poolside spot to enjoy the sun and a good book.

During our year, Sarah and I learned so much about living life under the reign of a queen and what a wonderful woman she truly was. There was so much that I wanted to know about her, such as: "What exactly does she do?"; Where does she get her money?"; "What do the people of the United Kingdom really think of her?" Each day the papers were filled with stories of William and Harry and their lives doing what boys are bound to do when surrounded by unlimited booze and beautiful girls. The papers also included stories about their late mother Princess Di and all the conspiracy theories still lingering, as papers looked to continue to profit from her death by publishing never-before-seen photos taken minutes after the car crash that had killed her. Those were all stories that sadly filled space and sold lots of papers and were much more common than positive stories about the Queen and the Royal Family. I guessed the public had grown tired of reading about the Queen opening another new hospital or airport terminal.

The Queen had had to endure many difficulties and criticisms over the years that had brought embarrassment to her and the monarchy—much of the criticism resulting from the behavior of her children and all their failed marriages, as well as the public's perception of how she had handled Princess Di's death and her lack of publicly paying the proper respect. The Queen was a tough woman, and she had endured, and some say she had rebuilt the monarchy into a more modern, transparent, and popular institution. Her faith in her people was reenergized when she was overwhelmed by the deep affectionate response to the death of her own mother, who had often been referred to as "the Queen Mum."

In 1992, Windsor Castle suffered a serious fire, and there was a huge uproar by the people when it was discovered that the castle did not have insurance and the taxpayers would have to pay to rebuild the damage. The tragedy set in motion a series of events that resulted in the Queen paying income tax and providing a more transparent picture of her personal finances. The new attitude of financial transparency made it much easier to speculate on how much the Queen was really worth, how much she made each year, and how much the monarch cost the general public each year. The Queen agreed to pay income taxes at a suggestion from John Major, because he felt it might help her public image. Intelligently, the Queen negotiated a deal that, as long as her assets were passed on to succeeding royal generations, they would be untouchable to the inheritance tax of 40 percent.

Listings of the world's richest people often mistakenly include the Queen of England as the world's wealthiest woman. In their estimates, they mistakenly include all of the royal palaces, crown jewels, furniture, and priceless artwork in each palace. The last auction for a Leonardo da Vinci painting was for around $8 million. If the Queen really needed money, you might think she could sell one of her six hundred Leonardo da Vinci paintings. But technically she couldn't, because those items actually belonged to the State, and the Queen couldn't sell the paintings on eBay if times got tough for her.

However, the Queen had inherited a huge sum of money when her father had died and also when her mother had passed away in 2002. But she was not the richest person in Britain. According to the *Sunday Times* newspaper, she was only the 177th richest person in Britain, with an estimated wealth of approximately $500 million. Notable names higher up on the list included Sir Paul McCartney and J. K. Rowling, who had become regarded as the richest woman in Britain from sales of her Harry Potter books. A large majority of the Queen's wealth and income came from her extensive stock portfolio of mostly blue-chip companies. She bought and sold shares through an anonymity known as *Bank of England Nominees*, which also dealt on behalf of other incredibly rich investors, such as the Sultan of Brunei and the Saudi Royal Family.

Even though the Queen did not technically own royal establishments such as Buckingham Palace or Windsor Castle, she did own her share of property that was not considered state owned, such as her huge Balmoral estate, which had been purchased by Queen Victoria with her own resources and passed down to the next royal generation. Somehow it had been decided that, even though Windsor Castle was considered one of the monarch's private residences, officially the property was owned by the state, so the Queen had to pay for the huge rebuilding cost after the great fire in 1992. Since it was determined that the Queen had to pay, she had decided that she needed additional revenue streams and opened Buckingham Palace up to the public for tours when she was not staying at the palace.

British passports were officially issued in the name of Her Majesty, so the Queen did not actually need a passport and did not have one, but all the other members of the Royal Family did—even her husband, the Duke of Edinburgh. But who paid for all the Queen's trips, cars, boats, and airplanes? In the new age of financial transparency, it was made clear what the Queen and Royal Monarchy paid for themselves and what the taxpayers paid for. According to Buckingham Palace, it cost taxpayers 62 pence ($1.24) per person each year. The biggest bulk of cost picked up by taxpayers was travel, with Prince Charles and his wife the Duchess of Cornwall incurring the highest travel expenses. Hundreds of thousands of dollars were spent on what were called "staff reconnaissance visits," which actually cost more than the Queen's visits. In response to the public opinion that the monarch's wealth and business affairs should be more open and accountable, the Queen had scrapped her royal yacht Britannia but still used the royal train a few times a year. She did own a helicopter, but no airplanes; instead she chartered a British Airways plane when flying. The airline did take out every other row of seats to give her more legroom.

Royal spokespeople wanted it made clear to the public when discussing royal finances that the goal was not to run a low-cost monarchy but to instead run a value-for-your-money monarchy. They liked to point out that that miniscule annual cost to each taxpayer produced a huge return on the investment in the form of all the tourist dollars that flood into the country from tourists who specifically visited England and London for a chance to observe Royal traditions firsthand by witnessing the changing of the guard or by visiting Windsor Castle or Buckingham Palace. Those tiny expenses were a great deal less for British taxpayers compared to what we Americans paid to support the president or to impeach him if needed.

So, what did a woman whose face was featured on money and postage stamps, who had a national anthem that requested God to save her, actually do? Not an easy question to answer, because the Queen preferred to be observed rather than questioned, and you couldn't just walk up and ask her questions. The Queen had never given journalists a full interview. She was fully aware of the criticism she had endured during the previous two decades, with the majority of coverage given to the family as the result of some misadventures of the younger Royal Family members, allowing many to forget what the Queen actually did.

Even at eighty years young, the Queen had learned to become much more media savvy, and it seemed the royal palace was constantly conducting focus groups and research on what activities and roles the public would like to see the Queen take on. Technically, the Queen could dissolve Parliament and get rid of the Prime Minister if she felt it was needed, but everyone knew the Queen would never consider pushing the country into a constitutional crisis.

The Queen had grown into the role of a grandmother to all of the country. She was a soft-spoken woman who seemed to be more famous for really saying nothing at all. She had never caused any controversy with anything she had publicly said, but she had been criticized for not saying anything more political. She had been a constant in a sea of change for the country. Prime ministers had come and gone—over eleven of them—but she had always been there. She still opened parliament each year, gave a Christmas message to the people, hosted dinners for foreign leaders, and made worldwide headlines when she traveled outside the country.

Sarah and I found great joy when reading in the papers the occasional story about the Queen doing something common, such as taking a taxi to go see the newest, hot theater production, giving us hope that when we went to the theater, we might see the Queen actually sitting in the royal box. When an English man or woman finally wins Wimbledon again, I'm sure she will be there to present the trophy, even if she lives to be as old as her mother, who died at the age of 101.

With her son Charles remarried and her grandson William well on his way to finding his future wife, the Queen had prospered in those years of calm and had risen to the occasion to comfort the country when needed, especially during the Tube train bombings; she had also congratulated the country on a job well done when it was announced that London had beaten out its rival Paris to host the 2012 Summer Olympics.

The Queen's popularity had been restored and was at its peak; a recent Buckingham Palace poll showed that 81 percent of the people wanted to maintain the Royal Family versus dumping them all and moving toward a republic. The Queen must be commended for her incredible job in "image management." She even carried a cell phone in her purse, just like the rest of the country, and seemed to understand that the actions of her grandsons were just part of growing up and maturing.

The British may poke fun at America's incredible obsession with the Royal Family—especially since we are a country founded on the act of telling off royalty and cutting all ties—and the British may say that the monarchy was for the tourists only. But the British were just as obsessed as we were. If the Royal Family had suddenly disappeared as if it had never existed, there would have been a huge void, and suddenly, being British would have had a whole new meaning.

The same poll that showed overwhelming support of the Queen also showed that only 32 percent of the people felt that Britain would still have a monarchy in fifty years. Fifty years was a long way off, but only a blink of the eye when you think about how long the monarchy had been part of English history.

- Chapter Sixteen -

Please Don't Empty the Museum

✦

I could not stop smiling as I exited the Russell Square Tube station and walked down the diagonal path that cut through the center of Russell Square. I was still thinking of the phone call I had received from my mother and of how when my parents returned home after their trip, they would be asked by friends and family how it was, and part of their answer would be "and then we met the Queen," as if all the tourists in England got to meet the Queen. I was out-of-this-world jealous, and I thought to myself that if my parents got to spend the day feeling special, I was going to go to the one place that I, too, felt like someone special. I was just about there.

The smile on my face was finally starting to fade as I exited the square and passed by Huron University, where I spotted Ray, the school provost, standing outside talking to a group of students. He spotted me, waved, and yelled, "Off to the pub for an early one?" That brought the smile back to my face.

His endless enthusiasm and energy as well as humor made him such a popular person, constantly attracting people to talk to him. Later in the year, while riding on the Tube with me, Ray would share a personal thought with me on how he was saddened but comforted in his later stages of life because, after having always been a popular choice to speak at school, weddings, and graduations, he was a popular choice to speak at the funerals of good friends and family members.

I escaped the temptation to stop and talk to Ray, because I was on my way to feel special. I made a right turn at the end of the street and entered my favorite place to study, visit, and actually feel like a celebrity. I could do all of that at the most famous and controversial museum in the whole world—

the British Museum. As I entered through the front gates, I made my way through the large school and tour groups standing together in the courtyard, as their chaperones tried to keep them all from wandering off in the wrong direction. I could hear languages from all over the world being spoken by the groups. I kept walking and entered the front doors of the museum, walking right in. One of the best parts of visiting the British Museum was walking right in. The museum was absolutely free and an incredible gift for all those lucky enough to visit London.

With my first-semester final exams quickly approaching, I needed to spend some serious time catching up on my studies. With all the distractions of London, Europe, and our new friends, it was becoming difficult to keep up. Entering the museum and walking straight into the Great Courtyard, I stopped and marveled at the 3,312 glass panels; each was a different size, and when they were placed together, they gave the large indoor space an outdoor feel to it—something I greatly appreciated on rainy, miserable days. Next, I continued straight into the breathtaking reference library, known simply as the Reading Room. Upon entering the Reading Room, I was instantly overcome with its large size and gold-detailed, domed ceiling, which was painted in a light blue that enhances the gold trim, making it soft on the eyes and giving the room a warm and inviting glow.

It was tough not to feel smart in the library, with the three-story-high rows of books lining the circular dimensions of the room. Studying in the room made me feel special and almost like a celebrity, because even though the room was a functioning library, many tourists walked the aisles of long rows of desks all day long as they admired the enormous room. I often found myself the subject of tourists' photos, as they snapped a picture or two of me surrounded by and engaged in my textbooks, almost as if I was a staged prop in the library for them. The librarians would quickly run over and remind the tourists that talking and taking pictures was not allowed in the library.

I enjoyed sitting at one of the many old desks and chairs where the likes of Mohandas Gandhi, Karl Marx, Vladimir Lenin, H.G. Wells, and Oscar Wilde had sat in the library at one time. When I needed a study break or just a slight change of scenery to work on memorizing long, mathematical equations, I would walk the long halls of the many rooms of the museum, occasionally stopping to admire an exhibit. I could walk the museum with my eyes closed and still easily navigate my way through the halls, stairs, and many rooms—a talent I had developed during the hundreds of hours I had spent there.

Some mornings I would clear my head with a quick walk through the museum upon it opening and before beginning my studies. Often I had many of the rooms and exhibits all to myself to marvel at the Moai statue from Easter Island, the Rosetta Stone, Egyptian Mummies, or the carvings from the Athenian Parthenon.

The museum had been enshrined in controversy because of the items that, in one way or another, had found homes in the museum. Many of the countries where the artifacts originated had asked for the artifact back, especially items like the Parthenon Marbles. The museum had provided the artifacts a safe and well-maintained home for many years, and through the British Museum Act of 1963, the museum was legally prevented from returning any item from the museum. It was true that if the museum had to give everything back, the museum would be just an empty building. In its then current state, the museum was an amazing place, and as long as the museum was free for all those who entered, it was tough to argue for sending all the items back to the countries they came from.

My grandmother had dreamed of one day visiting the museum, but she did not live long enough to experience her dream. I thought of her every day as I entered the museum. My grandmother had wanted just one day to experience the museum. I was lucky—I had over a hundred days.

The Marathon, Part II

Finals would begin in a week, and I still had plenty of time to mentally prepare myself for the upcoming tests, but at the moment I was sitting on an extremely packed train, regretting that I did not have more time to physically prepare myself for the physical test that would begin in just under a half hour. I looked out the window with concern, as the morning sprinkle of rain started to come down a little harder. The train pulled into the Greenwich station, I exited with thousands of others, and we all made our way through Greenwich Park in a sea of nervous energy, heading for the starting line of the London Marathon.

I quickly realized that I was way underdressed for the event. Even though the race was a well-known and respected sporting event, as well as the second-largest marathon in the world, the race was more of a large party and celebration. The majority of runners dressed in full costumes and ran the event to raise money for a charity of their choice. I did not have a costume on, and I did not have the name of a charity printed on my chest, which made me feel out of place.

The race began, and I started making my way along with the other forty thousand runners. Even though it had only been fifteen days since the Paris Marathon, and as the name of the sport implied, I had skied across the entire country of Norway, the festive atmosphere of the race immediately lifted my spirits, and I felt strong. I passed the twenty runners who were all running in a long sewn-together giant millipede, carrying plastic buckets to collect money during the race from the half million people lining the course. I also passed Lloyd Scott, a national hero in England for his charity work, raising close to $10 million for cancer through what he called "extreme charity fundraising events." In 2002, Lloyd completed the London Marathon in six days, earning him the official world record for the slowest marathon. His slow pace in that marathon was due to the fact that he had been wearing a 110-pound, deep-sea diving suit. He was back at it again, but that time, since the race fell on St. George's Day, he had dressed as St. George, wearing a full knight's armor suit and pulling a three-hundred-pound, twelve-foot-tall dragon behind him.

The first five miles of the race were fun, as all of the runners checked out all of the other runners' costumes. I was doing well; I had passed a guy who was dressed as a golfer and hitting a plastic golf ball along the course as he pulled his clubs behind him. I had also passed runners dressed in full costume as Papa Smurf, Darth Vader, Homer Simpson, and a full-size phone booth and a guy running the race completely backward, who held the world record for fastest marathon run backward. The crowd support was enormous, and most of the pubs were packed wall-to-wall with well-wishers, cheering and toasting all the runners as they passed by. The route passed close to the Mayflower Pub, where the pilgrims had first assembled to set sail for America, but because they were low on money, they had decided to move the ship to Plymouth to avoid having to pay mooring fees.

As I neared the halfway point of the Tower Bridge, I passed Katie Austin and Gordon Fryer, who, along with Katie's father, were running the race; the men were in tuxedos and Katie was in a wedding dress, complete with running shoes. The couple stopped at the Tower Bridge, and after a full wedding ceremony, they got back on the course and finished the race, raising close to $30,000 for charity. The groom, Gordon, joked to the local press before the wedding ceremony, "At thirteen miles, it has got to be the longest walk down the aisle."

The rain had stopped for most of the race, but at mile fifteen, the skies opened, and "it was raining cats and dogs," a phrase whose origin was thought to be early seventeenth-century London, where heavy rain had occasionally carried dead animals from the filthy street. Running in a heavy, cold rain was one of the most miserable experiences in life, and the heavy downpour quickly thinned out the large crowds along the course as they headed into the nearest warm pub. The thought of joining them was becoming more appealing, but I was in the final stretch of the last six miles—the point where most runners started to question why they were doing this to their bodies.

Once again, I was beginning to feel that running three marathons in such a short period of time was insane.

The rain stopped just as I passed Cleopatra's Needle along the shore of the Thames River and rounded mile marker twenty-five. Big Ben and the Parliament Building came into sight. I completed the last mile as wet as a seal and feeling like I was wearing cement blocks for shoes, but once again I raised my arms into the air in a sign of victory as I crossed the finish line on The Mall in front of Buckingham Palace.

I found Sarah and my parents, who were all huddled under an umbrella at our designated meeting spot. The race had been an incredible experience, and even with the heavy, cold rain, I had enjoyed every minute of it.

God Bless America

"Thank you for doing this with me," my mother leaned over and whispered to me.

"Mom, it's nothing. Sarah and I enjoy doing this, and we wanted to come here sometime anyway. Sarah and I love being able to spend this time with you and Dad," I said as the usher showed us to our seats.

There was one place that my mother loved to go with my father and her three sons, and that place was church. It was Sunday morning and my parents' last day in London before heading back home to tell their friends about meeting the Queen. We were spending the morning enjoying Sunday mass at the magnificent St. Paul's Cathedral.

The church dated back to the seventeenth century and had been rebuilt many times over. After the Great Fire of London in 1666, Christopher Wren had been awarded the honor of designing the rebuilding of the cathedral on the existing foundation. The new structure was finally completed in 1708. Even though the structure was targeted during the Blitz, and because its large size made it easily identifiable from the sky, the church never took a direct hit and survived the bombing. A bomb did hit the cathedral directly, but it was on a time delay, and it never exploded—confirmation of divine intervention, perhaps? If the bomb had detonated, the cathedral would surely have been totally destroyed.

Usually, royal marriages took place at Westminster Abbey, but the church had been used for the royal wedding of Prince Charles and Lady Diana Spencer, because it could seat many more people, giving the church the honor of being the setting for the fairy-tale wedding, which had been watched by millions of people around the world.

The church was one of London's most visited tourist sites, and many American tourists visited the church specifically to see the American Memorial Chapel dedicated in 1958 to the American servicemen and women who had died in World War II. Many European tourists visited the church to see and experience the Whispering Gallery, which was high up in the interior of the dome. Because of a quirk in the dome's construction, you could whisper directly into the wall and even the slightest of whispers could clearly be heard directly on the opposite side of the dome from where the whisper originated.

As the choir sang, I enjoyed the moment of being there with Sarah and my parents. I gazed up toward the heavens, taking in the church's amazing ceiling.

The church was packed with several hundred people, but the majority were tourists who wanted to see the church free of charge. Even though Europe was filled with some of the most beautiful, historic, and important churches in the world, churches throughout much of Europe were mostly empty. In many European countries, going to church had fallen out of fashion, and attendance had declined in the previous twenty years. It was not uncommon to hear Europeans say that the churches were for the tourists.

Like most kids, I had not chosen my religion while growing up, instead I had inherited it from my parents. I considered my parents to be highly religious, but not in a judgmental or prejudiced way. My parents had tried their best to make religion a part of our lives, and there was nothing that made my parents happier than the news that Sarah and I made it to Sunday mass. Even though there were many beautiful and historic churches in London, we always discussed going each Sunday, but more often than not, we found a reason not to go. When we did, we found the church mostly empty.

One Sunday morning, we had attended mass at St. Martin-in-the-Fields Church on the northeast corner of Trafalgar Square. The service had been sparsely populated, and most of those there were elderly people. The church had enough history in it to fill a phone book and was completing a major restoration project. Halfway through the service and almost as if on cue as the clergyman asked those in attendance to open up their hearts and wallets to assist the church, a steady stream of water began to rain down from the ceiling, and the ushers rushed to find large buckets to catch the falling water.

It was widely reported that "Christian Europe" was not very Christian anymore. The English were no longer a deeply religious society, and the large historic and architecturally impressive churches had become seen more as a relic of days past, when religion had meant something to the English. Marriage was on the decline as more and more English and European couples chose to live in monogamous relationships and sidestep the church altogether, avoiding an expensive wedding. Americans would be shocked by the high number of babies officially born out of wedlock, especially in northern Europe, where religion was of little or no interest to the people. If Europe continued to position itself as a counterweight to America, and America was religious, then Europe would not be religious.

Europeans had a difficult time with Americans thinking of themselves as a secular society in which religion does not dictate political decisions; our presidents are sworn in on a Bible, and they often end important speeches to the nation with "And may God bless America," the likes of which you would never hear out of the mouth of a European political official. In America, our money has the words "In God We Trust" printed on it. Presidential candidates had to prove their religious credentials to have any chance of winning the White House. George Bush used the phrases "leading a crusade against evil" and "with the help of God, we will win this war" in a speech on the war on terrorism. Europeans were shocked and used it in their argument that the war in Iraq was just a large, faith-based initiative from America. Europeans like to point out that Osama bin Laden and Taliban leaders and their representatives use similar language, with phrases such as "With the help of Allah, we will crush the infidels." Europeans have a difficult time understanding what religion really means to Americans and its influence on everyday life in America.

My explanations of the subject did not help, because I often found myself contradicting one statement about religion in America with another. Around 95 percent of Americans claimed they believed in God. Close to 80 percent of Americans viewed themselves as Christian. Millions of Bibles were bought or given away as gifts each year in America. Over 90 percent of Americans claimed to own at least one Bible, with the average household owning four. At last count, Sarah and I had five Bibles stored somewhere in multiple boxes deep in our storage closet at home. Most of them had been given to us as we passed through religious rites of passage in our lives from baptisms, confirmation in the church, or first communion. But how religious were Americans really? Many Europeans point out that as a heavily religious society, we should have a better track record of following the Ten Commandments—number six, "thou shalt not kill," being an important one. Some of the biggest shoot-'em-up killing spree headlines come out of America.

It was also reported in Europe that a Gallup poll demonstrated that less than half of Americans were able to name the first book of the Bible—I couldn't. Only one-third of Americans knew who delivered the Sermon on the Mount—got me there as well. Sixty percent of Americans could not name five of the Ten Commandments, while 80 percent could name all the ingredients in a Big Mac. I could name all the ingredients in a Big Mac, but I could only name nine of the Ten Commandments. I forgot "Thou shalt not covet," but in my defense, I don't really know what that means.

On the other hand, *The Da Vinci Code* was one of the best-selling books in America in recent years. It caused a huge uproar and a cottage industry. A huge number of books debunking the book's religious themes were published, all because of one little sentence on the first pages of the book that states, "All descriptions of artwork, architecture, documents, and secret rituals in this novel are accurate." The word that Americans seemed to forget in the statement was the word "novel"—a novel is a work of fiction, and in that case, not a religious text.

In true American fashion of being an incredibly mobile society, we changed jobs, spouses, and homes on a regular basis. Americans had also become increasingly mobile with their choices of religion; almost half of Americans had changed from the denomination of their childhood to another denomination, such as in my case. Many had changed to a new faith, and a growing number had dropped their faith all together. Religion was no longer a matter of inheritance in America; it had become a matter of choice. The religious marketplace in America had become incredibly competitive, especially in the marketing toward younger people. Churches were trying new tactics, such as opening doors to gays and lesbians and serving beer during Bible study, literally taking the edge off of religion in an attempt to acquire or retain new members.

As an American, I was still trying to understand what religion really meant to America and what the future holds for religion in America. Would we, too, end up like Europe? And if so, would it then cause Europe to quickly find interest in religion so as not to be considered "American"?

The younger generations in America saw how religion caused so many conflicts in the world—someone had to be right, making everyone else wrong—and that worries me. I secretly hoped that the Buddhists had it right. Buddha looked like an interesting guy to hang out with in the afterlife, as he might sit us all down and tell us where we all went wrong. I also saw hope in the future of religion in the youthful, smiling faces of the couples in church who were looking to gain approval to get married in that church or have a baptism. Sarah and I were once two of those people, often going out of our way to make sure the priest noticed us by sitting in the front rows of the church every Sunday before our wedding.

Saying that Europe was no longer religious was not entirely true. Even though the churches might be empty in many parts of Europe, the mosques were full, and, unlike churches, many more were being built.

- Chapter Seventeen -

When in Greece, Do as the Greeks Do

✦

With finals just a recent memory, it was once again time to put the books away, earn another stamp in our passports, and find some warmer spring weather in southern Europe. Sarah and I were "taking a holiday" and flying to Greece for the week. Sarah had been to Greece before, and I had never been, which meant that I was awarded the window seat on the flight.

We landed in Athens, and the sensation of the warm, early afternoon sun energized and excited us as we dug through our bags to find our sunglasses, before exiting the airport to jump into a taxi that would take us to our hotel. The airport had been filled with advertisements for an event to be held shortly in Athens called Eurovision. A taxi pulled up alongside the curb in front of us, and it also had a large advertisement for Eurovision painted on the side.

As we got into the taxi, I asked Sarah, "What do you think Eurovision is?"

"Not a clue," she said.

"Hello, my friends. How are you? Where are you from?" the taxi driver said, as he tried to get a good look at us in his rearview mirror while speeding away from the curb, with my right leg still sticking out of the car. "Sorry about that, my friend. Where we headed?"

I told the taxi driver, who was becoming more charming by the second, the address of the hotel, but he did not say a word.

"I don't think he heard you," Sarah leaned over and whispered to me.

"I'm not sure if you heard me, but—" The taxi driver cut me off before I could finish my sentence, saving me from the embarrassment I was bringing on myself by talking so loudly.

"Sorry, my friends, but I'm not sure I can take you there," he said.

"You can't?" I asked.

"No, I can't. Ah, how do you say in English?" He was motioning his hands to indicate that he was trying to think of a word, and then it suddenly came to him. "Demonstration," he said; he smiled with satisfaction that he had successfully remembered the English word. "Yes, there is a demonstration, and the city center is temporarily closed. But every problem has one hundred answers, and we only need one," he said with a friendly smile, as he took his hands off the steering wheel, picked up a map and a cell phone, and shifted the car into a higher gear—all while steering with his knees. His solution was to get us as close as possible and let us walk the remaining mile to our hotel.

We rolled our suitcases through the narrow streets of Athens in search of our hotel. There were no cars on the streets, the shops were all closed, and the streets were mostly empty.

"Wow, this is strange. What do you think is going on?" I asked Sarah.

We had booked a nice hotel in the shadows of the Acropolis in a popular tourist area, but the only sign of life was the occasional police officer flying by us on a motorcycle and large buses full of riot police trying to keep up with them. We finally reached our hotel, which was a big relief, since the road just ahead was blocked by a group of firemen putting out a small fire at the front of what appeared to be a small bank.

The cool air of the hotel lobby felt good, because my shirt was just about completely soaked with sweat from carrying all our bags through the streets under the hot afternoon sun. Sarah collapsed into a chair as I went to check us in. I gave the hotel clerk our reservation number and credit card as I peeked out the window and down the street.

"Is everything okay?" I asked with curiosity in my voice

"Yes, Mr. Ryan. Everything is in order," she said.

"I meant, is everything okay outside," I said.

"Yes, Mr. Ryan," she said.

"Well, what happened, then?" I asked as I looked at the firemen still spraying water on the fire, noticing that all the other storefront windows were smashed. "What smashed all the glass windows?"

"Oh, that is nothing," she said, shrugging her shoulders. "It will be cleaned up shortly, and the shops will reopen. Thank you for being our guest, and enjoy your time here with us."

I believed the Greek people invented the shoulder shrug. If you asked them why Greeks did the things they did, they answered with a shrug of the shoulders and replied, "Because we are Greek. We do things differently."

From our balcony, we could see the small destruction of smashed storefront windows and hear sirens blaring in the distance. We got more reassurance from the hotel concierge, who almost comically continued to answer my questions with her standard and continued reply, "Oh, that is really nothing." Little did we know that she was telling us the truth. It really was nothing; just another day in the life of being Greek, where protesting was part of the culture.

Our arrival to Athens had been greeted by a thirty thousand-strong, massive antiwar, antiglobalization demonstration, including a quite common element to many demonstrations: a small group of anarchists. The demonstration was being held near the city center and in central Syntagma Square. The anarchists had seized the opportunity in the large mass of demonstrators to throw rocks through many of the storefront windows and even tried to burn down a few banks, including the one next to our hotel.

We walked down the street, trying to avoid stepping in broken glass, but we were curious to see the extent of the damage. The riots were over, and the majority of the participants in the demonstration had filled the small cafés and restaurants within the area, their signs and banners rolled up and placed under the tables; all were talking enthusiastically, as if their hometown football team had just scored a big victory. It was interesting to see the diverse selection of banks and storefronts that had been damaged. The large McDonald's had received some damage to their windows, as had the Lacoste store and many of the European chain clothing stores. Strangely, the Nike store and the huge Starbucks next to our hotel had received no damage whatsoever, even though all the other surrounding storefront windows had been heavily damaged.

For a country that was known for moving slowly, a long, steady stream of trucks quickly entered the area, boarding and measuring the storefront areas for replacement glass, leading me to wonder if maybe the anarchists were really part of the storefront glass replacement union and they felt it was time to find some more work. Within two days, all the storefront glass had been fixed. Large and destructive demonstrations like the one that had welcomed us to Greece were scary to witness, but they were part of the Greek culture and perfectly harmless to any tourists who visited Greece, as long as they stayed out of the way. Demonstrations and protests were common enough that they no longer made international news. And because tourists were never the targets of such misadventures by a few bad apples, the United States State Department did not have any travel warnings for Greece.

Parents had protested in their younger years, and they felt it was perfectly acceptable for their kids to skip school to join in on the occasional demonstration. Greece was considered the birthplace of democracy, and you can't have a democracy without the right to raise your voice in protest if needed. The locals didn't seem to mind and found no aggravation when their lives were disrupted by demonstrations, simply altering their routes of travel when trains and roads were temporarily closed because of protestors.

The next morning, the bright, warm sun shone through our hotel room windows, enticing us to wake up and start enjoying the warm weather and the day, so we got out of bed to explore the city. The streets were quiet, as the shops that catered to tourists had not opened. We slowly made our way toward Syntagma Square to have breakfast and see the changing of the guard before making our way to the Acropolis, where we would spend the morning exploring the magnificent ruins.

For many years, Athens had been thought of as a smog-filled mess of a city that most tourists literally spent hours in just to see the Acropolis as quickly as possible before escaping to the many cruise ships taking them to the heavenly Greek islands. When Athens was awarded the Summer Olympics, many criticized the selection and said that the Greeks would never be able to host the Olympic Games successfully. For a while, it appeared that the critics might have been right. But just in time, the Greeks had pushed aside their well-known, it-will-get-done-tomorrow attitude, and the city was magnificently transformed. The 2004 Summer Olympics were a huge success and gave a massive boost to the city's tourism.

During the preparations, the metro underwent a huge transformation, and it was still apparent that it was a great source of pride for the Greeks, because it was the only place in the entire city where graffiti was not found. The rebuilding of the metro had been terribly behind schedule, because the workers kept having to stop work on the extension of the tracks; they kept finding new archeological finds every time they started digging. Professional archeologists had to be brought in to survey the area each time a new find was made.

The temperature was quickly rising as the sun shone down, and we snapped picture after picture of Greek soldiers marching in formation. Each was dressed in the famous uniform that included white tights, a kilt, and pom-pom-covered clogs and balanced a large, heavy, wooden gun over his shoulder. The soldiers marched in front of the parliament building, directly in front of the Tomb of the Unknown Solider. They marched back in forth, arms raised high in the air, opposite legs also rising high into the air and held for a split second before lowering and moving forward. After the ceremony had ended and Sarah and I had debated whether the changing of the guards had any value besides entertaining the tourists and frustrating the locals with street closures, we walked a short distance to the entrance of the Acropolis and climbed our way up the sloping and winding gravel pathway to the top, for an up close view of the Parthenon.

At night, the Acropolis was beautifully lit up, providing a great view for the diners eating at the many great Greek restaurants circling it. Each night, we drank Greek wine, dined on *souvlaki* and many different Greek olives

that went perfectly with the wine, and enjoyed the incredible night view of
the Acropolis. After stops for pictures at the Temple of Athena Nike and the
Theatre of Herodes Atticus, we made our way down for a cold, Greek beer
and an early lunch before the afternoon's activities.

A short distance from where we were eating lunch, a brand new Acropolis
museum was slowly being built. The soon-to-be-completed glass and cement
building had added another piece of propaganda in the twenty-five-year
old campaign by the Greek government to have the 160-meter long strip of
marble depicting the Panathenaic procession, which had originally adorned
the Parthenon before Lord Elgin had removed it two hundred years before
and sold it to the British Museum.

We spent the afternoon on a guided bus tour to the nearby coast to view
the ruins of the Temple of Poseidon. The temple was built high up on the
cliffs facing out to the sea, a fitting site to worship the god of the sea. Lord
Byron, the English poet and national hero to the Greeks, set in motion a
terrible tradition when he carved his name into the stone ruins. A couple of
people in our tour group were trying to add their names to the thousands
of other tourist names carved into the ruins while our tour guide was not
looking.

There was still so much to see in Athens, but it was all starting to blend
together, and we decided it was time to get out of the big city and head to the
islands and decided to divide our remaining time between the Greek islands
of Paros and Santorini.

We boarded the ferry to take us to the islands as the locals traveling back
home rushed onto the boat ahead of us and fought over the better indoor
smoking sections of the ship, while the few tourists who were boarding looked
for the better outdoor sections offering the best views. The boat ride to Paros
would be short, because it was one of the closer islands. As the ship pulled
away from the docks, the combination of the saltwater breeze and the smell
of the suntan lotion that Sarah was using to cover my face in a white, gooey
mess reminded me of past spring break vacations.

"How old is this lotion?" I asked. It seemed to disagree with my skin.

As soon as the large ship sailed out of the harbor, a series of announcements
were broadcasted throughout the entire ship. We had to listen to a long series
of loud emergency instruction announcements. The announcements were
made in first Greek, then Italian, then Spanish, then English, and finally
French. If there were ever a real emergency on board the ship, the order
of language in announcements would determine who got the seats on the
lifeboats and would most likely survive. Even though the announcements
were made in French last, there is a good chance the French would just push
their way onto the lifeboats and would all be saved.

"Didn't your mother ever teach you how to clean your ears?" Sarah asked; she was satisfied that there was no way I could get any rays of sun on my fair skin and had moved on to the cleanliness of my ears. "Wow, you've sure got big ears," she said, reaching into my ear with one of her sharp nails to pry away the small bit of wax that was annoying her.

"That's it. I'm out of here," I said in protest, as I got up and out of harm's way. "I'll go get us some breakfast."

"Sounds great. After breakfast I will clean out those big ears of yours," Sarah said in a devilish voice that suggested that she meant what she said.

As I stood in a long line to place an order, I looked through all the various euro coins that I would shortly need to pay for the food. The picture on the national side of the 2 coin caught my attention. The coin had been minted for Greece's transition from the drachma to the euro, and the picture on the coin depicted the nymph Europa being abducted by Zeus, who had taken the form of a white bull and raped the nymph. I found it slightly amusing that Greece got away with the national side of the 2 depicting a Greek god as he dominated Europa, the nymph Europe eventually got its name from.

The transition to the euro by Greece and the other participating European Union members was an amazing story itself. The event was considered to be the biggest logistical undertaking in Europe since World War II, and it was very difficult for the twelve initial countries to convert their currencies to the euro because a nation's currency was part of its history, identity, and national pride. The Greek drachma was the oldest currency on earth, and its long streak officially ended on January 1, 2002, at the stroke of midnight; all business transactions had to be completed in euros, or at least listed in euro prices. All the participating countries had given themselves a honeymoon period, when both the old and new currencies were accepted, except for the Germans, who felt they did not need a practice run. At midnight on January 1, 2002, the German deutsche mark had been made completely obsolete. The Germans proved everyone wrong, and the immediate transition was a success.

The burden of the transition to the new single currency was placed in the hands of banks and businesses, and a huge undertaking of preplanning had to be completed to have all the newly minted euros in place in ATM machines and in cash registers for the January 1 transition. There were widespread stories of banks having to reinforce their old floors to be able to store the newly minted and heavy coins. In predictable fashion, the French banking employees' union threatened a nationwide strike because of the extra work they were being asked to perform to get the new currency in place. But the single currency made it much easier for businesses and tourists to travel from country to country within the euro zone without having the headache and added expense of exchanging money at each border.

I was a little concerned that we were the only tourists to disembark when the boat made its stop at the island of Paros. The island had been recommended to us because of its smaller, less-developed tourism industry, promising us a slightly more authentic Greek island experience versus the larger, more popular islands that catered predominantly to large numbers of tourists. Paros was made up of smaller villages tucked between hills, vineyards, and olive groves. Our hotel was just a short walk to the town and small harbor and provided views of the small and colorful fishing boats that bobbed up and down in the small waves.

The owner of the hotel greeted us warmly, thanked us for staying there, and said we would be treated like family. We smiled in appreciation at the compliment, and he continued, "No, trust me. You will be treated like family. You are the only ones staying here besides my family at the moment. We are just opening for the season, and you are our first guests, so you are now family."

I thought back to my Greek professor saying I must ask for half off the nightly rate, but I did not have the heart to ask because we were family. The owner carried our bags to the room for us as we followed him through the small and narrow winding outdoor path, passing a small swimming pool that had a wooden sign tacked on the wall, informing visitors that the pool was closed every day from three o'clock to five o'clock for the siesta period.

After all the walking we had done in Athens, it was nice just to lie in bed and watch television while listening to the waves on the beach. All the channels were in Greek, and we watched the Greek version of *Deal or No Deal*, since you did not really need to understand the Greek language to know how the contestants were doing.

Paros lacked the historical sites, extensive shopping, and luxury hotels that many of the other Greek islands were known for, but we could not put a price on the way we were treated in the mostly empty seaside restaurants by the staff who showed great interest in where we were from and how we liked Greece. We dined on grilled octopus and fish that the boat captains literally brought in and handed to the chef right in front of us.

We enjoyed the misfortune of two English women who were sitting a few tables away from us at an open seaside restaurant. They had mistakenly ordered a large glass of the strong, Greek, aniseed-flavored liquor known as ouzo; they gasped for air after each took a large initial gulp of it. It was tough to blame them for their mistake, because the alcoholic drink was so popular with tourists. The restaurant placed the drink option on the menu directly next to other popular drinks such as Pepsi, lemonade, water, and iced tea. I did wonder for a second whether we should warn them when we heard them ask out loud, "I wonder what this Ouzo drink is?" But that would have been no fun, and when in Greece, do as the Greeks do.

We spent our last day renting a Jeep convertible and exploring the rest of the island and its many beaches. After dropping off the car, we grabbed a bottle of cold, white wine and navigated our way to a flat area of rocks along the shoreline to watch the sun set into the breathtaking turquoise-colored waters. Sarah looked so beautiful wading into the shallow waters with the backdrop of the small, anchored fishing boats that still bobbed up and down in the water in the slight breeze. Even though it was a perfect day, I could tell she was a little sad. When I asked her what was wrong, she said, "I was just thinking that the last family vacation I had had with my parents and sisters was when we all came to Greece together." I completely understood the significance of the moment and why it made Sarah feel the way she did. A family tragedy forever had made experiencing a vacation with her entire family ever again impossible.

- Chapter Eighteen -

A Second Honeymoon

✦

The next morning we boarded the same ferry that had dropped us off on the island. The ferry had slightly more passengers than it had had on the first leg of the trip, but we were still able to easily find a spot in the sun to enjoy the views of the passing islands as the ship made its way to Santorini. It would be a couple of hours before we would get our first glimpse of the magnificent caldera. With all the stress of school and finals, it was nice to have the time to get away and relax. Sarah had saved up a good amount of vacation time so that we would be able to live "the European life" of more frequent and longer vacations.

It was no big secret that Americans were given, and took, the fewest vacation days of any nation on earth. The number of mandated holiday and vacation days that the government requires us to take was a frightening zero, while the United Kingdom government required twenty days of vacation, France required thirty days of vacation, and Germany required twenty-four days of vacation and ten holidays. Not only did Americans take the fewest number of days off from work, but we usually only took two or three consecutive days off, or mini vacations. If we asked for two consecutive weeks off, our bosses would most likely tell us, "Go ahead and take two weeks off, but don't come back," so we stuck to the "keep it short so I don't get fired" or "I'll be gone just long enough that they don't realize they don't really need me" vacations. When we finally did take some time off, we couldn't seem to get away from our Blackberrys or laptops that usually accompanied us and were often found sitting right there next to us at the pool.

It seems we Americans had come to identify who we were as individuals mostly by our work. We were scared to lose our jobs, because that would mean a temporary loss of our identities. Often, the first question out of our mouths when we met someone at a social gathering was "What do you do for a living?" I have often been tempted to answer this question by saying, "Oh, I'm a drug dealer" because I feel it would lead to a much more interesting discussion than describing the activities of work.

All that hard work that we Americans did was probably part of the reason why we die three years younger than Europeans on average. We celebrated the successes of our work by often turning the richest and most successful businesspeople into huge celebrities. Money was our scorecard on how we were doing, and we couldn't help but take a peek over at our neighbors' to see what new car was parked in the driveway or to envy them when a delivery truck was parked outside their houses, dropping off new flat screen televisions. What I found so strange was that, even though work was so important to us, most of us were still searching for our dream job. The French might all hate their jobs, but at least they were home early enough each night to drink a glass of wine and complain about why they should be the boss, when we were still all at work trying to become the boss.

The ferry made its way through the Santorini caldera, and I was speechless at its beauty. I tried to take a picture that would capture it, but it was impossible. High up the sides of the volcano walls of the caldera, you could see numerous whitewashed buildings, all seemingly stacked on top of each other.

"Isn't it gorgeous?" Sarah asked. "Amazing. Absolutely amazing."

Since we had taken seats on the front deck of the ship to enjoy the view, we were the last to depart through the rear of the vessel. We stood in a long line in the sweltering heat, waiting for a taxi to pick us up. When we finally made it to the front of the taxi line, there were no taxis left. Finally, a taxi pulled up, and we asked an Australian couple in line behind us if they wanted to share the taxi so they would not have to wait in the sun any longer. They appreciated our gesture and accepted the invitation wordlessly, handing us each a cold beer. I had always loved Australia. How could you not enjoy a nation of people who always had a cold beer close at hand?

The four of us piled into the small taxi together. Sarah did not feel like drinking a beer, but instead of giving it back, I commandeered it from her and was trying to balance Sarah on my lap while holding a beer in each hand. The taxi driver was a mostly white-haired man who strongly resembled Ernest Hemingway in his older years. The taxi dashboard was overrun with numerous religious statues and icons that competed for attention. The driver asked the Australian couple which hotel they were staying at and then asked Sarah and me the same question.

With brutal honesty, and to the point of comedy, the driver said, "Your hotel is very good, and your hotel is not so good." Thankfully, he had pointed at us first.

There must be a rule in Greece that the older you were, the worse you were allowed to drive, because our driver sped along the road, weaving in and out of traffic as if we desperately needed to get to a hospital in a life-or-death situation. He accelerated quickly into oncoming traffic on a two-lane highway, passing three cars and two buses before swerving back and slamming on the brakes to turn safely into the hotel entrance and drop off the Australian couple.

Any hope that the taxi driver had been kidding were quickly squashed upon the Australian couple seeing their hotel of choice. The hotel itself was not bad-looking; it just did not have views overlooking the caldera like many of the other hotels on other parts of the island. I thanked the Australian couple for the beer that I was mostly wearing on my shirt and Sarah was wearing on her back. They offered us "good luck" in making it to our hotel, and the driver sped off. Within a minute, we were once again passing the same cars, buses, and trucks that had just barely avoided smashing into the rear of our vehicle.

When we pulled into the parking lot of our hotel, the first thing we saw was the amazing view overlooking the deep blue water. The hotel was reasonably priced, and the room came with a small kitchen and large balcony that looked out over the water. Reaching the main section of the hotels, shops, and restaurants of the town of Oia required that we walk one hundred yards down a small dirt path that would someday be home to a large luxury hotel. The view was amazing—it felt as though we could just walk right over the cliff and directly into the sea. After inspecting our room, we put on our bathing suits and made our way to the pool that had been built into the side of the cliff. Sarah started trying to put more suntan lotion onto my white skin, which was turning slightly pink as I unfolded my towel and placed it over the chair. As I straightened out the corners of the towel, I looked up and caught the glance of a man directly across from me on the other side of the pool who appeared to be giving me a nasty look.

"Sarah, did you see the look that guy just gave me? I wonder what his problem is?" I said.

As I continued to fold the ends of my towel around the back of the chair, it hit me that the towel I had brought was a beach towel with the St. George flag printed on it—the official flag of England. The man looked Italian, and with the World Cup starting in just a few weeks, he was mistaking me for an Englishman.

"Bloody hell, I should walk right over to that bloke over there and let him know our boys are going to do a real number on 'em in the cup," I said with my best British accent.

Sarah acknowledged my joke with a smile and said, "All right, love, you do that, then. I'm getting it on with the sun at the moment."

"Wow, nice English accent, but I still hate how you easily turn a nice golden brown color while I turn into a lobster in seconds. Does that oil you're putting on even have any sun protection in it?" I said.

We spent the rest of the day playing cards and drinking Greek beer while sitting around the pool. A group of actual English people who had obviously been drinking way too much did show up at the pool and get into it with the Italian man when he complained to the hotel staff about all the noise they were making.

Later that night, we walked along the small stone walkways past some of the most luxurious hotels in the world, each one built right on top of the next and all whitewashed in bright white with blue window trim and doors. Many of the hotels had pools that offered infinite views into the distant sea below. On our way to dinner the first night, we stopped in a small market store.

"Wait a minute. There is something I want to pick up," I said to Sarah as I slipped into the store. Sarah was slightly amused when I exited the store carrying a box of dog treats.

Many of the island shopkeepers and restaurant owners had adopted dogs as pets, but the animals usually spent their lives in the street outside the owners' shops or restaurants. Since Santorini was an island, the dog population could easily be controlled. Each owner usually placed a collar on his dog to identify that it had an owner.

We picked a restaurant that offered nice views out over the sea so we could look at all the cruise ships coming into and out of the harbor in the far-off distance. Greece was one of the few places in the world where yes actually meant no, because the Greek word for yes (*neh*) sounds very much like no, and the Greek word for no (*okeh*) sounds very much like okay. "Honeymooners? *Neh*? Very good!"

Because of our youthful looks and my overly sun-soaked face, many of the restaurant owners, hotel clerks, and shopkeepers mistakenly thought that we were honeymooners enjoying our first few days of marriage on the beautiful and romantic island. I thought, *If it gets us a better room, better meals, or some sort of discount or upgrade, then sure, we are honeymooners.*

At the end of the evening, we wandered slowly back to our hotel, enjoying the view of the moon in the sky as it illuminated the whitewashed buildings hugging the side of the cliff. As we passed each sleeping dog, we stopped and placed a couple of dog treats next to him before walking on.

The next morning, we made our way back down the dirt path to a small café overlooking the caldera to have some coffee and egg croissants and read the newspaper while we waited for the shops to open. On the way to breakfast, we passed two dogs, who approached us with their tails wagging. As the small shops selling jewelry, artwork, and souvenirs finally opened for the day, we made our way out of the café. To our surprise, the same two dogs were still there, two others had joined them, and all four of them were following us. As we walked down the street, the four dogs became six, and six became eight, before we finally ran out of dog treats. For the rest of our stay on the island, we became the Pied Pipers of the dog world, with a small procession of dogs following us whenever we walked through the narrow streets. It gave us a sense of power, as many people moved out of the way when they saw us coming, and shopkeepers smiled in disbelief.

In the afternoon, we stopped at a small art gallery and instantly fell in love with an oil painting depicting the beautiful and unique scenery, with the whitewashed and blue painted buildings clinging to the sharply inclined sides of the island. The artist explained that each of her paintings had been painted on small wood planks taken from an old wooden floor at her grandfather's winery on the island.

"My grandfather says to me quite often, 'I don't get it. You slap a little paint on my old wooden floor and are getting rich off of it while I am breaking my back trying to make wine that nobody will buy.'"

After making our selection and thanking the woman, we left the gallery and made our way back to our hotel to change into some new clothes for the afternoon's activity.

"You do know what the *real* problem with globalization is?" I asked Sarah rhetorically.

"Oh, great. Here we go again. Can't we just have a nice hike and enjoy the view and warm weather?" she asked.

I often started conversations during long car rides or walks through the park with statements like "You *do* know what global warming could do to the tourist industry." or "You know what will happen if gas prices continue to rise?"

We were hiking together along a steep path that, if followed correctly, would lead us to the town of Fira for an afternoon of exploring the area. We passed many small hotels and churches on the way. We had misjudged the distance to the town, and the hot sun and lack of water made us thankful, upon our arrival into Fira, to still be alive and relieved that we had money to take a taxi back to our hotel. We walked through the town as we looked for a taxi to take us back to the cool swimming pool we were dreaming of, when we spotted our taxi driver friend, who appeared to be either dead or asleep at the wheel of his taxi in the middle of the street. The tourists in rental cars and on mopeds gave the strange sight a curious look as they drove around, while the locals did not even seem to notice and passed right by him.

We could not find a taxi, so we started walking toward a bus stop we had spotted on the outskirts of town. Just as we were about to reach the bus stop, a small car pulled up and an elderly lady got out right in front of us, arguing with the driver.

"Taxi. You need taxi?" the driver shouted at us with a smile.

"Yes," we said with a hesitant look, as the woman continued to yell at the man.

"Get in. I will take you to where you want to go!" he bellowed.

We got into the taxi and sped off, leaving the elderly lady standing in the dust that the car kicked up.

"What was that all about?" I asked the young driver.

"Oh, that was my mother. She is angry, because I stopped to pick you up and made her take the bus home," he said nonchalantly.

"You just kicked your mother out to pick us up?" I asked. I was starting to feel bad for accepting the ride, because it was still very hot out. "Will a bus be stopping at that stop soon?" I asked, hoping that the answer would be yes.

"Buses will be stopping there later in the day," he said. "She is tough woman. She will be fine."

We thanked the taxi driver and asked him to hurry back to pick up his mother.

"And don't pick up anyone else along the way until you get your mother home," Sarah added to our instructions.

Our last night on the island was spent enjoying our new power as the leaders of the island dogs. We rewarded them for their undying loyalty with even more dog treats. We dined on swordfish and fried octopus and enjoyed a free drink of ouzo with the restaurant owner, who, just like all the others, had mistaken us for honeymooners, or Sarah suggested that maybe he feared the pack of dogs waiting for us outside the restaurant.

The next morning, we got out of bed as the sun was still rising and made our way to the waiting taxi that would take us back to the ferry for the trip to Athens to catch a flight back to London. I was a little disappointed, but Sarah was relieved when we discovered that the taxi driver who was there to pick us up was not the same older driver who had originally dropped us off at our hotel and had been asleep at the wheel of his car in the middle of the street the day before. Our taxi driver made his way to the ferry terminal, taking the same winding road that had taken us to our hotel.

At the highest point on the island, we could see the sun slowly rising above the horizon on our left-hand side, and on our right-hand side, we could see the full moon slowly dipping below the horizon. It was an amazing sight that Sarah and I looked at in wonder before the moment was disrupted by loud honks of a car, as the taxi driver who had originally dropped us off (and who I secretly wished had picked us up) whizzed right past us at a high speed, cut directly in front of us, and within inches of our front bumper, narrowly avoided a head-on collision with another taxi driving the other way. Our young taxi driver let out a small curse while shaking his hand in the air. We could not understand what he said, but we could guess.

After a long day of taxis, ferries, airplanes, and trains, we finally made it home and climbed into bed for a good night's sleep.

"So, what was your favorite part of the trip?" Sarah leaned over and asked as I turned off the light.

"The part where you did not ask me if we could take one of those stray island dogs home with us as a friend for Sydney," I said.

- Chapter Nineteen -

Roll That Cheese!

✦

A Short Story

For one full day during the month of May, the lunatics were let out of the asylum to gather in the English countryside at the top of Cooper's Hill to chase a seven-pound round block of Double Gloucester cheese down a steep and treacherous hill at the Cooper's Hill Cheese Rolling event. Actually, the lunatics were not let out for the yearly tradition, but the participants who showed up each year to compete in the event should be considered insane and probably locked up.

The Cooper's Hill Cheese Rolling competition was held each year near the town of Gloucester, England. The event got its name from the intimidating hill on which racers lined up at the top to chase a rounded, seven-pound block of Double Gloucester cheese as it rolled down the hill at speeds of up to seventy miles per hour. The first person to successfully descend the steep, two-hundred-yard incline and cross the finish line—conscious or unconscious, dead or alive—was declared the winner.

The event had gained fame around the world due to the many television and Internet highlights of bloody, dazed, and bruised participants somersaulting downhill like skiers, living a nightmare as their bodies were tossed like rag dolls. As racers tried to keep pace with the rolling cheese, the carnage of broken limbs and unconscious racers piled up in the wake of the cheese. Thousands of spectators lined the sides of the hill and chanted "Roll that cheese!" in anticipation of the start of the men's or women's race.

Adrenaline junkies from all over the world routinely showed up to "give it a go" and risked life and limbs, as injuries were an expected part of the event. There were so many injuries that ambulances waited at the bottom of the hill during the event to peel off the injured competitors and take them to the local hospital. Races during the event had been delayed, because all the ambulances had yet to return from the hospital after transporting a high number of casualties from the previous race

It seemed like a silly idea to risk life and limbs when the only prizes were bragging rights and the seven-pound block of Double Gloucester cheese for each winner. But what did I know? The tradition was some two hundred years old.

- Chapter Twenty -

Where's My Gnome Gone Run Off To?

✦

It was late May, and spring was well into its early transition to summer.

"Any extra tickets?" a woman whispered suspiciously in our direction as we walked past her on a small path leading to the grounds of the Royal Hospital in the Chelsea area of London.

The woman did not look like your typical ticket scalper, with her bright yellow polka-dotted cocktail dress and matching yellow hat, black shoes, and enough pearls on her neck and wrist to fill a jewelry store.

"I can't believe people are actually scalping tickets for this," Sarah said, starting to feel slightly underdressed.

"For once, I actually planned ahead and purchased tickets when they went on sale," I said.

"Crazy. All this for a garden show," Sarah said, looking down at her ticket.

"Don't even think of it," I said, as I snatched her ticket from her hands.

"Oh, come on. That woman back there probably has more money than the Queen. I'm sure I could get some serious money for this ticket. I did notice our bank account was running low again," she said, looking back to see if she could spot the woman still standing on the path.

It was a beautiful night, and we were spending it together enjoying another event in the summer social season, the prestigious Chelsea Flower Show. The show was immensely popular in London, and rightfully so. If football was the national sport, gardening was the national pastime, and the English proudly displayed their "green thumbs" as a true badge of honor. The garden show sold out months in advance and received extensive television coverage during prime-time viewing hours each night during the five-day show. The English had somehow found a way to make gardening very interesting, because I had watched the television coverage of the garden show almost each night that it was on. My father and grandmother, two gardening enthusiasts, would consider the show pure heaven.

The Chelsea Flower Show had a long history—just like almost everything else in the country—and dated back to 1852. The show's success was due to the organizers finding a way to improve it every year. We followed the tradition of the London summer social season and purchased two cold, ice-filled glasses of Pimm's, a gin-based alcoholic drink that has a spice and citrus taste to it and was usually mixed with lemonade or ginger ale. How could you not love a garden show where, in five days, eight thousand bottles of Laurent Perrier champagne and twenty thousand pints of Pimm's were consumed?

We walked around the grounds with a Pimm's in one hand and the digital camera in the other as we admired the amazingly detailed and luxurious gardens that had been shipped in from France, Japan, Africa, New Zealand, and many other countries from around the world and had taken weeks to build on the grounds of the show—many of them costing over $100,000. The show was referred to as the equivalent of the catwalk at a fashion show for the garden design community. Prior to the show opening, it was customary for the Queen to walk through the grounds and admire the gardens before the awards were handed out.

England had been in a drought for many months, and one of the themes of the show was water-wise gardening. With English gardeners facing a water hose ban—or, as the English refer to it, a hosepipe ban—in the coming summer months, many of the garden designs incorporated elements that would retain water. But in true English fashion, the opening of the show was greeted with a massive dousing of rain, causing much flooding in many of the gardens.

"Where are all the garden gnomes?" I asked Sarah, but not loud enough so others would hear me.

"You're right. Where are all those cute little garden gnomes? The English love their garden gnomes. Have they all been stolen?" she asked.

Garden gnomes were a popular accessory in English and European gardens, with their little red hats, white beards, and pipes in hand. Gnome-hunting was a term used to describe the sport of stealing garden gnomes and releasing them back "into the wild." Some stolen garden gnomes had even experienced around-the-world trips; videos of their exploits were placed on popular Web sites like YouTube. The American travel company Travelocity picked up on the pop culture phenomenon and featured an ad campaign with a garden gnome traveling around the world. Sadly, gnomes had been banned from the prestigious Chelsea Flower Show, because the show's organizers claimed that serious garden designers did not use gnomes in their gardens.

A Night of All Things Kitsch

After a week of hard work and studying, it was time to relax and spend the weekend with our friends. Upon returning from Greece, we had quickly discovered what the Eurovision fuss was all about. The evening was described to us as a night of tearaway skirts, lesbians kissing, sequined G-strings, and complete and utter, televised tastelessness. I had to be honest—the description of the event caught my interest, and we decided to have some friends over to eat, drink, and watch it together so they could tell us everything we needed to know about it.

Eurovision was an annual singing competition held in Europe that was a celebration of pop music and all things kitsch. If the American television shows *The Jerry Springer Show* and *American Idol* had a child together, the result would be Eurovision. The annual occasion routinely attracted more viewers for the one-night event than the Super Bowl did in the United States and was considered one of the most-watched nonsporting events in the world. The biggest difference between the events for the Super Bowl and Eurovision television viewing audiences was that even though both events ran close to the same time in length, Eurovision had few commercials, while some Americans watched the Super Bowl simply to watch the commercials specially created for the occasion that costs millions of dollars to produce and air during the event.

Eurovision started in 1956 as a way for war-torn Europe to come together during the rebuilding. Over the years, the event's format evolved, but the idea had stayed the same. Each participating European country held their own singing competition and sent the winner to represent the country in the Eurovision contest. The show was aired simultaneously across Europe, one act immediately following the next. The performers usually sang a pop song with a catchy chorus to it and attempted a stunt—e.g., two girls kissing or tearing away skirts to reveal thongs underneath—to differentiate each performance from the others and make a strong impression on the one hundred million-plus viewers watching the event in a pub or at a gathering of friends with an alcoholic drink in hand.

By far, the majority of the songs were sung in English—the French being some of the few to not perform in English. Once all the acts had performed, the voting began. The winner was selected through a point system that was determined by the general public voting via cell phones and home phones.

The catch was that we couldn't vote for the country our phone was registered in, so we could vote for any country but England. After all the acts had finished, there was a short break before announcers in each participating country revealed how many votes that country was awarding to each country, on a scale from a high of twelve points to a low of one, based on the call-in or text voting from that country.

When the votes were awarded, almost every country communicated to the rest of Europe on television in English, with France once again being the exception. The country of origin of the winning act was awarded the honor of hosting the event the following year. A Greek act won the event the year before and was therefore hosting the event.

The winner did not receive a trophy, and usually their music careers did not go any further, but in years past there had been some notable winners and participants. In 1974, an unknown band from Sweden by the name of ABBA won the contest by singing what would soon be a huge hit, "Waterloo." Olivia Newton-John had represented Britain; Julio Iglesias had represented Spain; and Celine Dion had represented the "Canadianesque" country of Switzerland.

I flipped the burgers on the barbeque, Sarah filled up our guests' drinks, and Sydney looked for the next willing person to scratch her ears. We all laughed together as another act followed the norm of executing the tearaway skirt trick on the performer and backup dancers. What made Eurovision so interesting was that even though the voting was one hundred percent democratic and transparent, so-called political voting and regionalism seemed to heavily influence who won each year. It was well known that it did not take much singing talent to win the competition, just a couple gimmicks, and maybe more importantly, good standing in the eyes of other Europeans— especially neighbor countries whose citizens liked to vote for each other.

It was difficult to think of Eurovision as a simple singing contest when you heard stories about things such as Serbia-Montenegro dropping out of the contest because Serbian voters and Montenegrin voters could not come to an agreement and decided to withdraw to avoid escalating tensions. Especially with a referendum to vote on independence for Montenegro, which would split the two former Yugoslavian territories, scheduled for the day after the competition.

Even though England had one of the better performances, because of its decision to assist the United States in the war in Iraq, the European voters used the competition as an opportunity to display their displeasure against England and awarded the band only twenty-five votes, placing them nineteenth out of the twenty-five participating countries. If the event was a barometer of true feelings of Europeans, France fared much worse than England, and it showed in the votes; both came in at the bottom of the standings, with France receiving just five votes and Israel receiving only four.

The real shocker of the night was the unexpected runaway success of the Finnish band Lordi, which performed their contagiously catchy tune, "Hard Rock Hallelujah." The blue-eyed, blond-haired band members had dressed in their usual gruesome gothic monster troll costumes, obviously influenced by the American rock band Kiss. The win ended Finland's forty-year streak of losing when the band received 292 total votes to Russia's 248-point performance, which included ballerinas and a woman in all-white body paint emerging from the center of a grand piano as if being born—weird, but memorable.

Prior to the contest, Finland had not been too happy with the group's entry, and even the president of Finland had gotten involved and tried to use her influence to get the group dropped from the contest. She had felt that the band's look and act had a negative impact on the youth of the country and was concerned that the act would diminish the country's reputation abroad, because the lead singer often sang while wielding a chainsaw. But after the win, the group returned to Finland to a hero's welcome. The lead singer of the band summed it up best following the remarkable turn of events a week after the competition: "Being a hero is easy. You just have to win the Eurovision song contest, apparently. Until a few weeks ago, the whole nation was against us totally. They did not want us to represent Finland. Now all the magazines in Finland are printing Lordi masks for children. There's not much logic going on inside. But let's face it, people are stupid."

Watching the event with our new friends from all over Europe was special and sort of made Sarah and me feel a little European. It was no big surprise whom everyone wanted to vote for, even though they openly admitted that their own country's entry into the contest had hardly deserved the vote. A television audience of 110 million watched the Finnish victory, which caught the attention of the American television company NBC, which was considering bringing a version of Eurovision to America to compete with the show *American Idol,* where each state would nominate an act to compete against all the other states. Living in Illinois, I will vote for Michigan, Indiana, Ohio, and Wisconsin—but don't expect any votes from me, Texas.

Fahrvergnügen

A few weeks before, Denis and I had been walking out from a morning session of swimming laps at the pool when he had handed me a small white envelope. As soon as he gave it to me, I knew what it was: a wedding invitation. For weeks,

Denis had been giving me updates on his wedding plans while we drank our morning coffee in Russell Square. We had laughed together, because many of the frustrations Denis was experiencing during his wedding planning with Jenny were very similar to the frustrations that Sarah and I had experienced. Denis described how the wedding reception was planned for a lodge high up in the mountains in southern Germany. As he described the setting, every German stereotype played through my head, with the wedding guests dressed in *lederhosen*, clinking large steins of beer together as they toasted, sang, and danced to old German folk songs.

Denis said it would be an honor if Sarah and I could attend. Even before Denis handed me the invitation, I had known that Sarah and I would not be able to, because the date on which they had chosen to get married was the same date of the wedding of another friend back in the United States that Sarah and I were heading home to attend. Denis had told me that even though he had only known me for a few months, he felt like I had been a friend for all his life. Since Sarah and I would not be able to make the wedding, we decided to all drive together to Wales for a weekend to get out of the city, have a nice meal, and spend some time together.

We decided to simply get into the car without making any hotel reservations and see where fate took us for the weekend. Denis and Jenny pulled up to our flat in a small, white, two-door Volkswagen that looked like it probably had some good stories to tell. Jenny had driven the car from Germany two months prior to moving in with Denis while he finished his MBA. Denis felt that he had to apologize for the appearance of the car, but since Sydney was coming with us and would most likely get into a few mud puddles on the trip, we actually felt better that the car was a little beaten up.

Since the car had been made for the German market, the driver's side was on the left instead of the right, causing a few stares from drivers passing us by on the right side of the front seat in the car where Sydney was sitting upright looking out the window providing the appearance that she was the one driving the car.

Wales was a small country located in southwest Great Britain. Our destination for the weekend was the Brecon Beacons National Park, a three-and-a-half-hour drive from London. We all tried to think of someone, something, or even a stereotype of Wales, but none of us could, so we were all traveling with a clean slate for first impressions of the country.

Sarah claimed her ancestors were from Wales, which Denis and Jenny found very interesting. Really, they were just trying to be nice and show sincere interest until I told them that, in every country we had visited in Europe so far, Sarah had claimed some of her ancestors had been from there.

Sarah had punched me in the arm to show that she did not appreciate my mocking her ancestry.

Three hours into the drive, we were tiring of being in the car. Denis started to drive a little faster to cut down the drive time, causing the old Volkswagen engine to strain from the added stress. Since it was officially Jenny's car, she was getting annoyed at Denis's treatment of her "old friend," and as couples often did during a long car ride, they began to argue.

Jenny had joined in on the pact to always speak English in front of us so we would not feel excluded and also so she could improve her English as quickly as possible. But Jenny's English was not nearly as good as Denis's, and she was badly losing the argument. In an effort to try to keep up, she was once again using the phrase "how do you say," as she literally thought each rebuttal out loud. Since I was sitting in the backseat directly behind her on the passenger's side, I tried to feed her English words to help her in the argument. But it was no use. Denis was a good debater, and I actually thought his argument was stronger than Jenny's, so we decided on a strategy of just calling Denis English swearwords and phrases most often overheard in the men's locker room in a high school. Their argument was going nowhere fast, so I finally told them to finish it in German. With Jenny finally on even footing, she seemed to make a quick comeback, as she was doing most of the talking.

They finally kissed and made up just as we arrived at the Brecon Beacons National Park. We were all tired of being in the car, including Sydney, who, it appeared, had picked up on the scent of open grass fields and was getting excited. The area was not much of a park, rather it was more of a giant landmass over five hundred square miles and full of picturesque scenery of rolling hills and small farms, with sheep gracefully grazing on many shades of green grass. The park had over thirty thousand inhabitants living on the large farms and in small villages and towns, which had interesting names like Llanddeusant, Crickhowell, and Llanfrynach.

Since no reservations and spontaneity was the theme of the trip, we had no agenda and no final destination. A small rainstorm unexpectedly rolled in, so we pulled into a tiny pub on the side of the road to wait out the rain. We entered the pub and spotted four farmers in mud-covered work boots sitting at the bar. It was obvious we were tourists, and they turned their heads for a good look at us. The sight of Sydney threw them off as to exactly where we were from.

"The dog can sit up here with us at the bar, but you scoundrels will have to sit over there in the measly corner and keep quiet." It took us all a second or two to comprehend the joke through the bartender's thick Welsh accent as he whistled for Sydney to come to him.

We waited out the storm with a pint of beer, and Sydney took turns sniffing the farmers' boots. Once the rain stopped, we took the farmers' recommendation and made our way to the town of Crickhowel to do some hiking. We could walk across large areas of the countryside designated as open land for the public, we just had to remember to close each gate we passed through to keep livestock in. Sydney had to always be under observation so that she did not disturb or scare farm animals or wildlife. By law, a farmer could shoot a dog that attacked or injured any of his animals.

After enjoying a nice walk through the countryside, we decided to start looking for a place to stay for the night, because it was getting late. By the time we arrived back in town, the visitor's center had closed for the evening, so we were on our own. Each bed-and-breakfast or inn sign we drove past, we inquired about available rooms for the night. We randomly drove down the area roads looking for signs advertising a place to stay.

"All right, everyone, keep your eyes peeled for a place to stop and ask," I said to the group.

"Keep our eyes peeled?" Jenny repeated the phrase, which she had obviously never heard and did not understand.

"'Keep your eyes peeled' is an expression used to mean 'keep alert' by keeping your eyelids peeled back so you don't miss what you're looking for." I was not sure if she truly understood my explanation; it looked like she was trying really hard not to blink, and she had a bug-eyed look on her face.

Every place we stopped was completely booked. The desk attendant at one place even said, in a not-so-polite tone, "Don't you know the Hay Festival just started?" I later learned that the Hay Festival in the nearby town of Hay-on-Wye had nothing to do with actual hay but was an extremely popular literary festival that drew almost one hundred thousand visitors for the ten-day event, which Bill Clinton had once described as "the Woodstock of the mind."

So much for spontaneity, we thought, as disappointment and frustration set in. It was looking hopeless that we would be able to find a place to stay for the night, and we were not looking forward to a long drive back to London. Sarah was the most disappointed of us all and took charge, calling as many hotels as she could find in our small Wales guidebook. We all sat silently in the car as we started the drive back to London.

Sarah finally broke the short silence with screams of, "I did it! I did it! Turn the car around because I found us a place!"

We were relieved that we had been spared the long drive back to London when we had just gotten to the park. Sarah had found us two rooms at separate hotels. We decided who would stay at each hotel based on the simple fact that one allowed dogs and the other did not. Denis and Jenny dropped us off at our hotel first. We pulled off the main road and onto a small dirt road that had large trees planted perfectly on each side, leading up a hill to a large and beautiful white hotel overlooking the valley. Sarah and I secretly smiled at each other, because the hotel had allowed dogs and the other had not, letting us avoid the awkward conversation of deciding who got to stay here.

We waved good-bye to Denis and Jenny as we walked through the front open hallway leading into the hotel. Honey, the resident Golden Retriever, greeted Sydney with a wag of the tail and a quick sniff. In no time, the two of them were outside taking turns chasing each other on the large front lawn. Denis and Jenny returned, and we sat outside on the hotel's terrace, enjoying a nice glass of wine as we watched the sun set in the distant valley.

The hotel was hosting a large wedding, and because of a last-minute cancellation, one room had become available for the night. It was apparent that the wedding guests were already drunk, as we could hear them trying to shout down the music coming from the bagpiper who had been entertaining the guests. A few minutes later, we watched the bagpiper storm out of the hotel and drive off as fast as he could.

The hotel had an international award-winning restaurant in it, and the four of us dined together under soft candlelight, enjoying Welsh lamb and beef with roast potatoes, Yorkshire pudding, and rich gravy, before ending the meal with some sticky toffee pudding. The meal was amazing. The chef came out to our table and told us how the meat we had enjoyed had been raised at the hotel's farm a few miles away.

As we enjoyed being together, Sarah told the story of how the two of us had bungee jumped off a bridge into the river below while tied together by our feet in New Zealand. Sarah told Denis and Jenny how she had made me promise her that if she did the jump with me, I would never climb Mount Everest. The story was fitting, because the name of the restaurant was Everest, after Sir George Everest, whose name had been given to the world's highest mountain in honor of his pioneering map work in the Himalayas. The hotel had a special connection to Sir George Everest, because he had been born in the hotel in 1790.

After dinner, we retrieved Sydney from our room and sank deep into the soft leather chairs and couches that surrounded the large and cozy fireplace in the bar area, and the hotel manager brought us a complimentary bottle of wine for having to listen to the loud wedding guests in the nearby ballroom. The wedding guests were so drunk, they felt they could sing better than the band and were trying to prove it.

The next morning, Denis picked us up and took us over to the hotel they had spent the night in so we could all have breakfast together. Sarah and I were relieved to find out that the hotel they had stayed in was also quite nice and appeared to be an old castle.

We would spend the day climbing a large hill or small mountain so we could get a view of the surrounding area and enjoy the sunny weather, and we were anxious to get going. We climbed higher and higher as Sydney chased us back and forth, having the time of her life. We could not fault her if she thought she was back in her native country of Ireland. We came upon a large flock of sheep grazing on the lush grass on the side of the mountain. A thousand eyes were on Sydney as the large flock of sheep cautiously watched her and slowly began moving away from her. The sheep had also caught Sydney's attention, and something in her genes seemed to be telling her something.

Wheaten terriers had originally been bred as all-purpose farm dogs that were used for herding, guarding, and watching the livestock. Sydney quickly picked up that the sheep were more afraid of her than she was of them. She desperately wanted to sniff them to find out what they were. She tried moving downwind from them to sniff the air. Sydney then tried a slow, sneaking approach, followed by a quicker, more aggressive approach. But each time, the herd of sheep managed to keep the same distance from her. Sarah called Sydney back, as she was afraid that Sydney's behavior would result in a farmer shooting her.

"Come on, Sarah, let's see what she can do," I said. "This is probably her only chance in life to use those herding skills of hers for real."

I allowed Sydney to investigate the sheep a little longer, until Sarah finally put an end to it and overruled me. In the tone of *"You better get over here now,"* Sarah snapped her fingers and called Sydney's name. Sydney reluctantly released her eyes' lock on the sheep. After a second or two of stubborn hesitation, she obediently walked over to Sarah, sat down next to her, and waited to be told it was okay to start walking again.

After a long day of hiking and after all the fresh country air we had enjoyed, we rode in tired silence back to London. Just as I was about to fall into a nice afternoon nap, a thought entered my mind.

"Oh, my God. Oh, my God," I said in disbelief.

"What is it? Is something wrong?" Denis asked as he looked back at me from the front seat.

"No. Everything is great, my German friend. I just realized that we are doing some serious *fahrvergnügen*," I said.

"What did you say?" Denis and Jenny asked. Denis said it first, since it took Jenny slightly longer to produce the English.

"*Fahrvergnügen*. We are doing some legitimate *fahrvergnügen*! Come on, what kind of Germans are you two?" I said with a laugh.

Denis and Jenny were quite interested in where I had learned the German word *fahrvergnügen* since my depth of German was about three words deep. I explained to them that in the late 1980s, Volkswagen had used the word as part of an American ad campaign, telling Americans that it meant "enjoy driving," and in some commercials using the tagline "*Fahrvergnügen*: It's what makes a car a Volkswagen." Denis and Jenny told us that the word was mostly used by older generations to describe a better time or golden era. I think they were really happy that I had learned another German word.

- Chapter Twenty-One -

Que Sera, Sera

✦

"Hello! Sarah, I'm home," I shouted, as I took off my jacket and braced myself for Sydney's welcome home bounce that would arrive any second.

"Auuggghhh! The Italians are driving me crazy," I heard Sarah say from the other room, as Sydney jumped over the couch, well on her way to fulfilling her loyal duty as the welcoming committee.

From Sarah's strange but not surprising greeting, I knew exactly what kind of afternoon it had been for her. As part of Sarah's job, she had to coordinate, track, and manage a project that involved collaboration between people in the United States, India, Italy, and Scotland. She spent a good amount of time on the daily calls playing the role of translator, first deciphering the broken English herself and then re-communicating it to the entire group. She had told me once that she secretly suspected that the Italians sometimes pretended that their English was not as good as it really was, to make up for the fact that they had not started their part of the project or that they were days, if not weeks, behind. I was so proud listening on the phone as she patiently played the role of ringleader in her globalization circus.

"Come on, the weather is great. Let's go to the park for a walk," I said to Sarah, as she continued to pretend to pull her hair out in frustration.

Spending time together walking through Kensington Gardens and Hyde Park had become a daily ritual, rain or shine, and with summer just about here, the park did not close until ten thirty at night, providing us with plenty of time to enjoy it in the evening. Back at home in Chicago, our after-work ritual had evolved into dinner in front of the television, followed by watching more television in silence because we were tired from working all day, followed by more television in bed before falling asleep.

Because the weather in London was, on average, warmer than Chicago, we could enjoy the park every day of the year. Our walks through the park together were starting to become very meaningful, and it had became something we eagerly looked forward to each day.

We passed through the black ornate metal gates leading into Kensington Gardens. I reached down and unclipped Sydney from her leash, letting her free to roam the park to sniff, chase, bark, and, most importantly, look for her boyfriend. Yes, it was true—Sydney had found a boyfriend at the park. Each time we went to the park, she searched for him off in the distance. His name was Tenor, and he was an Irish Setter with a radiant brown coat that made it obvious that he was well looked after. Unfortunately, like every bachelor, Tenor usually played hard to get, and after giving Sydney a friendly greeting each time he saw her, he would go back to doing what he loved the most—hunting squirrels.

It was funny to watch the two dogs, Sydney following directly behind Tenor as he tried to lower himself down into the low grass and quietly sneak up on one of the many squirrels living in the park, who had strayed just a bit too far from a tree. Tenor was always just a step too slow, and the squirrels seemed to find a safe tree to climb, out of harm's way.

During our walks through the park, we talked about some silly things, such as replays of my encounters during my morning walk through the park to exercise Sydney, when I was constantly mistaken for a local and asked for directions to famous landmarks close to the park. I noticed that if I gave directions with my American accent, it often led to a ten-minute talk with the stranger or strangers about what I was doing in London and why I had a dog with me. I was getting good at giving directions in a fake English accent to the point that I really enjoyed people stopping me to ask me for directions, which in hindsight, I guess, defeated the whole purpose, really. It was truly a challenge to not sound more Irish, Scottish, or even Australian than English. There were times when I had really sold some fellow Americans with my fake accent; I would say things like, "Oh yer Americans I see, very good. Never been, but I've heard good things about the place. Very good things." which usually put a smile on their faces as I walked away.

However, what really made the walks through the park memorable were the serious and personal talks about things we had never shared with each other before. Those memories and stories were bringing us even closer together as a couple. Sarah and I had shared so much with each other since we had first met, but we had never really talked about the day that her mother died. We walked through Kensington Gardens, watching Sydney dance in and out of the long uncut grass that romantically hid couples enjoying an evening dinner together on blankets, eating cheese and sipping wine as they wondered whose dog had found their picnic to be the most interesting thing in the world.

Meanwhile, Sarah talked about the worst day of her life. Her mother had had a heart condition that was not immediately life threatening but needed to be addressed sooner rather than later. Tears streamed down her soft cheeks, and I could tell that she was discussing an element of the event that she had thought to herself but never said out loud to anyone. She described her anger at how the doctors had acted like it was a simple surgery and no big deal and how they had treated her as if it was silly that she was worried about her mother. She was angry that her mother's surgery had started so late in the day, because the surgeons had been working on a ninety-year-old woman, whose surgery had delayed that of her mother and, quite possibly, had caused the surgeons to be a little tired and not as mentally sharp as they could have been. She was angry that they had been told that the surgery would only take four hours and then nobody had come out to tell them anything until eight hours into the procedure. But most of all, she was angry that she had not gotten to say good-bye to her mother.

She described how, upon the doctors telling her, her father, and her sisters the devastating news and feeling like her whole world had just come crashing down on her, she had locked herself in the bathroom and thrown up. Then she had finally gotten the courage to go in and see her mother's body and spend a few minutes alone in the room with her. She had held her mother's still-warm hand one last time as she had sat in silence, thinking to herself that that moment would probably be the last quiet moment for the rest of her life.

From that day on, her mother would never age another day for the rest of Sarah's days, burned into Sarah's memory forever. I often wondered what I had been doing that day and at that exact moment when Sarah's world had come crashing down upon her and her sisters. I wished I had made a real effort to get to know Sarah's mom when I had had the chance. I wished I could have had just one more opportunity to walk right up to her and talk to her, something I never did other than a casual hello or good-bye. I wished I could remember what her voice sounded like. Those "I wish" feelings were easy to say then and unfortunately would always have to be "I wish."

I had never shown Sarah the letter that I had written to her mother. Someday I would, and she would probably smile at me, cry a little, and then smile some more. But I felt it was best to just listen to Sarah, hold her hand, and enjoy that day's walk in the park and hope that there would be many more walks like that as our year abroad brought us closer and closer as husband and wife.

Dear Carol,

Today is one of the greatest days of my life. Today is the day that I begin the journey of marrying my best friend. Even though you are not able to be here to share this day with us, you are in our hearts.

I am writing you this letter to make you a promise. To promise to take care of Sarah for the rest of her life and to be the husband that she deserves.

To promise to keep her safe and out of harm's way at all times.

To promise to do whatever it takes to give our marriage the best possible chance.

To promise to be faithful to her in every possible way.

To promise to show Sarah the world and to encourage her to continue to explore everything that life has to offer.

To promise to be there when she needs me, especially during the tough times.

To promise to help Sarah continue to grow into the incredible woman that she has become.

In return, I ask that you continue to look out for her and to help keep her safe when I am unable to.

I wish you were here to share this magnificent journey with Sarah and me. My family welcomes Sarah into our family with open arms. Thank you for the incredible gift of Sarah.

Love,
Garrett

- Chapter Twenty-Two -

The Marathon: The Final Chapter

✦

Since I'd had the window seat on the last flight and neither of us had been to Sweden before, Sarah was awarded the window seat on the flight. As the plane started its descent, I leaned over Sarah's lap and tried to peek out the window to catch my first glimpse of Stockholm, Sweden. It was exciting to be visiting Sweden for the first time in my life, but there was also an argument raging inside my head, and a clear winner had yet to emerge.

The purpose of the trip to Stockholm was not just to be tourists in the city but also to take care of some serious business—the business of running the Stockholm Marathon. The marathon would be my third and final race in an eight-week period, and I honestly did not know if I had the courage to show up at the starting line in just over twenty-four hours. Denis had talked me into joining him on a three-day bike trip from London to Paris the following weekend, and a serious injury during the race would most likely force me to cancel the trip, which was something I desperately wanted to avoid.

I had been dedicating the majority of my free time during the weeks to extra studying so Sarah and I would have the weekends free to do as we pleased, which left me with very little time for running after the London Marathon. The left side of my brain was encouraging me to sleep in, enjoy Stockholm, and forget about the race. The right side of my brain was making the argument that, since I had failed to catch the bird flu sweeping across the United Kingdom, break my leg cross-country skiing in Norway, or wear out the rubber tread on the bottoms of my running shoes, I should run the race. I was leaning toward the right side of my brain, since its argument was based on fate. Being a strong believer in fate, I felt that fate wanted me there at the starting line. I also knew that I would be disappointed if I decided not to run the marathon once I saw all the other runners taking over the city for a few hours during the race.

Sarah and I had developed an appreciation that just about every major European city had a train that made traveling into the city from the airport easy and cheap—Stockholm was no exception. It was impossible not to notice how nice and clean the train was as we rode it into the Stockholm city center. Our hotel was easy to find, because it was the official hotel of the race and all we had to do was follow all the other people wearing running shoes and carrying suitcases as they exited the train and made their way down the street.

The Stockholm Marathon was not steeped in history or tradition like other marathons, but the once sleepy race had grown in size and stature and routinely attracted some of the best professional runners from all over the world. The days of a Swedish runner winning the race were most likely over, at least for the men's race, which was now commonly won by runners from Kenya or Zimbabwe. But unlike most marathons, which usually took place early on a Sunday morning to minimize traffic disruptions, the Stockholm Marathon took place on a Saturday afternoon, providing participants the opportunity to sleep in late before the start of the race and be able to celebrate their accomplishments later in the evening.

After picking up my race number bib and timing chip, Sarah and I set off to get lost in the city of Stockholm and enjoy the day as tourists.

"I hope Sydney will be okay," Sarah said, as she slipped her hand into mine and we crossed the street to walk along the edge of the water in the direction of *Gamla Stan*, or Old Town.

Once again, we had faced the obstacle of finding a willing participant to watch Sydney for the weekend. I had taken on the challenge and come up with another brilliant idea to solve the problem. I had offered our home in central London for a long weekend to a good friend, who was also an airline pilot and routinely flew between Chicago and London for a major airline. He accepted my offer of a free place and was flying his wife and young son over for the weekend. In exchange for the free place to stay, all they had to do was watch Sydney for us.

Our first afternoon in Stockholm was spent exploring the narrow, medieval streets of the Old Town area of the city, which was on a small island with narrow passages that gave it the mixture of adventure and charm that every tourist looks for. Postcards failed to truly capture the atmosphere and feel of the place. Old Town was filled with numerous historic sights that were packed tightly together along with souvenir shops, bookstores, cafés, and restaurants that had once been medieval cellars.

After adequately exploring the area, we followed one of the narrow streets to the water's edge and wandered aimlessly, crossing the occasional bridge and enjoying being casually lost as we soaked in the beauty of a city that seemed to have been perfectly planned, with miles and miles of accessible waterfront for everyone to enjoy. As we walked, I told Sarah about the 1986 assassination of the Swedish prime minister, Olof Palme, and how he had been shot and killed one night while walking home from the cinema with his wife. Multiple arrests for the murder had been made, but none of the arrests or convictions had held up over time, and the murder was still considered unsolved and overflowing with tantalizing material for conspiracy theorists to work with.

Our first afternoon in Stockholm had been so perfect that we didn't even mind the angry looks the occasional bike riders commuting to and from work gave us when we accidentally drifted into the designated bike lanes on the sidewalks that seemed to be everywhere in the city. Late in the afternoon, we sat down in a small café for a cold drink and a snack. The soft, indeterminate background noise of the city, along with the warm, salty breeze blowing in toward us from the sea, put us both in a relaxed and lazy state of mind. We slipped on our sunglasses, leaned back in our chairs, and sat in the sun, enjoying the chic European atmosphere of an outdoor café.

Unfortunately, the relaxing silence did not last as long as we hoped it would. The sound of loud, American rock music echoed off the nearby buildings and seemed to grow louder and louder by the second.

"What is that?" I asked Sarah, as we curiously waited to see what was interrupting our relaxation.

Whatever it was, it was coming around the corner quickly. Seconds later, a large group of high school students drove by. They were standing in the back of a large, decorated, flatbed truck, dressed in Mardi Gras-style outfits, shouting, singing, and waving at the people sitting in the café or passing by on the street while dancing to the loud music that blasted from large, rock concert speakers placed in the back of the truck. It was obvious that they were pretty drunk. A few seconds later, another flatbed truck with a different set of students drove by slowly.

For the next couple of hours, as Sarah and I continued to explore the streets of Stockholm, a wide variety of flatbed trucks with ten to fifteen students in each one drove past us; all of the students were having the time of their lives. They were high school students celebrating graduation by participating in a perfectly acceptable tradition of taking to the streets in the backs of decorated flatbed trucks with their close friends, dressed in Mardi Gras outfits, with beers in one hand, as parents on the sidewalk and friends in other trucks snapped pictures of the seemingly random procession through the streets.

Sarah and I found the students' fun to be not too out-of-the-ordinary for a group of friends celebrating an important rite of passage. But what I could not stop shaking my head at were the beers in the students' hands and the obvious drunkenness. Sarah and I agreed that if we had rented flatbed trucks and driver to drive us all around public streets to celebrate our high school graduations with cans of beer in our hands, we would have been in unimaginable trouble. Threats of revoking college admission would have been made, driving privileges would have been yanked, and a stern what-were-you-thinking message would have been severely inflicted upon us all. The scene really had an impact on us and showed us just how different the attitude toward drinking at the age of eighteen was in Europe compared to the United States.

Later that evening, Sarah and I found ourselves back in the Old Town area, but that time, we were looking for an Italian restaurant we had been told about, so I could load up on some pasta and carbohydrates the night before the big race. It was easy to find the restaurant, because everyone else had had the same idea and there was a long line out the door. The restaurant was trying to serve as many people as possible, and not wanting patrons to see the long line and look elsewhere for a meal, decided to hand out free glasses of cheap red wine to give the crowd of people the appearance of an outdoor cocktail party instead of an intimidating line for a meal.

When we were finally seated at a small, red-checkered tablecloth-covered table for two, we found ourselves packed in tightly with surrounding tables of groups of people, which made us feel as though we were all dining at one enormous table. The restaurant owner thanked us for waiting and promised a great meal as he handed us the menus.

The restaurant resounded with the sounds of various languages being spoken all at once. It was difficult to distinguish them, because they all seemed to blend together into one sounds-Greek-to-me mishmash.

A group of three men and women from England were sitting at a table directly behind us, and their loud voices occasionally drowned out the other tables' conversations. The three men had also entered the marathon, and it seemed like their girlfriends had joined them for the weekend to watch them run. I decided to refer to them as Larry, Curly, and Moe from *The Three Stooges,* because they did not look like marathon runners and also because they were behaving childishly, competing amongst themselves to see who could impress the women the most. I could not help but listen to their conversation, as they took turns bragging to the three women about their training programs for the race or lack of training for the race. Larry claimed that the farthest he had run was fourteen miles, leaving him twelve miles short of the full race distance. Curly was not impressed, as he had run a mere ten miles. Moe topped them both with a claim that, not only had he only completed a long run of ten miles, but he had not done any running in over a month.

Sarah and I ate our pasta and tried to have a nice conversation, but I could not concentrate, and I kept drifting back to the conversation of The Three Stooges and their girlfriends, who were daring one another to have a pint of beer or two. I asked the waiter for our bill, using the international Ugly American Tourist "check, please" hand signal. The waiter, who was all the way on the other side of the room, witnessed the signal, understood it right away, and sprang into action to turn the table over to another waiting group of people. As we got up to leave, I looked over at the group of men, who had elevated their attempts at trying to man up one another by ordering shots of liquor that the waiter was carefully passing out.

"See you tomorrow, guys," I said to Larry, Curly, and Moe as I passed by their table.

"Cheers!" the guys answered in unison, each raising a shot of clear liquor. On our way out of the restaurant, we passed The Three Stooges' girlfriends smoking and giggling about how there was no way the guys would finish the race alive.

The next morning we slept in before making our way downstairs to the hotel race buffet—a nice, hearty, American-style breakfast. Then we returned to the hotel room so I could change into my running shorts, which still had salt lines on them from all the sweat I had produced during the last marathon and which I had forgotten to wash. I said a small prayer to the shoe gods that my shoes would not fall apart until after the race as I laced them up and walked out the door.

The starting line of the race was next to the Stockholm Olympic Stadium, where the 1912 Summer Olympics had been held. The marathon course looped twice through the city before finishing inside the small stadium. It was early June, and the weather was warm but not too warm, making the afternoon start to the race perfectly fine.

When the race began, I ran down the left-hand side of the course, looking for Sarah. Somehow I had confused which side Sarah would be standing on during the early part of the race, and by the time I came upon our first meeting spot, I had to keep running so as not to be trampled by the large mass of runners. I tried to wave to her, but it was no use; she was concentrating on the runners running along the right-hand side of the course. I finally gave up and continued running.

The race passed through many architecturally interesting neighborhoods and expansive green parks before passing the clean, blue water of the harbor area that provided a slight ocean breeze that pushed the runners along and made it a little easier to run. The course was mostly empty of spectators, but in a few places, many locals lined the edges, looking on with curiosity and occasionally yelling out some words of encouragement. I thought they were words of encouragement, but I was not sure since they were in Swedish. The faces of the spectators appeared eerily similar; the vast majority had beautiful Scandinavian features: tall and skinny with fair skin, a small nose, blond hair, and blue eyes.

Halfway through the race, something in the corner of my eye caught my attention. It was Sarah running along the side of the course, desperately trying to catch up to me. I had run right past her and not even noticed.

"Here, I got you this," she said as she handed me a bottle of water she had purchased. "Wait! Don't drink that," she said. She quickly grabbed the bottle of water, as I was just about to take a long, refreshing gulp from it. "I almost forgot—I accidentally purchased sparkling water. Here, drink this instead." She handed me another bottle of water. I cautiously sipped it to make sure it was not sparkling water, and then drank the rest in three seconds. I had developed a taste for sparkling water during meals or on hot, lazy days with a slice of lemon, but the thought of drinking sparkling water during a marathon made me feel queasy.

The first loop, or thirteen miles, of the race was easy, and my legs felt strong. I was somewhere in the middle of the pack; the leading runners passed me at mile marker twelve during their second and final laps. But at mile fifteen, I could feel my legs start to tire, something that usually happened around the twenty-mile marker. I had run the first half of the race at a slower pace to try to conserve my leg strength for the end, but I was beginning to worry that I would be in serious trouble in just a couple more miles. I needed a distraction, and I tried to find a song on my iPod to provide me with some inspiration. *Why did I not download the theme music from* Chariots of Fire *or* Rocky *before the race? Either song would be perfect right now!* I thought.

My head was down, and as I continued to fidget with my iPod, not paying attention, I just about ran into the backs of three slower runners, who were right in front of me. I was just starting to get the words out of my mouth to apologize to them when I made the connection that the three runners were the English guys from the night before—The Three Stooges: Larry, Curly, and Moe.

"Are you guys going to make it?" I asked, after apologizing for almost running them over. Larry and Curly did not answer, but Moe gave a thumbs up, slightly bumping into the other two, causing them to waver like dazed boxers seconds before doing a face-plant onto the boxing ring mat. For a split second, I thought I heard one of them say to Moe, "So, you think you're a wise guy, do ya?" The sight of the three guys with their ghost white faces and dark stains on their white shirts, which looked like vomit or blood, made me feel slightly better that someone on the course was in far worse shape than I was.

The question "Why am I doing this?" made its first appearance earlier than I had expected at only mile seventeen and lasted well into mile twenty-three before my brain decided it was tired of running, took pity on me, and numbed the needle-like pain shooting through my thighs. The just-arrived temporary numbness allowed me to run slightly faster than I had for the previous six miles, making it feel very good to make the last turn into the Olympic Stadium and finally cross the finish line, where, for the last time, I raised my hands into the air in triumph.

Three consecutive marathons—never again!

Two On The Rocks, Please!

In the evening, Sarah and I celebrated my victory with a nice dinner at the Pontus by the Sea restaurant. Petter had recommended the restaurant to us, and it was obvious why. The restaurant was located in an old customs house and faced out toward the archipelago. The place was also the country's oldest brewery, and the copper brewing vats had been creatively worked into the design of the upscale atmosphere. The best part of the place was the outside lounge, where we sat on comfortable couches and waited for a table while enjoying the view of the setting sun and drinking a beer.

We were eventually seated at one of the best tables that provided great views of the islands and the small ferryboats heading out toward them. The waiter greeted us with *akta svensk gastfrihet* or genuine Swedish hospitality and started out by introducing himself and telling us about the night's specials—we thought. If it were not for the blank nobody-is-home look that I held on my face as he continued speaking to us in Swedish before apologizing to us in English and graciously starting over, he might have never known we were not Swedish. As Sarah and I both had blondish hair and blue eyes and dressed with more of a European look, we were constantly being mistaken for being Swedish while in Stockholm.

"I am going to do it," I said to Sarah as I closed my menu and put it down on the table.

"I wouldn't, if I were you," she said, still looking over the menu.

"I'm going to do it. I don't care what you say. I'm going to order reindeer," I said, trying to project confidence in my voice about what I was about to do.

"I hope it is not Rudolph the Red-Nosed Reindeer, or else you could seriously ruin Christmas for millions of little kids," Sarah said.

When our dinner was finally brought to the table, Sarah's dish of grilled zander, a fish that had been freshly caught in the immediate area and served with shrimp and a hint of horseradish, instantly gave me order envy; hers looked so much better than my reindeer fillets.

"What were you thinking? We're surrounded by water. Your reindeer probably came from Finland," she jokingly said, refusing to give me a bite of her fish.

The reindeer fillets were very tender and delicious and served with fried onions and a red wine gravy sauce, so my order envy diminished slightly.

After dinner, we made our way over to a unique bar in Stockholm, where the phrase "on the rocks" had been elevated to a whole new level. In the large lobby of the Nordic Sea Hotel, we found the Absolut Ice Bar. The entire bar—the walls, ceiling, tables, and bar—was made out of large chunks of ice taken from the Torne River. A large glass window let tourists passing by in the hotel lobby see what was going on inside the frozen ice bar, as if it were an aquarium.

Upon entering the small entrance to the Ice Bar, Sarah and I were given oversize, silver space age-looking, hooded parkas lined with soft, fake fur. After completing our new outfits with large, black, ski gloves, we were allowed into the refrigerated passageway leading into the small ice bar. The barroom temperature was kept at a constant twenty-three degrees Fahrenheit, and the cold air quickly penetrated your entire body. We walked up to the bar and ordered two sugary, fruity drinks filled with—what else?—Absolut Vodka, served in a glass also made entirely out of ice. There were no bar stools to sit on, since your bottom would melt the ice, so we had to stand while the bartender made our drinks.

As soon as our drinks were ready, the bartender slid them down along the bar as if we were in a Western cowboy movie. Sarah was caught off guard and, with her large, oversize gloves on, was not able to catch her drink. We all watched it fly over the edge at the end of the bar and crash down onto the floor.

"Oops, sorry about that," Sarah said, her face turning red, even in the cold air of the ice bar.

"It happens all the time. Let me pour you a new one," the bartender said to our relief—each drink was costing us about twenty dollars. After snapping a couple of photos of us in our Eskimo parkas and deciding together that the novelty had worn off (we were both freezing), we finished our drinks and headed home. It was almost eleven o'clock at night, but there still seemed to be just a little bit of daylight in the sky. The summer solstice was just a few weeks away, and the daylight in Stockholm would soon extend beyond eighteen hours.

IKEA or Bust

The next morning, on our last day in Stockholm, we boarded a turn-of-the-century, steam vessel for an early morning tour of the nearby Archipelago islands. During the winter months the ice froze, making it possible to skate or ski to and around the small islands. The guide on the ship introduced himself and explained that he would be giving the tour in English, Swedish, and French, and then failed miserably at making a joke that produced no laughter and very little acknowledgment. It did not help that the Swedish usually told jokes with a straight face. Swedish people were known for being quiet and respectful, which made me wonder how they succeeded at doing business with southern European countries, where several people shouting and speaking at the exact same time was considered part of the art of conversation.

Before visiting Stockholm, my initial idea of the city was that it was just the capital of a cold, Nordic country. *My idea of Stockholm could not have been more wrong,* I thought, as I looked out from the side of the ship over the water toward a city that was dynamic, beautiful, continental, and cosmopolitan. There was so much that Sarah and I admired about Stockholm and Sweden. The air and water was clean and clear. The sun shone often and the trains were easy to navigate. Everyone was good-looking and healthy. Vacation time was plentiful, with a statutory maternity leave of one year at close to eighty percent of salary. Even spanking a child was against the law in Sweden. There was nothing I could find to dislike about Stockholm and Sweden, until Sarah reminded me that the world's largest IKEA store was located just outside of Stockholm in Kungens Kurva—finally, a chink in the armor of the great country of Sweden.

The world was constantly changing and evolving as the spin cycle of globalization took its effect on everyone, and Sweden was no exception. It was becoming more difficult to tell what was Swedish anymore. Volvo and Saab were owned by American car companies. The best Swedish hockey players played in the American hockey leagues. IKEA's headquarters had moved to Denmark. The Swedish Bikini Team was just a fabrication of American beer marketers, and the Nobel Peace Prize—the most prestigious of the six Nobel prizes, which had been named after the Swedish chemist and inventor—was awarded in Oslo, Norway, not Sweden, where the other five Nobel awards were handed out. Globalization had definitely helped the Swedish people, but the last truly Swedish icon, the Swedish lifestyle, was dramatically changing because of globalization.

Just a few years before, the British newspaper *The Guardian* proclaimed Sweden the most successful society the world has ever known. The Swedes were proud of their classless society but still enjoyed climbing the social ladder. The Swedes had been able to find great economic success, using a mix of capitalism and socialism that was sometimes referred to as capitalism with a touch of humanity and equality. The joke was that even the very rich had a difficult time making ends meet when the income tax was levied at 110 percent.

Sweden still had some of the world's highest taxes, but it also had the most generous welfare benefits. But just like other European countries, Sweden was also struggling to remain competitive in the world while still being able to fund its generous social model, which was truly a source of national pride. The difficulty in upholding the system worried many European economists as the weight of the aging population began to build up.

To stay competitive in the world marketplace, Sweden had had to find ways to cut high labor cost. There was no better place to witness that than at IKEA. Even though the gap between high and low salaries was much smaller than in most economies in the world, it was very expensive to hire a worker in Sweden, so companies were always looking for ways to get around hiring workers. IKEA had mastered that with the self-service business model for a large retailer. At IKEA you select, locate, load, and assemble the furniture yourself. The only human contact with a store employee was usually with the clerk at the checkout counter.

The Swedish people who did find themselves gainfully employed were also witnessing the erosion of the Swedish vacation. Sweden had been at or near the top of the European vacation rankings, with close to seven official weeks of vacation time off and many people enjoying a five-week continuous vacation in the summer. Traditionally, Swedes used the majority of their vacation time at the same time, usually beginning in July and lasting into August. The last day of work before the long vacation time off used to be considered national news as television crews greeted employees outside the gates of the large factories to interview the workers and ask them how they would be spending their weeks of time off. For Swedish companies to stay competitive, vacation days, if not weeks, were going unused by employees.

It was difficult to get excited about the not-too-far-off day when we would all make our own lattes at Starbucks, put together our flat-pack furniture from IKEA, and diagnose and treat our health ailments on WebMD, because corporations had discovered that self-service was much cheaper on the bottom line. I just hoped we all still had some vacation time left to be able to enjoy a cup of coffee, fill our homes with comfortable furniture, and keep our bodies healthy. Thanks, IKEA.

- Chapter Twenty-Three -

Did You Hear About the Guy Who Tried to Ride a Bike to Paris from London?

✦

It was five thirty in the morning on a Friday and less than a week since I had crossed the finish line at the Stockholm Marathon. I was alone in the elevator at the Earl's Court Tube station, riding it down to the platform for the Piccadilly Line trains. With plenty of room in the empty elevator, I was bending over, touching my toes, and trying to stretch out my leg muscles, which had not quite returned to normal. Since returning to London from Stockholm, I had avoided my daily routine of taking the long flights of stairs at each Tube station and had instead opted for the cramped, unreliable, and mostly dilapidated elevators at each Tube station to help my leg muscles heal faster. Physically, my body was happy for the change, but mentally, I was regretting it, because I seemed to be developing a phobia of small, cramped, dilapidated, and unreliable spaces.

Many of the London Tube station platforms were buried deep in the ground and required a long elevator or escalator ride to reach them. When traveling to and from class each day, I usually took the long, winding, spiral staircases to reach the street level as part of my marathon training regimen. It was difficult to make it to the top of each staircase while keeping a steady and constant pace without my legs severely burning with fatigue and begging me to stop. Many of the Tube stations had warning signs posted at the stairwell entrances, warning against taking the stairs, most likely because of the tremendous physical effort required. I was surprised to encounter others on the usually empty stairs making the journey as well. Usually the poor individuals were resting along the handrail trying to catch a breath and often asked me how much farther they had to reach the top when I encountered them while descending the stairs.

To my absolute horror, I occasionally encountered people trying to haul large suitcases up the long staircases—a feat better suited for a donkey. I always stopped and assisted them, which caused me to arrive at class late, dripping with sweat and smelling like a high school gym locker. While accepting praise from the individual after helping him carry his suitcase to the top, I usually tried to let the person know I was an American. I thought every little bit of American kindness helped the cause. I often wondered why those out-of-their-mind people were punishing themselves by attempting the backbreaking feat, which was the equivalent of walking up the stairs of a ten-story building. It was not until the early developmental stages of my elevator phobia that I began to understand why they might be doing it.

The first train of the morning pulled into the Tube station at 5:35 AM. A lone head peaked out of an open door of the train, far down on the empty platform. I instantly recognized the head looking down at me and gave a wave as I boarded the completely empty train just before the doors closed on me. I walked through the empty train cars until I found Petter, waiting for me. I greeted him with a half-awake good morning and sat down in the seat next to him. I told him the highlights of the weekend trip to Stockholm, with special emphasis on how much Sarah and I had enjoyed his home country of Sweden.

Then we sat in silence while the train traveled around a long curve and produced a deafening shrieking noise as the wheels of the train strained to keep the train on the track. After the noise subsided, Petter pulled out a white sheet of paper and unfolded it.

"Hey, Garrett, it says here, in our trip itinerary that Denis sent me, that we drive from London to Newhaven on day one, and then on day three, we drive to Paris," he said. "I thought we were riding the bikes the entire trip?"

I could not help but laugh at Petter's question, because I, too, had noticed the word "driving" on the trip itinerary. Sarah had also noticed it and questioned me about whether I was really planning a "boys' weekend" and why we were driving and not riding. Since I knew Denis much better than Petter did, I was more familiar with Denis's use of the English language, and I knew what he was really saying.

"Wherever you see the word 'drive,'" I said, "replace it with the word 'ride.'"

Denis's English had improved dramatically since I had first met him, but there were some phrases he still said wrong, such as "Will you make me a picture?" when he wanted me to take a picture for him, or "I invite you," which meant he wanted to pay for me. He often used that phrase when paying for a pint of beer or for a coffee at Starbucks. I felt it was rude to constantly correct his English, and since I did not speak any German, who was I to criticize him? As Denis's English steadily improved, mine became worse, because I had made a habit of using the same phrases when talking to Denis. Sometimes I wondered if Denis knew the phases were not exactly correct but still used them because I used them, and he did not want to correct my English.

Petter and I arrived as planned at six o'clock in the morning at Denis's house. Denis was standing out in front with the biggest smile I had ever seen on his face, ready to begin the trip. Petter and I placed our saddlebags on our bikes and checked the bikes one last time in our final preparations for the three-day trip to Paris.

Denis and I had envisioned recruiting a sizable group of friends to join us on our bike trip. More often than not when asking friends if they wanted to join us, their first response was, "You do know you can't ride a bike to Paris from London?" After explaining that we were aware that the English Channel made it impossible to ride a bike to France from England, and that we would be taking a ferry across, the reply was always "Thanks, but no thanks." The only reason Petter had agreed to join us was because we had asked him after buying him three pints of beer. When Petter did not ask us if we knew that we couldn't ride a bike to France from England, we instantly knew he was the right man for the job.

For the most part, London was a very bike-friendly city. But to ride a bike outside of the parks and through the twisting and turning streets of London took some serious courage and insanity. The morning rush hour was quickly building up, and the streets were filling up with numerous large and intimidating, red, double-decker buses packed with commuters; the buses often drifted uncomfortably close to the bike lane. At times, I found my face just inches from the face of a complete stranger on a bus looking over at me as I tried to ride and hold my breath so as not to pass out from the heavily toxic fumes from each bus.

By seven o'clock, the temperature had risen to the mid-seventies. We had only traveled three miles, because of the heavy street traffic and because we had to constantly stop and recheck the map to try to avoid most of the heavily congested streets and stick to small residential areas.

By eight o'clock, the temperature had risen to the mid-eighties. We had only traveled about five miles, because we had gotten lost, Petter's chain had fallen off, we had gotten lost again, and then we had stopped for a bathroom break in a large, unsuspecting bush in a small park.

By nine o'clock, the temperature was in the mid-nineties and we had only just crossed the Thames River and stopped at Greenwich. It was too tempting, and I suggested we make a pit stop at the large Starbucks in front of us. To my luck, everyone agreed, and we slowly waddled in for refuge in the air conditioned cafe for an iced coffee.

The temperature leveled off at ninety-five degrees by around ten o'clock in the morning. The riding became easier when we finally made our way to a designated and conveniently marked bike path that we would follow to Newhaven for the ferry over to France. We felt as though we were finally making progress, because the city had given way to green fields and storybook English cottages with finely manicured gardens. The path was mostly paved, but occasionally, it turned into hard-packed gravel. We had to pay attention cautiously to the few cars that we encountered on the mostly deserted roads, as they passed us at high speeds while barely making an effort to share the road; then they showered us with the small gravel, rocks, and dust that the tires kicked up at us, causing the pain of dozens of bee stings.

We rode up a large, rolling hill via a narrow, tree-covered path that provided some much-needed shade. It took us two hours to finally reach the top, where we stopped for a rest. Looking down the steep embankment of the hill, we saw a golf course in the distance with what appeared to be a horse lazily grazing halfway up on the side. I took out my camera and turned to Denis.

"Can you make me a picture, Denis?" I asked.

Denis put down the map that he had been studying with a worried look on his face and snapped a picture of Petter and me in our silly-looking bike shorts that we wore to provide extra padding between our bottoms and the bike seats.

Farther off in the distance, I could just see the carriageway—as the English called it—or the highway leading to the coast. I was not sure if it was the heat or the salt in my eyes from sweating, but it appeared that not a single car was moving; the roadway looked more like a parking lot than an expressway. Denis and Petter confirmed that it was the expressway, and we all agreed that we were glad not to be stuck in that traffic. Seeing the traffic backed up as far as we could see made us appreciate being on bikes in the fresh air with an amazing panoramic view to enjoy, but at the same time, it began to worry me.

Even though France was just a short distance from England, French workers could still cause chaos to the expressways in southern England at a moment's notice. On average, French ferry workers strike two to three times a year without any prior notice, preventing trucks from crossing the channel to France, as the ferries had to stop and wait until the strike ended. The trucks quickly become stranded and piled up, clogging the roads. Unsuspecting motorists soon found themselves spending the day in their cars, often having to sleep in them, with no place to go until the strike ended and the trucks started moving again, unclogging the small, two-lane highways.

I was trying to explain to Denis why we should be concerned by the incredible traffic jam, but he was not listening to what I was saying; instead he was busy looking over the map and checking his watch. Denis finally put the map down and told us he was also worried about the snail's pace at which we had been traveling so far. He explained that we must arrive in Newhaven by five o'clock in the evening for the last ferry departure of the day to France. If we missed the ferry, we would have to spend the night in Newhaven and would be a half-day behind schedule, because we would not reach France until late the next morning.

Denis presented us with two options. Option one was to ride our bikes as fast as we could up and down the rolling hills in the ninety-degree sweltering heat, and maybe, just maybe, we might make it by five o'clock. Option two was to ride downhill for twenty minutes to the nearby town and take a train to Newhaven, arriving within an hour and providing us with two long hours to sit down at an outdoor pub and drink cold beer while enjoying the cool ocean breeze.

At three o'clock, we were sitting down at the outdoor pub comparing our farmers' tans from our socks, shirts, and shorts. We toasted Denis for his brilliant idea. It was tough to decide which we were enjoying more—the ice-cold beer or the cool, ocean breeze? We all agreed that they complemented each other quite well and were the perfect way to make it through a record-setting heat wave of an afternoon. We were also relieved to find that the French workers were not striking at the ferry terminal.

Just before five o'clock, we walked our bikes over to the ferry check-in area. We had needed to arrive by five o'clock, because our bikes had to be placed deep in the ship where all the trucks were parked during the four-hour boat ride to Dieppe in northern France. After handing over our bikes to be loaded on, we proceeded to the customs area to board the large ship.

We were considered foot passengers on the ship, because we had not arrived in a car or truck, so we waited patiently in the small customs line that was moving as fast as the standstill highway traffic we had witnessed earlier in the day. There was good reason for the painfully slow pace of the customs workers as they carefully studied each passenger's passport or identification card—the month-long World Cup soccer tournament would officially start in just one hour.

The World Cup was held every four years, and it was Germany's turn to host the tournament, making them, along with England, one of the favorites to lift the cup in victory. Many European countries had put various measures in place to try to significantly reduce the number of incidences of hooliganism abroad. England was without a doubt the leader, because they had all but invented the international pastime of hooliganism at football matches. England has an unparalleled number of hardcore fans that would travel thousands of miles whenever and to wherever their teams were playing abroad. As part of the preparation for the World Cup, England was requiring close to 3,500 known hooligans to turn over their passports to local police before the tournament started in an attempt to prevent them from traveling to Germany during the tournament. All but two hundred had complied, and the police were intently watching every airport, seaport, and Chunnel train in the hope of arresting them if they tried to leave the country.

The ferry pulled away from the dock, and we found three comfortable seats in the bar area of the ship and enjoyed the view of the huge White Cliffs, which consisted entirely of soft chalk. As the ship sailed farther out into the English Channel—or *La Manche*, as the French called it—the tall cliffs appeared to sink right into the sea. The spacious bar lounge on the vessel seemed to be the most desirable location on the ship, because of the many television screens. When word got out that the televisions were not working and would not be turned on, the bar quickly emptied; most of the passengers decided to take their drinks outside on the deck to smoke and enjoy the warm, early evening sun. Later during the ferry ride, the bartender quietly told me that the televisions did work, but they were under strict orders not to turn on any of the first World Cup games, because they did not want any trouble on the boat in case passengers did not like the outcome of a match.

Denis had scolded Petter and me when we had first arrived at his house in the morning, because he had felt that we had too many changes of clothes in our saddlebags and that the extra weight would slow down our riding pace. I gave it right back to Denis when he pulled out a small but heavy radio that he had brought with him on the trip so that he could listen to the German team match while we rode the ferry over to France. Denis had decided to leave behind extra changes of clothes and instead opted to wear pretty much the same clothes for three days just so he could listen to the game on the ferry—he was a truly dedicated fan of his national team.

Denis left Petter and me behind and went outside onto the deck so he could listen to the game. For the next two hours, it was easy to spot where Denis was sitting, because half the ship's passengers were following him around, also trying to listen to his radio while he moved around the ship to improve the reception of the radio. When the match ended, Denis joined us back in the bar. It was obvious that Germany had won their first match, because Denis returned with a round of drinks that he had purchased for us all; then he proceeded to buy us another round.

The ferry finally arrived into the port of Dieppe, France, and we followed the line of truck drivers who were descending into the belly of the ship to get into their trucks and exit. The truck drivers started up their engines well before the ship was completely tied up and ready for them to disembark, filling the large holding area with diesel fumes. When the heavy doors finally did open, Denis, Petter, and I got onto our bikes, slowly wedged our way into the line of trucks, and rode off the ship. I don't know if it was the beer we had drunk on the ship or the large amount of toxic truck exhaust fumes we had just inhaled, but my brain had me riding my bike on the left-hand side of the road. I realized my mistake after coming face-to-face with a large truck that blared its horn at me as it drove toward the ferry to board for the return trip back to England.

We rode through the dark, empty streets of Dieppe for twenty minutes, while Denis worked the rust off his French asking for directions. We finally found our hotel, and after checking in and inspecting our small bedroom filled with bunk beds, we headed out for one last beer for the night.

We purchased three beers from a small store that was closing up and found a small square surrounded by mostly closed stores and restaurants to sit down in. We felt that, because we were three guys on a guy's weekend, we should be drinking beer at ten o'clock at night rather than sleeping. We were exhausted from the day's riding in the hot sun, and after sitting together on a small wooden bench mostly in silence for ten minutes, we decided we would still be men, even if we were in bed fast asleep by ten thirty on a Friday night.

We slept with the air conditioning on the entire night, and the next morning, I did not notice how hot the temperature was in the early morning hours until we made our way to the small lobby that was being used to serve the free continental breakfast and had no air conditioning.

Many great things have come out of Europe, but the continental breakfast was definitely not one of them. I was finding it difficult to put together a filling and power-packed breakfast for another excruciating day of riding a bike in a sweltering heat when my choices were coffee, tea, juice, pastries, croissants, cheese, and jam. I tried to get as creative as I could with the limited options, but I somehow managed to walk out even hungrier than I had been when I had walked in.

The large and growing pain in my stomach was quickly erased by an even worse pain that gave new meaning to the phrase "pain in the butt." At the beginning of the trip, I was really worried about my legs being too sore to ride a bike all the way to Paris. My legs were fine; it was my butt that did not want anything to do with sitting back on a bike seat for a second straight day. Every little bump in the road sent a sharp pain shooting up my spine from my buttocks. I had found a new respect for the competitors in the Tour de France bike race, whose seats most likely did not have half the padding that mine did.

Still, the second day's early morning ride was off to a much better start than the first day's ride. Compared to London, it was easy to navigate the streets of Dieppe. When we encountered a car on the road, the driver would slow way down and carefully pass us as if we were on the endangered species list. We did make one early stop, because I was not the only one who had been disappointed with the morning's breakfast. We stopped at a bakery that had halted us dead in our tracks with its intoxicating smell of fresh bread spilling out the front door and onto the road.

It was amazing how close France and England were to each other geographically, with just twenty miles separating them at their closest points, but how dramatically different the two countries were in language, culture, and architecture. As the morning sun rose slowly into the sky, we rode past many small farmhouses and French manors, which were popular in the Normandy area. Many of the buildings' architecture included the French eclectic style of tall, steeply pitched roofs with eaves with prominent towers topped by conical roofs—an architectural style with which American soldiers became very familiar.

The second day of the trip required us to ride close to one hundred kilometers. Denis had originally estimated that it would take six to seven hours of riding to reach the town of Gournay-en-Bray. But that was before he had seen the pace we had traveled on the first day, and I was starting to suspect that he was watching for train station signs just in case we needed to do a little cheating again.

The first half of the day's ride was done on an old railroad line that had been converted to a forty-kilometer-wide, flat, and perfectly paved surface, which allowed the three of us to ride parallel to each other, occasionally alternating who rode in the middle. With plenty of time on our hands, our conversations covered a whole range of topics.

Denis told us about how he had spent a summer as a bicycle guide tour, taking American, German, and English tourists on weeklong bicycle rides through southern France. He explained how his boss had told him that the feedback from clients on his first trip was that he lacked any interesting knowledge about the sites they rode by each day. His boss had told him that he needed to do a better job or look for a new one. Denis had felt that a more interesting tour route was necessary. But the route he had to take mostly covered a great deal of flat land and avoided steep hills, because, other than us, who wanted to spend their vacations riding a bike up and down steep hills in the blazing summer heat of France? Denis had not wanted to lose his job, and he had been happy when the second group of clients he had guided for a week had reported to his boss that Denis had provided amazing insight on the area and sites and they had all thoroughly enjoyed the trip with him.

Denis paused for a minute, waiting for Petter and me to finally ask him what he had done differently on the second trip. With a sly smile on his face, he told us how old, half-standing barns had become great historical sites, or better yet, were haunted by local ghosts. Fields with no significant historical value had become the settings of fierce battles fought to the last soldier standing before victory was declared. Clients' cameras had been quickly pulled out for a shot of a tree that Denis had told them was the meeting place of young forbidden lovers who later paid the price for their sins by being hanged there. Everyone was happy—the tourists, Denis, and most importantly, Denis's boss.

- Chapter Twenty-Four -

Je Ne Veux Plus Monter Ma Bicyclette

✦

(I Don't Want to Ride My Bike Anymore)

The morning ride through the Normandy area of France was as perfect as we could have hoped for; we had a smooth, flat, and car-free trail to follow, which was all but impossible to get lost on. The afternoon ride started with our sights set on riding the remaining distance to the city of Gournay-en-Bray by day's end. We were relaxed and in good spirits, mostly due to the two glasses of wine that we had each enjoyed with our lunches. Even though we were dressed from head to toe in bike-riding clothes and equipment, the waiter still brought glasses of cold wine instead of cold water to our table when we had first sat down.

The smooth, flat, riding surface of the old railroad line came to an end ten minutes into the start of the afternoon's ride, and the end was marked by a sign in English that simply stated "end." The vacation was over, and we once again stood straight up on our bike pedals, pushing down with all our leg strength as we slowly and painfully climbed the first looming, intimidating hill of the day. The road was steep and winding, and a constant flow of cars carefully passed us by as we made our way higher and higher up the precarious path toward the top. During the long, strenuous climb, the three of us slowly developed distance between us, with Denis in the lead, me in the middle, and Petter bringing up the rear.

I flipped through my bike gears, desperately searching for relief for my muscles as the incline intensified. The journey was made worse by my not really knowing for sure how much farther I needed to ride before reaching the top and the end of the torture. My bike chain began to make an alarming grinding noise, instantly stopping my experiment of pedaling in a lower gear, out of fear that my bike chain would fall off, leaving me stranded along the road with only Petter while I tried to find a way to fix it.

The view of Normandy in the distance below was our only reward during the steep climb. We were pedaling our bikes not far from a place that I had always wanted to visit—the D-Day beaches of Omaha and Utah, where so many American soldiers had lost their lives during the beach landing invasion as the campaign to liberate Europe had begun.

The road became even steeper, and upon deciding that my body would be much happier if I gave up and just walked my bike to the top, I carefully dismounted. As I pushed the bike up the hill, my mind wandered, as it often did during a long run or marathon race, which helped to relieve the monotonous and difficult physical activity. I thought about the D-Day beaches and war movie visuals of the events on the beaches. That thought brought back discussions about the attitudes and opinions of war that Sarah and I had observed and heard since arriving in Europe.

With the ongoing war in Iraq led by American forces, the subject was all but impossible to avoid on television, in newspapers, and in discussions in the pubs. From the onset, France had taken the lead in the European resistance to the Iraq invasion and the war that had immediately followed it. As a result, heavy anti-French attitudes had taken root early and peaked with stories of french fries being renamed "Freedom Fries" in the House of Representatives cafeterias in response to France's unwillingness to assist in the efforts. The French embassy quickly pointed out that french fries were actually a Belgian creation. Many Americans also demanded that we remind the French again that if it were not for us, they would be speaking German, a point that, even decades after the war had ended, we Americans still liked to remind the French of whenever we did not see eye-to-eye on foreign policy strategies.

Caught directly in the middle of the conflict between the United States and France was the small Normandy region of France, an area that was very pro-American for what America had done for them—liberated them—as well as what we did for them then—supported their local economy by visiting the numerous war cemeteries and beaches in the area. I had always wanted to visit the beaches where so many young men had become heroes but not come home. I would have liked to walk along the rows and rows of perfectly aligned white crosses that stretched into the horizon and overlooked the English Channel to quietly and personally say "Thank you."

Sarah and I had only been in Europe for six months, but I was surprised that, through many discussions with friends and through observation of the European media, I was beginning to understand why most European countries were so reluctant to join in the fighting. With a large and growing Muslim population throughout much of Europe, invading, participating in the war, or even supporting the war being fought on Islam-dominated soil was just bad business. War had also had a long and painful history in Europe, and as a result, the European continent had gotten out of the business of fighting wars and had replaced it with welfare.

A country could either have universal health care or a dominating military; it was impossible to have both, even if it was a rich country. Europeans often used the phrase "bombs or babies, which one is more important?"—a tough antiwar argument to dispute. In Germany, it was almost impossible to travel through the country without running into reminders of its embarrassing past and the constant message that "this can never happen again." Germans didn't just oppose the war in Iraq; they opposed any kind of war and look to the promotion of peace to be an ongoing campaign to help the country deal with its burden of guilt. For the citizens of Europe, war was not something that was fought off in distant places or in films and on television. Millions and millions of Europeans had been killed during World War II on European soil. Because of that alone, Europeans were skeptical about any war as a solution to a conflict.

There also seemed to be a mentality in France and throughout much of Europe that the world would always have a crazy, evil dictator causing problems for his own people and neighboring countries, and if you searched hard enough you could find an endless supply of them. When one evil dictator was replaced or defeated, another one was ready to take his place on the global stage somewhere else, and the whole process seemed to start all over again.

France did owe a great deal of gratitude to the United States for what it had done to liberate its people, but did that mean that France must forever fall in line with every United States foreign policy decision? Was that what freedom was all about? Americans might never understand that France's actions were part of a campaign to prevent further planting of many more white crosses in American military cemeteries, and the French might never understand Americans' belief that freedom was not free and sometimes required fighting in distant places where soldiers can't speak the local language and might even feel that the culture was archaic, if not downright backward.

Finally conquering what seemed to be an endless uphill climb brought on a much smaller feeling of accomplishment than I had thought it would when I had started the climb, because I had cheated and walked my bike up most of the hill. I looked down the long, twisting road in front of me, but Denis was nowhere to be seen. I turned around and looked back down the road I had just walked up, but Petter could not be seen. I hopped back on the seat with a slight groan from the soreness in my butt, tightened the chin strap on my helmet, and tested the front and rear brakes before pushing off with my feet and pointing the bike downward.

The bike instantly responded to the steep slope and quickly accelerated. The rush of wind against my sweaty head and face brought much-needed relief in the ninety-degree heat. Faster and faster the bike sped as I navigated down the steep road, cautiously watching for cars driving up the hill. It felt as though it had taken many hours to reach the top, but only thirty seconds to reach the bottom, where I found Denis sitting in the only shady spot he could find on the side of the road.

"That was great! Let's do it again!" I shouted to Denis in my best twelve-year-old kid voice.

"What was so great, the uphill or the downhill?" Denis said with a smirk on his face.

"Very funny," I said, still using my twelve-year-old voice.

A few minutes later, just as Denis and I began to worry about Petter's status—alive or dead—he came barreling down the hill, his body wobbling ever so slightly as he tried to spit out the large mass of bugs he inhaled on the way down. Petter came to a stop in front of Denis and me and took his helmet off to pour some water on his head.

"What's up with you two?" Petter asked, referring to how strange Denis and I looked sitting so close to each other in an attempt to both fit under the small, shady spot that the only tree remotely close was providing us. "Is there room for one more underneath there?" Petter asked, after we told him we were planning to stand there until the sun went down.

Our teenager-like giddiness of once again being united as friends after successfully slaying the monstrous hill faded when we realized that the first hill was only one of many to come that afternoon. For the next three hours, we rode in a painful silence, pushing our bodies in the sweltering heat up and over the hills. At times, we rode in a straight line, one after another, but often we found ourselves spread out.

During one long, flat stretch, I thought that the heat had finally gotten to me, because a mirage seemed to appear right in front of my eyes. A man on a bicycle pedaled right past me with a small boy holding onto the back. They both wore blue berets, and what appeared to be two loaves of bread were strapped onto the back rack. Just before the man and small child were out of sight, the small boy turned around and smiled at me. The experience made me feel as though I had just lived the famous black-and-white photograph by Elliot Erwitt of a French father and his son riding together on a bicycle, both wearing berets, with the small boy smiling as he looks back. The French tourist board used the image in an advertisement to encourage American tourists to visit the French countryside and not just Paris, before traveling to other major European cities.

We were only about two hours away from the day's destination of Gournay-en-Bray, and the large hill climbs seemed to have taken mercy on us, becoming fewer and less frequent. The hot afternoon sun had already peaked, and even the smallest drop in temperature brought on a welcome relief. We were riding on a bike trail through a small nature preserve that ran alongside what looked like a large, man-made pond. Denis signaled that we were stopping, and Petter and I stopped alongside him.

"Is it happy hour yet?" I asked, wondering why we were stopping.

"No, it is time for swimming," Denis said.

I looked over at the marshy water that was far more green than blue and then back at Petter to judge his thoughts on the proposition. From the look on Petter's face, I could see exactly what he was thinking, which was the same thing I was thinking.

"Denis, I think you're on your own with this one," I finally said.

"Your loss, not mine," he said, as he quickly took off his shirt and shorts and made his way into the water in just his underwear.

Even though it was still hot as hell and a cool dip would have felt great, I knew I made the right decision when Denis's first step into the muddy waters resulted in his right foot sinking deep into the muddy bottom.

"I look forward to scraping all the leeches off you when you come out of the water!" Petter yelled at Denis, who looked like he was having second thoughts, before diving headfirst into the muddy sludge.

"Come on in, you babies! The water is great!" he yelled.

We ignored his feeble attempt to persuade us to join him and watched him do the backstroke, pushing himself farther away from the water's edge.

All the noise Denis was making had attracted the attention of the many people who were enjoying the nature trail, and they stopped to stare at Denis, who had reached the middle of the green lake; they shook their heads in amazement before continuing their afternoon hike.

Petter walked over to the edge of the pond and pulled out his camera phone to capture what could be Denis's last few minutes of life before the green pond boogeyman took offense to Denis's trespassing and gobbled him up. But before Petter could snap the picture, he slipped on the muddy embankment and slid halfway into the pond, accidentally baptizing his phone in the muddy waters.

"Shit, shit, shit!" Petter shouted. Hearing Petter curse like that at his misfortune reminded me of the American traits that he had acquired while living in the United States.

Petter cleaned the mud off the small screen and surveyed the damage to his new phone. To my surprise, he pulled out another cell phone from his pocket and frantically dialed a friend to ask what he should do to fix his wet phone, before I could ask him if it still worked or not. As I sat there in the shade on the cool grass, I could not decide what amazed me more—Denis's courage to swim in the most disgusting, green, pond water I had ever seen or the number of cell phones Petter seemed to be carrying.

Denis's adventurous swim finally came to an end, and to the disappointment of both Petter and me, Denis emerged from the water leech free. We were once again back on our bikes and in the home stretch. The swim seemed to have recharged Denis, and he again rode far in front of Petter and me, stopping occasionally to show us which road we needed to turn on before riding up ahead of us again.

Petter and I rode side by side as we passed large farms on both sides of the road. I could tell that Petter was sick and tired of riding, because I was sick and tired of riding and we were both hunched over the fronts of our handlebars. Petter was quickly fading, and the last ten miles of the day were going to be tough. Taking a train was not an option. Every time I said something nice about Sweden, Petter seemed to perk up and ride a little faster. The Swedish national team would be playing their opening World Cup match in just over two hours, so I told Petter how I thought they would surely win their first match. He smiled and rode faster. I told him how beautiful I thought the Swedish girls had been. He rode even faster. I told him how amazing I had thought Sweden was and how great their hockey players were. The final comments made him ride the fastest I had seen him ride all day; he smiled and adamantly agreed with the final compliment I had given Sweden.

We coasted into the day's final destination, of the small town of Gournay-en-Bray, which had probably seen better days and seemed to be suffering from being too far from Paris and not being close enough to the tourist sites in the Normandy region.

Denis went into the hotel to collect the room key while Petter and I found a safe place to store the bikes for the night. We all met back in the modest hotel lobby and made our way up to our room. Denis had booked a spacious triple room with three single beds. We entered the room, and Petter immediately checked to make sure the small television worked so we could watch the Swedish World Cup match. After the television properly turned on and displayed a picture along with sound, the three of us proceeded to simultaneously collapse into our individual beds, resting in silence as we enjoyed the feeling of the soft mattresses supporting our exhausted and sore bodies.

Petter asked if he could shower first, because he did not want to miss the start of the football match. As it was his country playing, he had the honor of the first shower. The restful silence was broken by the sound of Petter turning on the fan in the bathroom, which sound was immediately followed by Petter sticking his head back out the door.

"Denis, are you kidding me? This is a bike trip. We need a shower," he said.

The thought of a room without a shower caught my curiosity, and I got up from my bed to see what Petter was talking about. The room Denis had booked did not have a shower—just a bathtub with a small hose attached to the nozzle.

"I want to take a shower, not a bath, Denis," I agreed with Petter.

I had been looking forward to a hot, relaxing shower and not having to squeeze my sore six-foot frame into a four-foot tub to take a bath.

"This room is only costing you twenty euros a night. Deal with it," Denis said, emphasizing the "deal with it" part.

"Nice, Denis." I could not help but compliment him on his very American response to Petter's very American complaint against a European tub rather than a stand-up shower.

We rested in our single beds, which were situated in a row, facing the small television. The configuration of the room made me feel as though we were three young brothers sitting in our bedroom together, hanging out and watching sports.

The match ended with Sweden cruising to a 2–0 victory, and Denis and I congratulated Petter on his team's success. I told him that I thought the best part of the match was not the two goals that Sweden had scored but the opposing fans chanting "You're just a furniture supplier!" in reference to IKEA. Petter did not appreciate my comment, but Denis found it funny and complimented me on my observation of the match.

We walked down the street to a small restaurant that the hotel concierge had recommended that we try. He had recommended it because it was the only restaurant still open and serving dinner. We sat down at a large round table outside on the sidewalk that provided us with a great view of the town's nightlife, which seemed to consist of two young, male teenagers riding loud, beat-up mopeds up and down the streets in the hope of attracting the attention of young female teenagers who were just as bored.

The scenery might have been lacking, but the service and smell of the food made up for the annoying and smelly mopeds that sped by in front us. Glasses of wine were once again immediately handed to us with greetings of "Bonjour! Bonjour!" by the restaurant owner, who did not hold back his delight that we were visiting his restaurant as he thanked us in a unique mixture of French and English. One glass turned into two and then into three as Denis, Petter, and I dined on garlic, butter-topped steaks and potatoes, happy to be sitting on something other than an uncomfortable bike seat.

Every time the level of our wine neared the bottom of the glass, the owner sprang to life and refilled each glass, continuing to thank us for visiting his place of business. With a bottomless glass of wine in each of our hands, our conversation shifted to the theme of the meal—alcohol.

We took turns sharing stories about our first experiences with alcohol. Denis and Petter's descriptions of their early encounters and introductions could not have been more different than mine. Each of them had had their first tastes of wine as children, when it was offered to them by their parents in a severely watered-down version. Their early introduction had been part of a message that alcohol was something to be enjoyed and appreciated for its taste and not to be abused. That was very unlike my first early impression, or lack of impression; adults had constantly reinforced the message that alcohol was bad and forbidden, that giving into any temptations would ruin my chances of getting into a good college, and that I would be severely punished if caught drinking it.

Unlike Denis and Petter, the early do-not-touch message communicated to me and my friends by adults only increased our curiosity as to why it was so forbidden and eventually built up to a level at which we could not resist the urge to try it. Instead of viewing it as something to enjoy and appreciate for its taste, many of my friends used it as an expression of rebellion to solidify their coolness among our peers.

I had always found it contradictory that, in America, you were considered mature enough at the age of eighteen to make the life-changing decision to join the army, where you could easily find yourself fighting in a war, but you were not considered mature enough to enjoy a beer or a glass of wine until you reached the age of twenty-one. It was hard to argue that the risks associated with fighting in a war were far less dangerous than those associated with drinking a cold beer or a glass of wine at a high school graduation party.

The rite of passage performed by many Americans when they turned twenty-one was often visiting a bar at the stroke of midnight on their birthdays, and the goal was to try to consume twenty-one consecutive shots of liquor before the bar closed, while their friends cheered them on. Completing the feat provided validation and bragging rights between friends who succeed— if it did not result in a trip to the emergency room. Often the twenty-one consecutive shots of liquor ritual was the first step toward a substance abuse problem among college students in America, whereas in Europe, drinking was no big deal and not a source of rebellion, because students had been doing it for years.

The end of our meal was signaled by the arrival of an enormous cheese cart, which the restaurant owner rolled out to the table. I followed Petter and Denis's lead and filled my dessert plate to capacity with various cheeses, even though I did not have a clue as to what each one was. The French liked to say that they had a different cheese for each day of the year, and it appeared that the restaurant owner had half the year covered.

In America, it was extremely difficult to find unpasteurized cheese, as the extended shelf life of pasteurized cheese was required by all United States supermarkets. Even though the United States had five times the population of France, there were still more food-related deaths each year in France.

The Normandy region of France had close to twenty varieties alone of soft, creamy Camembert—with most of it unpasteurized. The wide variety of cheeses I had filled my plate with ranged from wonderful and full of flavor to all but inedible, causing me to wonder if it was rude to leave a fair amount of uneaten cheese on my plate. Denis and Petter had both cleaned their plates of cheese, and with no dogs in sight to come to my aid, I wrapped the uneaten portion in my napkin and secretly placed it in my pocket when no one was looking. It was not until I returned home and a strange smell began to crawl out of my laundry basket that I remembered that I had never removed the napkin of cheese from my pocket.

Day three of the itinerary called for us to "drive" the final ninety-five kilometers to Paris. Even though I knew that Denis meant we would be riding the final ninety-five kilometers to Paris, I leaned over to Petter and openly shared the thought, "Wouldn't it be great if we drove to Paris today?"

"Tell me about it," he said. "My butt is refusing to get on my bike seat this morning."

The torturous summer heat showed no sign of taking a day off as the temperature quickly made its way back up into the nineties. It was apparent that we were all sick and tired of riding a bike, and the thought of another eight-hour ride in the blazing heat dampened our spirits. We rode in silence rather than chatting away like schoolgirls as we had done during the two previous morning rides.

An hour and a half into the ride, we made our first stop in a small village made up of a church, a café, and a market store. We parked our bikes and walked into the café for a nice, cold drink and a snack. We purchased three drinks and some pretzels. Petter looked for a quiet place to see if his cell phone had dried out while Denis and I went back outside with our cold drinks and sat down to rest on a curb.

As Denis and I sat there on a curb in the middle of nowhere in northern France, trying to stay out of the hot sun, he told me about how the French referred to the sun with a masculine noun (*le soleil*) and *la lune* or the moon was a feminine word. But in German it was the opposite; the sun or *die Sonne* was feminine term, and *der Mond* or the moon was considered masculine. It was such a simple comment, but I found it fascinating. Before arriving in Europe, I had always wondered if two people from two distant countries and cultures could really become good friends. Petter and I had become good friends and connected fairly quickly, but I felt that that had mostly been aided by the fact that Petter had lived in the United States for so many years and had a true American side through which we could easily connect.

I thoroughly enjoyed the time I spent just sitting and talking with Denis, and a day without talking to him almost did not feel complete. Denis and I had often had silly conversations, such as when he had explained to me why Germans loved the American television star David Hasselhoff's music so much and when I returned the favor by explaining to him what the term "soccer mom" meant. But we also had many serious conversations, during which we had shared personal stories about growing up, first jobs, first cars, or first loves. In the brief time since we had first met, we felt that we had really made a connection, and I truly felt that Denis would be a good friend of mine for the rest of my life. Because we looked like we could be brothers, he was my long lost European twin.

As Petter walked back toward us, smiling because his cell phone was working once again, I asked Denis why European football players exchanged jerseys with their opponents at the end of the match, often putting them on immediately, even though the shirts were soaked with their opponents' sweat and blood.

"Exchanging your jersey with your opponent is to show him respect as a player and a person," Denis said.

I thought over Denis's response for a minute.

"Well, Denis, you are a good friend, but if we ever do make it to Paris, don't expect me to ask you to swap T-shirts—that's disgusting."

Denis smiled at my joke as we both lifted ourselves off the curb and got back on our bikes.

We only rode for an hour and a half before making another stop. What stopped us that time was not the deathly heat or a long uphill climb, but the intoxicating aroma of steamed mussels served in a white wine, garlic sauce. The smell came from the window of a small restaurant kitchen next to the road. We could not resist the smell and quickly found an empty table and waited for the waiter to bring us each a large bowl of our own to enjoy. The meal was unforgettable and would most likely have cost us three times as much if we had ordered it in a restaurant in Paris. Of course, we had to have a bottle of wine that complemented and enhanced the meal.

The meal topper was the knowledge the waiter provided us that a train station was only a ten-minute, downhill bike ride away. The bike trip was officially over—or at least the riding part. We decided right then and there that we were taking the train the rest of the way to Paris.

"Waiter, please bring us another bottle of wine."

- Chapter Twenty-Five -

My Cup Runneth Over

✦

"Oh, you Americans. You are so smart, so inventive, so creative!" I was thoroughly enjoying the compliment from a complete stranger whom I had struck up a conversation with while waiting in line to order a pint of beer. "But you stink so bad at football that you turned it into a women's sport (emphasizing the word "women's" to help make his point), and you now dominate it. Amazing!"

The second half of the compliment was not nearly as enjoyable as the first, but he did have a point. It was true that the United States' men's national soccer team had yet to make a headline on the sports page, but the United States' women's national team had been very successful, winning the inaugural women's World Cup in 1991 and the Olympic gold medal in 1996, when women's soccer first became an Olympic sport. While the United States' men's national team was hardly recognized by the majority of Americans, many of the women's team members had appeared in national ad campaigns for Nike and were even household names, such as Mia Hamm. In the United States, women's soccer was just as popular as men's in many high schools, and in college, it was the most popular women's sport.

Every four years for an entire month, the world—or at least five billion people in 189 countries—stopped showing up regularly for work, woke up at four o'clock in the morning if necessary, and climbed a mountain if necessary to go out of their way to find a television, any television as long as it worked—to watch a group of men kick around a small ball on a grass field. The event finally reached its climax when one in five people in the world watched one team hold up a small golden trophy as World Cup champions, instantly earning the status of national heroes in their home country.

Even though the month-long World Cup tournament took over much of the world's interest, it was hardly a blip on the sporting radar in the United States. The World Cup was the only truly international sporting event on the planet that brought together the attention and interest of the rich and poor, people of all ethnicities, and followers of nearly every religion. We Americans preferred the Olympics, in which we usually did extremely well in the medal count; we enjoyed sitting in front of our televisions watching the athletes' stories, which were presented to us with heart-tugging tales of overcoming tough odds, making sacrifices, and enduring hardships to become Olympic athletes—and get rich on endorsement deals. While we chose the Olympics, most of the world preferred the World Cup. Don't get me wrong, many countries would spend hundreds of millions of dollars to campaign for the chance to host the Summer or Winter Olympics, but if they had the choice between hosting the Olympics or the World Cup, they would choose to host the World Cup nine out of ten times.

It was easy to understand why the world preferred the game of football (or soccer) over all the other sports. The rules of the game were simple to understand and the sport did not require purchasing expensive equipment— just a round ball and a modest, flat playing surface.

Many children in African countries couldn't afford a real ball to play with and improvised by wrapping plastic bags tightly together to form a rounded ball. A few years back, while enjoying a stroll with Sarah along the beautiful beaches of the small island of Zanzibar off the coast of Tanzania, we had come across a group of children playing a game of soccer with what appeared to a ball made of dirty rags wrapped together with plastic bags. We enjoyed watching the kids smile and laugh as they chased the ball around. At the same time, the obvious poverty of their village and the lack of a real soccer ball to play with made us both feel guilty for staying at a luxury resort a half-mile down the beach, where one night's room rate could have purchased a hundred soccer balls.

The sport also does not require you to be a certain height or size to excel. One of the sport's all-time best players, Diego Maradona from Argentina, was barely five feet five inches tall, and the Brazilian soccer god Pele was only five feet ten. Finally, outcomes of games between countries were not dictated by economic wealth, so countries like Ghana, a small African country that I had difficulty accurately locating on a map (and I had been to the continent of Africa twice) could push around big, powerful, rich countries on the soccer field as they did when beating the United States 2–1 in a World Cup match.

Luck was on our side, our time in England coincided with the World Cup tournament, providing us with a chance to experience "World Cup

Fever" firsthand. Sarah and I both quickly learned that the experience of the tournament involved much more than just watching the actual matches themselves. We both showed early signs of World Cup fatigue weeks before the tournament even started, because it was impossible to read a newspaper, watch the news, walk into a pub, or shop in a supermarket without being bombarded with information or marketing campaigns from companies looking to make money from sponsoring the tournament. Pubs decorated their interiors with World Cup flair and postings of match schedules, and some even went so far as to shut their doors for two weeks to completely redecorate the interior and upgrade their televisions to new, large, high-definition, flat-screen TVs. Old women could also be overheard on the Tube discussing how to best treat a sports-related injury, such as the broken metatarsal that the English star player, Wayne Rooney, had tragically suffered just weeks before the tournament and hoped to have healed before the start of the tournament.

Sarah felt that the most interesting pre-hype for the tournament was the World Cup widows support groups that were forming. The groups were for women, who would soon be ignored by their boyfriends and husbands who would be dedicating a large amount of their time to sitting in pubs watching every match with "their mates," to find non-World Cup socializing activities during the month-long tournament to keep them occupied. A small group of pubs catered to those anti-World Cup groups by proudly announcing that they were "World Cup Free," strictly prohibiting viewing and even discussing the World Cup.

I felt that the most interesting thing was the fact that the players from Serbia and Montenegro were representing a country that no longer officially existed, because the country had split into two separate countries just weeks before the tournament but had qualified as a single country and was still required to play as one country. It seemed that everyone was directly affected by the tournament in one way or another.

When it was apparent that it was a slow news week in terms of World Cup news coming out of each country's training camp, it seemed the press literally made news themselves. A British tabloid printed an extremely unflattering photo of the German Chancellor Angela Merkel pulling on her underwear after swimming. The accompanying headline read "Big in the Bumdestag," a pun on the German parliament, which was called the *Bundestag*. The article was sprinkled with praise for her economic success, saying that Germany had experience a "much-improved bottom line" and referred to her as the "cheeky chancellor." German newspapers countered with claims that the printing of the picture demonstrated that the English were truly trash and that Germany would never print a picture of the Queen of England in her support stockings. Even David Beckham, the *GQ* cover boy and captain of the England team, could not avoid being baited into a confrontation with the European press, when he angrily addressed comments made by the German press that David's mother had "the smile of a peasant" and referred to his sister as being "lardy." The attacks did not end there, including claims that his wife, Victoria Beckham, was nothing but a "trophy wife" and that his son Romeo looked more like a girl and should have been named Juliet.

The pre-event smear tactic was popular in other sports, as Tiger Woods found out the hard way while playing for the United States team in the Ryder Cup against Europe. Stories in Europe circulated around a false claim that his wife's modeling past was linked to the world of porn.

The German Chancellor, Angela Merkel, had more pressing World Cup issues to deal with, because Germany was the host country for the tournament. Since Iran had qualified for the tournament, she was busy trying to persuade Iran's president, Mahmoud Ahmadinejad, not to travel to Germany to watch the Iranian team play, mostly because of his open hatred toward Israel. Since denying the Holocaust was against the law in Germany and punishable by jail time, she wanted to avoid a diplomatic nightmare, which would take away Germany's limelight for hosting the tournament, if Ahmadinejad decided to travel to Germany to attend the event.

The additional pre-tournament hype in England was greatly aided by the belief that England had put together one of the best English teams to qualify for the tournament in decades. We could physically feel the collective weight of the country's hopes and expectations of winning the World Cup on our shoulders while walking the streets of London. The public and press talked so confidently about the fact that England would prevail that I began to worry about what would happen if the English team didn't bring home the Cup.

Prior to our arrival in England, Sarah had never heard of any of the players on the England World Cup team other than David Beckham. By the start of the tournament, she could name many of them; eventually, I could name them all. During the weeks leading up to the tournament, not only did we learn their names but, without really trying, we learned about their favorite foods, the cars they drove, the types of beds they slept in, and the women who slept in their beds with them.

A guilty pleasure that most of England enjoyed, admittedly or not, was following the exploits of the football subculture of the "WAGs," or "Wives and Girlfriends," of England's national team. In a move that he must have regretted, the England national team's coach had invited the wives and girlfriends to join them for the tournament at the Baden-Baden training camp in Germany. A bigger mistake—or possibly a perfectly planned public relations stunt—was the decision to book the WAGs and the press that had been sent to cover their shenanigans in the same hotel.

The small spa town of Baden-Baden, located in western Germany close to the Black Forest, eagerly welcomed the WAGs and their luxury shopping lifestyle. In anticipation of capitalizing on the opportunity, the local stores stocked up on additional Prada, Gucci, Dolce & Gabbana, Fendi, Hermes and Dior items. Restaurants and bars stocked up on the trendy, expensive champagne brands for the WAGs' post-shopping drinking binges. Economists sat back and watched to see if the English football WAGs could single-handedly boost the German GDP, while the business owners of Baden-Baden prayed to the soccer gods that the English team would do very well in the World Cup tournament, keeping the WAGs and their credit cards in town as long as possible.

The press did not disappoint and provided a daily stream of what types of bikinis each WAG wore that day, as well as who was getting along with whom and which girls were trying to out-bling the others. Nightly drunken episodes of the WAGs filled newspapers back in England the next morning, featuring pictures of them dancing drunkenly, dressed in high-end designer dresses. Special emphasis was always given to the daily activities of Victoria Beckham, even if she seemed to be enjoying a far less active lifestyle—if not a downright boring one compared to the other WAGs.

While Victoria Beckham, a former member of the pop group the Spice Girls, given the nickname "Posh Spice," was arguably the queen bee of the WAGs, her husband David Beckham was undoubtedly leader of the team on the field and held the honor of being the captain of the team. Their marriage elevated them both to a dizzying status in the world of celebrities. David Beckham had admirably connected the different audiences from sports, fashion, and style under the umbrella of "Beckham mania."

In the United States, it was common to hear people refer to David Beckham as the Michael Jordan of Europe. The two sports gods had many similarities. The two obvious similarities were that both could do amazing things with a ball and both had earned hundreds of millions of dollars while building a global following. The biggest difference between the two was that Michael Jordan had been considered, for many years, to be the best player in the world in his time, while David Beckham had never been talked about as the best player in the world; he was more of a specialist who was known for his passing skills and his free kick mastery. But while kids in America dreamed at night in their beds of "being like Mike" on the basketball court, much of the world wanted not only Beckham's on-field skills but also his mojo; they even went as far as to copy his latest haircut style, even when it was the rebellious Mohawk.

Prior to the England national team leaving for the 2006 and 2002 World Cups, David and Victoria had hosted a star-studded going-away party at their mansion, which was known as "Beckingham Palace,". The 2002 dress code called for "white tie and diamonds." In 2006, Victoria had wanted to top her 2002 going-away party, so she spent over one million dollars on the 2006 party and set a dress code that called for "full length and fabulous." The guest list included Tom Cruise, Elton John, Sharon Osbourne, Liz Hurley, members of the Royal Family, and many more A-list celebrities. The food had been prepared by the Michelin-starred, celebrity chef Gordon Ramsey, and Robbie Williams and soul legend James Brown had entertained guests with their music. The highlight of the night had been the charity auction, in which American rap mogul Sean "Puff Daddy" Combs had auctioned off a chance to spend a weekend with him in New York. Twenty-year-old England star player Wayne Rooney had outbid Sharon Osbourne, with a shocking winning bid of $300,000—even though Wayne was technically not old enough to drink in a New York City nightclub.

USA! USA! USA!

There was nothing that really got under the skin of Europeans more than the chant of "USA! USA! USA!"

"Can't you Americans come up with something better? What does chanting three letters over and over really mean? There is no story or history behind such a simple chant. You're really just being overly obnoxious." Those were common comments that were harmlessly thrown my way by friends and strangers. From the start of the tournament, the United States' men's national team had sputtered and fizzled out quickly with an early 0–3 loss to the Czech Republic. Their tournament hopes ended with a 1–1 tie with Italy and finally a 1–2 loss to the tiny African nation of Ghana. Even though the United States' men's team was not producing the results that the few Americans who had interest in the World Cup had hoped for, the British press did not waste the opportunity to take a few cheap jabs at Americans and printed a few entertaining and harmless anti-American remarks about the United States' team's performance. My favorite was an article in the *Guardian* newspaper with the headline "Over-excited, overweight, and over here." The article had been written to poke fun at America's lack of interest in the event and made the suggestion that the few American fans who had attended the United States' team's matches in Germany could easily be identified, because their seats were surrounded by piles of discarded hamburger wrappers and they all wore FDNY T-shirts. The article went on to point out that far more

American journalists had covered the preseason launch of *American Idol* than had covered the World Cup. It also reported that the lack of interest in the sport and tournament had inspired a company in the United States to sell T-shirts with "What World Cup?" printed on the front.

Coming into the World Cup tournament, the United States' men's team had had a respectable world ranking, but their performance in the tournament was a disappointment, and by no means the expectation. While the other World Cup teams paraded to and from training sessions and matches through the streets of various German cities in their team buses with their countries' flags proudly draped over the sides, the United States' team traveled in a bus without a flag on its side and usually tried to keep a low profile. No fans lined the streets to cheer them on, because the streets were closed to traffic, and a large convoy of police vehicles escorted the team bus through the streets.

It was not easy being a member of the United States' men's national team during qualifying matches. Even home matches in the United States against neighboring countries like Mexico had the atmospheric feeling of an away match, because many Mexican citizens lived in the United States and attended the games. For most of the year, the United States' men's team members were unknowns to foreign fans and could go unnoticed and even walk the street as common people. But when they put on the national team jersey and walked out onto the field, they were often seen as public enemy number one by hostile home fans. Chants of "Osama bin Laden! Osama bin Laden!" were common during their matches. Dodging projectiles thrown from the fans in the stands was part of many matches. Team members literally needed to develop "thick skin."

As a country that had dominated the world's popular culture for better or worse, the United States lagged far behind in the world's most popular sport. I found it amusing to hear smart, educated people discuss theories as to why the United States, with its enormous population and its well-organized youth sport infrastructure, was still unable to produce a group of men to compete in and win a World Cup. My favorite was a theory from a friend who felt that since "sixty percent of Americans are overweight, you have to cut the eligible population accordingly," our minimal "soccer-fit" population hindered our chances of producing world-class soccer players. Usually, remarks such as those were supported by the commonly accepted thought that Americans greatly preferred American football because men needed to be "big and fat" to be star players, and most Americans identified with supersize athletes.

I tried to explain to friends and strangers in the pub that, in the United States, soccer was immensely popular with young kids—both boys and girls—and that the suburbs of America were filled each weekend with soccer games where proud parents and grandparents stood on the sidelines, furiously snapping pictures of the kids chasing the balls around with their new friends. But around age ten, that scene fades out. Those same kids seemed to lose interest in the sport and would rather play more mainstream sports that have reached critical mass on television such as baseball, football, basketball, and even hockey. Some even migrated toward skateboarding or snowboarding. Preteens saw those sports and X-Games activities on television where soccer was nowhere to be found; they aspired to be like the athletes they saw on TV and in advertisements.

Game On!

Since the United States team had quickly exited the tournament, Sarah and I decided that we would throw our support behind England and Germany. Supporting England was an obvious choice, but cheering for the German team was more of a requirement if we wanted to spend time with Denis and Jenny and all of our other German friends. Both the English and German teams got off to a good early start and both played well enough to move on to the quarterfinals of the tournament. I found it a strange experience to look out the pub window during an English World Cup match and see very little traffic, if any at all, on the usually heavily congested streets.

Sarah and I stood shoulder to shoulder in packed pubs waiting to erupt in joyful celebration when England scored or ended the match with a victory. The feeling of being part of the sea of England supporters desperately pleading for another victory was great and made us feel as though we were part of something big, something special. When England crashed out of the tournament in dramatic fashion with a semifinal loss to Portugal, in a match that had been settled by penalty kicks, Sarah and I were truly devastated. We had bought into the English confidence that anything short of a World Cup victory would be disappointing. England had earned a well-deserved reputation of choking when it came to delivering a victory through penalty kicks. So when the match with Portugal ended in a tie and the penalty kick phase of the game started, we too felt the pain that destiny was no longer on England's side. England once again choked and only scored a single goal in four penalty kick tries.

The blame game quickly followed in the wake of the final defeat. The media placed blame far and wide, blaming everything from coaching decisions or tournament player selections to referees or hot game-time temperatures, even throwing in all the distractions from the WAGs' endless shopping and bad girl behavior.

The German team's dreams of winning the World Cup were dashed shortly after England's, with an 0–2 loss to the eventual tournament winners. Germany had entered the tournament with a good team and had been helped out by the fact that every match was a home game for them, because Germany was host country of the tournament. For Sarah and me, watching the German team play was just as special as watching England play, because it provided a slightly different and unique perspective to the experience of the tournament.

We watched the German matches with Denis and Jenny and our other German friends, Max and Felix. We watched each match at a small pub that was close to school and had plenty of seats. As Germany progressed further and further into the tournament, the word spread among other Germans living in London that this was the place to go to watch the German matches. With each additional win by the German national team, the number of German supporters who came to the pub to watch each match grew larger and larger, making the atmosphere fun and exhilarating for us to be part of, even if most of the room's conversations were in German.

At the start of the match between Germany and Sweden, a male German supporter attempted to pass out small German flags to the growing crowd of complete strangers who were there to support Germany. When the stranger made his way over to where we were sitting, he reached out to hand Jenny a flag. She turned down his offer, quickly sending him away. I could not understand the reason she had given him for declining his offer, because she had spoken to him in German. I finally turned to her and asked why she had turned him down. Jenny said that she did not think it was right to wave a German flag in England.

I was taken aback by her response, because it was my first experience of Denis and Jenny being part of the German "guilt generation." Decades after the war had ended, they had both been born into a generation that still had to bear the guilt of the atrocities of past German actions, even though they had had nothing to do with those actions. It made me feel sorry for them, because they both were such wonderful people and they truly represented what Germany had become. It was an educational moment, but at the same time, I wished she had accepted the flag and waved it proudly during the match.

The month-long World Cup tournament of "the beautiful game" ended literally facedown in the mud when the tournament's most memorable moment came in the final match. The French national soccer hero Zinedine Zidane, who had come out of retirement to represent France in the tournament, delivered a devastating and violent head butt to an Italian player who had provoked

Zinedine with a "yo mama" joke—an insulting joke that was widely accepted as part of the trash-talking heard constantly in American sports. I was further disappointed when the championship game was decided by penalty kicks.

"This is like deciding who the basketball champions are by shooting free throws," I tried to explain to Sarah, who was beginning to worry that I might throw our small, twelve-inch television out the window. "There are players who haven't even played yet and are still sitting on the bench. Keep playing!" I shouted at the screen in frustration.

Sarah and I watched together as Italy prevailed in penalty kicks. I could tell that she was glad the tournament was over and that the country would finally return to normal; she was suffering greatly from World Cup fatigue.

Italy emerged as the winner of the World Cup, but the European media unanimously crowned the tournament host country of Germany as the real winner. Even though Jenny had reluctantly turned down the offer of a German flag to wave to show her support on English soil, back home in Germany there was a spontaneous national embrace of the black, red, and gold colors of the *Bundesflagge*. It could be easily spotted being proudly displayed from car windows, homes, and on the backs of Germans, showing everyone that it was once again all right to be proud to be German. The overwhelming display of national pride, even though Germany had not won, proved that the country had taken a giant leap toward returning to normal. Sarah and I could not have been happier for Denis, Jenny, and all our other new German friends.

- Chapter Twenty-Six -

Paris en Juin Est Grand

✦

I have always found it fascinating that pop culture could inspire people to travel hundreds—if not thousands—of miles to experience a place that they had read about in a novel or that had been the setting of a popular movie or television show. It could be a baseball field cut into an Iowa cornfield or the landscape scenery in *Lord of the Rings* or *The Sound of Music* that made us want to get into our cars or head to the nearest airport and spend precious vacation time experiencing the locations firsthand. London was filled with a seemingly endless list of places that let us literally follow in the footsteps of some of our favorite and most beloved fictional characters. The latest additions to the pop culture must-travel-to-see list, *The Da Vinci Code* and Harry Potter, provided enormous material for sightseeing companies.

Sarah and I were walking down a train platform to board an early morning Eurostar train to take us to Paris for the weekend. Unless we had been deaf, blind, or drunk, we could not miss the enormous floor advertisements, wall posters, and continuous overhead announcements of the marketing movie tie-in between the Eurostar trains and *The Da Vinci Code* book and movie. The marketing campaign was called "Join the Quest," and one of the grand prizes included lifetime travel on the Eurostar trains. The campaign to get more people to travel to Paris or London on the Eurostar train could be judged a success purely based on the evidence that the number one lost and found item on the trains was Dan Brown's *Da Vinci Code*, as growing numbers of tourists took to the train to make their own *Da Vinci Code* pilgrimage between London and Paris.

"Excuse me, pretty lady, but do you know where I can find platform nine and three-quarters? I am meeting my friend Harry to say good-bye," I said to Sarah, sounding like Prince Charles and referring to the magical train platform that the young Harry Potter wizard and his friends boarded the Hogwarts Express from in the Harry Potter books and movies.

"You're at the wrong train station for that, buddy," Sarah said in more of a tough Brooklyn accent.

I had worked on the joke the entire morning, waiting for just the right moment to use it, only to have it flop badly because I could not correctly remember that in the Harry Potter books, the Hogwarts Express had left from the King's Cross train station rather than the Waterloo station.

It was Sarah's birthday, and she could not think of a better place to celebrate it than in Paris. Because it was Sarah's birthday, there was no point in asking who got the window seat for the train ride. The train pulled out of the station and gradually built up speed, ultimately reaching close to 190 miles per hour and making it possible to arrive in central Paris in only two-and-a-half hours.

We arrived in Paris's Gare du Nord station and made our way off the train and to the metro. As an extra treat for Sarah's birthday weekend, I had told her that I would carry all her bags for her. Her bag was much lighter than mine—a rare occurrence—and I wondered if Sarah had packed lightly because she was planning to fill the empty space with the spoils of a shopping spree. It was her birthday, so she made the rules, and if shopping was what she wanted to do, then shopping was what we would do.

The morning rush hour traffic on the metro had already ended, so we had plenty of space on the train as we traveled to the station closest to our hotel. Sarah sat down in an empty seat, fully looking the part of a Parisian in her summer dress and sunglasses, picked up a local newspaper that had been left on the seat, and tried to read it. I looked every bit the tourist as I stood in the aisle balancing all of our small suitcases. Sweat stains showed through my shirt from carrying all of our bags on and off the trains and up and down the metro stairs. I think Sarah was intentionally ignoring me because she did not want the other passengers to know that she was with the sweaty American Sherpa. *What a jerk,* I thought to myself. *Luckily, she is cute. And it is her birthday.*

The small hotel I had booked us was in the charming and elegant seventh arrondissement of Paris. That was one of the most expensive parts of Paris, but you could also find some small and inexpensive hotels there if you looked hard enough. I had always liked the area because of its proximity to the Eiffel Tower, which provided a unique illusion that the tower was right behind all of the narrow, low-lying side streets.

Sarah and I had decided that the weekend would not be a whirlwind tour of the city. Our goal, for the most part, was to avoid setting foot into a single museum or monument and to live like the locals did—relaxed and carefree.

After I changed out of my sweat-soaked shirt, we walked down to a corner café for a nice, long, Parisian-style lunch. It was a perfect, blue sky day, and we picked a table that was near the edge of the café and right next to a flower shop, where the owner had just decorated the sidewalk with the day's offerings of beautiful flowers.

We ordered two glasses of white wine and sat in silence as we watched the café slowly fill up with the lunch crowd. An American couple with four young kids began to argue with the waiter, who was trying to seat them at one of the worst tables with the view of the street severely obstructed by an awning flap and a large bush in a decorative planter. The husband and wife did not understand that the waiter was saving all the good seats for the regulars who would be showing up shortly but decided to take the table instead of leaving.

Sarah and I cringed as the couple quickly approached the "Ugly American" spectacle stage and the waiter ignored them for ten minutes while he greeted his regulars and sat them all down at the best tables in front. The couple's children grew restless and bored. The husband kept looking at his watch and murmuring to his wife that they would soon be behind schedule on the long list of sights they were trying to see.

One of an American's best skills was eating on the run, especially when in a hurry. But even when we sat down, we have an expectation of the timing and rhythm from the meal and service. But in Europe, the reality was that unless you had two hours, you shouldn't even think of stepping foot into a café for lunch. The husband was about to lose it, and he all but tackled the nearest waiter, proceeding to order drinks and food and request that the bill be brought with them.

Since Sarah and I did not have any other place to be, I did not mind when our food finally came some half an hour later, though I, too, was beginning to think that the waiter had forgotten we existed. We finished our meal, wisely ordered another glass of wine because we knew it would be another half an hour before the bill came, and sat back to watch the business crowd, who had also just finished their two-hour lunch, prepare to leave.

As we left the café, we watched in curiosity as the businessmen and businesswomen said good-bye to each other with kisses. Sarah and I strongly agreed that the double *bisou*, or two-cheek kiss, would be really uncomfortable if the person on the receiving end was a coworker or a client. If we had to regularly kiss coworkers or clients on each cheek every time we said hello or good-bye, it would take some getting used to. But that was what made the French French.

The afternoon activity was to sit on the lush green grass, literally in the shadow of the Eiffel Tower on the Parc du Champs de Mars gardens and take a nap, read our books, and people watch. As we walked under the four legs of the Eiffel Tower and made our way to the garden lawns, we discussed whether Paris should be considered a museum or a museum city because of the overflowing mix of architecture, history, and romance.

As Sarah sat on the grass reading her book, I was distracted by a group of young men playing a game of soccer. Sarah quickly picked up on my staring at them.

"You really wish you could go play with them, don't you?" Sarah asked me.

"Why would you think that?" I asked.

"You look like a dog watching a Frisbee get thrown back and forth, and it is killing you not to go chase it," she said.

Sarah was absolutely right. I was dying to join in on the fun, but I was too shy to ask and was secretly hoping that the soccer ball would be accidentally kicked my way, providing the opportunity to ask the Frenchmen, in English of course, if I could join them. But their game ended without the stray kick I was hoping for, and bored with my book, my focus drifted back to Sarah while she read hers.

"Did you know that my first hero was a Frenchman?" I said to Sarah, who was enjoying reading her book and feeling just like a local.

Without looking up from her book, she said, "Yes, I know that Jacques Cousteau was your first hero and has since been replaced by someone who gained fame for traveling to this very spot."

I sat there in silence, stunned that she had remembered that Jacques Cousteau had been my childhood hero and had since been replaced by Charles Lindbergh, who had become the first pilot to cross the Atlantic nonstop when he traveled from New York to Paris in his single-engine monoplane, the Spirit of St. Louis, in 1927.

"Unlike you, I do listen and remember the things you tell me," Sarah said through a half laugh, half smile, with her head still buried in her book.

For dinner later that night, we walked over to a nearby restaurant that had been recommended to us by—of all people—my parents. The restaurant was located far off any of the area's main streets, hidden away on a narrow street just a few minutes' walk from our hotel. It took us three wrong turns and a five full minutes of consulting our area map before we found it, adding to the building curiosity about how my parents had found the restaurant in the first place. We knew the place was probably good when we discovered that all the other area restaurants were empty but that one. To our dismay, we soon learned that the restaurant was completely booked for the night. We looked on in disappointment at all the wonderful empty tables lining the sidewalk and waiting for the night's regulars to fill them.

The restaurant hostess sensed our deep disappointment, and after watching us stand in silence for a second or two, she said in perfect English, "Actually, I just might have one table left, but it is right next to the kitchen." She did have one table left, and it was as close to the kitchen as you could get without actually sitting in the kitchen. Sarah was happy with the table, because she could watch the skilled chefs carefully craft each dish. The meal was one of the best I had ever eaten, and the service could not have been any better. The hostess even came over to make sure everything was great and apologized again for the table's location, even offering to take a picture of the two of us. I rolled my eyes at Sarah, with a do-we-have-to? look.

"Hey, it's my birthday," she said.

After dinner, we slowly walked hand in hand back to our hotel through the humid night, enjoying the view of the Eiffel Tower as thousands of lights flickered and danced above our heads from high up on the tower. Even the foreign-sounding police sirens far off in the distance added to the romantic atmosphere of the moment. The day could not have been more perfect.

Parlez-Vous Anglais?

The next morning, we got out of bed and did as the locals did. We walked over to the famous Poilâne bread company and picked up some freshly baked bread to spread jam on top of and eat for breakfast. Next we walked over to the local grocery store and cruised up and down the store aisles. I felt that one of the best ways to better understand a foreign place was to make a trip to a local grocery store and explore the selection of products and packaging, looking at where and how items were displayed.

Our next stop was on a quiet street on the Left Bank, where on Rue Léon Delhomme, the world's most famous cooking school, Le Cordon Bleu, was located. But since it was a Saturday, there were no students hard at work, hoping to someday earn *Le Grand Diplôme du Cordon Bleu*. We stepped inside so Sarah could steal a quick peek and marvel at the classrooms while dreaming of someday sitting in one of the room's chairs as a student. We purchased the long, white cooking apron with the school emblem engraved high up on the chest in the traditional blue that students wore.

We agreed that, while the locals most likely did not routinely enjoy a tourist-filled riverboat cruise up and down the River Seine, it was the perfect day for a boat ride and an excuse to get off our feet for an hour. The next boat would not leave for another half hour, so we sat down at a nearby café to order a cold drink and wait to board the tour boat. I don't know if it was the heat or my growing hunger for lunch, but when the waiter came to take our order, the words "Una cerveza, por favor" popped out my mouth. The waiter gave me a well-deserved "stupid American" chuckle as Sarah tried to fix the "Ugly American" situation I had brought upon myself, correcting, "I think you mean 'Une bière, s'il vous plaît.'"

"Yes, I will have one of those, please," I said, looking up at the waiter, slightly embarrassed.

While the waiter took his sweet time fetching my beer—probably waiting for it to lose most of its chill before bringing it to the table—I thought of the classic joke, "What do you call someone who speaks four languages? A Dutchman. What do you call someone who speaks one language? A Frenchman. What do you call someone who speaks no languages? An American!" It was true. In general, we Americans don't speak any foreign languages, or more correctly, a large number of United States-born citizens don't learn a second language during their lives.

Most Americans couldn't speak another language, and even though quite a few of us would have liked to learn to master another language, I feel we didn't make the effort because the financial incentive is not as strong to learn a second language as it is in Europe. English is the language of global business. No matter how much the fact upsets the French, English, for the foreseeable future, will be the language of choice. For many years, music, television, and films had helped spread English around the world. The Internet had become the new workhorse in helping to spread the English language. Europe spoke many different languages, but they needed a single language for doing business, and English has become that language.

The French had resisted the growing trend to use English. The use of English in French advertising was strictly monitored, and any common slogan in English, by law, also had to have a French translation alongside it.

The French had also made headlines with acts such as Jacques Chirac's walking out of a European Union Summit session when a fellow Frenchman had committed the heinous crime of addressing the audience in English. When Chirac had asked him why on earth he, the president of the French employers' association, had spoken English, the Frenchman had answered him by saying that the language of business in Europe was English.

I truly believe that if we spoke one language in my current home state of Illinois, another language in Wisconsin, and a third in Indiana or Michigan, many of us Midwesterners could probably speak all of them well enough to get by. If California were its own country, it would have the fifth-largest economy in the world, and if Californians spoke their own language, the rest of us Americans would have all learned that language so we could work or do business in California.

Those Americans lucky enough to be able to afford to travel outside the country quickly discovered that English was spoken all over the world, and we could easily travel the world and only rarely run into a situation where we could not communicate with someone in the tourist industry. To get a job in the tourist industry, the ability to speak English was pretty much mandatory. Many of the students I was attending classes with each day were there to get an MBA in London primarily because it would help them perfect their speaking and writing ability in English, making them stand out just a little bit more on their résumés and get the better jobs.

Many of the students could have stayed in their own European countries and received MBAs without paying any money out of their own pockets, but there was an economic incentive for them to learn English, and it was worth the cost. The reason the banners and signs held up by protestors and marchers throughout Europe were in English was not only so Americans could understand them when cameras were focused on them but also so Europeans could read and understand them, because English was the language they mutually understand.

Many Americans would love to be able to learn a second language, but while it is a luxury and not mandatory, the individuals who can speak another language in America will always be in the minority.

After enjoying the scenic, hour-long boat ride, it was time to do some shopping. Our first stop was at a department store, or a grand magasin, literally meaning "big store" in French—Printemps and Galeries Lafayette, located on Boulevard Haussmann. Earlier in the day, Sarah had made the remark that she had forgotten to bring a white bra, which she wanted to wear to dinner with her white dress later in the evening, and she needed to pick one up. Really, she was telling me that it was time to go shopping. French women spend a huge amount of money on lingerie, and Galeries Lafayette was more than willing to help satisfy the addiction with a twenty-eight thousand-square-foot lingerie shop.

I was afraid that, if I left Sarah alone, I might lose her in the sprawling store and spend the rest of the afternoon wandering around trying to find her. The lingerie department was packed with women running their fingers through the different types of fabric and unabashedly holding up sexy and revealing outfits for their friends and partners to give them their opinions on. The uncomfortable feeling of being surrounded by sexy Frenchwomen stocking up on outfits better suited for a strip club than for middle-aged women lasted longer than I wanted it to before Sarah found what she was looking for and we exited the store.

The shopping spree continued with a stop at a local bookstore and children's toy store to stock up on children's toys and books, which we would take back home, store in the closet, and someday use to teach French to the kids that we did not yet have. I could not help but notice the difference between the types of toys from country to country and what it suggested about European culture. The French wanted toys that helped to build a child's imagination, while the Germans preferred toys, such as Legos, that would possibly inspire them to become engineers. Unlike most American toy stores, there were no army soldiers, tanks, guns, or fighter planes, and there were very few action hero toys.

The anti-war and violence attitudes of Europe had trickled down to what toy stores made available to kids and parents. Strangely enough, in recent years, Belgium television aired a UNICEF commercial that showed the lovable, blue-skinned cartoon characters The Smurfs on the receiving end of a carpet bombing campaign as warplanes zoomed overhead. The campaign's purpose was to shock the public and drive home the message that war could happen anywhere. The advertisement achieved a high shock value, as the commercial ends with a Smurfette left for dead and Baby Smurf crying and orphaned.

While Sarah stood in line to pay for the French children's books, calendars, and bath toys for the kids that we did not have, I continued to look at all the French books sitting out on tables. I came across a book that I had heard about and stopped in my tracks to pick it up. Even though I could not understand a word of it because it was in French, I flipped slowly through the pages, my eyes locking in on the words that did not have French equivalents—"World Trade Center," "United Airlines," and "Pentagon." Thierry Meyssan's *L'Effroyable imposture* ("The Horrifying Fraud") was a best-seller in France when it was published in 2002. The English version was titled *9/11: The Big Lie*. The book made the argument that the horrific terrorist attacks of September 11, 2001, had actually been carried out by the United States government, which had wanted a *casus belli* that would support a military invasion of Afghanistan. I thought it was sad that so many great books never gained any traction, but a book that was filled with complete garbage had become a huge hit.

After we left the bookstore, my sweet tooth got the best of me, and we perused the huge chocolate selection at the Maison du chocolat before making our last stop of the day at the former residence of Coco Chanel—a favorite drinking establishment of Ernest Hemingway's—and quite possibly the world's best hotel, the Ritz Paris. We decided to see how the other half lived and stopped to treat ourselves to two outrageously expensive drinks in the hotel bar.

Sarah and I bathed in the cool air conditioning of the Bar Hemingway, sipping on a strawberry daiquiri and a mojito. As we sat there at the bar, I told her about the ongoing argument between the flagship Louis Vuitton store on the Champs-Élysées and the French Labor Union on whether the store could stay open on Sunday. LVMH Moët Hennessy, owner of the Louis Vuitton brand, had come up with a pure genius plan to circumvent the one-hundred-year-old labor law that severely limited business on Sundays. The company placed an artistic gallery on the top floor and claimed that it should be allowed to open on Sundays because it offered a cultural experience on par with other museums in the city that were permitted to open their doors on Sundays and take in all the tourists' money. Louis Vuitton ultimately won the court case, which handed them a tourist shopping monopoly on Sundays.

French for Red Mill

The highlight of the weekend had finally arrived—a night out at the most decadent of nightclubs, the world-famous Moulin Rouge. Even though it was a weekend of non-tourist activities, we had already broken the rule with a scenic boat tour, and while I'm sure the French would never be seen inside the Moulin Rouge, we figured there had to be a first time for everything.

The Moulin Rouge was easy to find on the Boulevard de Clichy, with its large, red, neon windmill perched on the roof. The show was advertised as a must-see spectacle that had been entertaining the masses since 1889. Maybe it was the Hollywood movie, the paintings of Toulouse-Lautrec, or the prospect of being surrounded by beautiful, half-naked women dressed in feathers, rhinestone sequins, and G-strings, but I could hardly wait.

As we entered the front doors, we admired the decorations at the entrance.

"Let's take a picture," Sarah said, diving into her purse for the camera.

We found an usher who was more than happy to take a picture of the two of us standing together like shameless tourists. We quickly regretted giving him the camera, because once he took the picture, the nice young man scolded us in a not-so-nice tone in English, "No picture-taking is allowed in the Moulin Rouge. You can have your camera after the performance has ended."

He handed us a ticket and pointed to a wide counter next to the coat check that looked like it held over a hundred other confiscated cameras. He was like a policeman working a speed trap. As we entered the main room,

I looked behind me and, to my utter disbelief, saw the same usher taking another unsuspecting tourist's picture and then confiscating the camera!

We had decided not to purchase the dinner and show experience and had booked just show tickets, which meant that we were given a table tucked on the far side. Our tickets had cost well over $100 each but included a bottle of fine champagne. The room was packed solid with a mixture of American and Japanese tourists who had just finished their dinner and were anxiously awaiting the start of the performance.

As the lights dimmed and the curtain opened to reveal a long line of beautiful women in lavish costumes, each wearing a black top hat, I leaned over to Sarah and whispered in her ear, "I give you the Moulin Rouge." The words came out more like a used car salesman than like a romantic lover, but either way, Sarah appreciated the moment.

The first song and dance routine ended, and Sarah and I agreed that it had been interesting but that the best was yet to come. The second routine ended, and we again agreed that the second routine was not as good as the first but the best was still yet to come.

Near the end of the third routine, Sarah leaned over and whispered, "How much did our tickets cost again?"

"More than the cost of our digital camera which we may never see again," was my reply.

The fourth act ended, and it was apparent that the best was not going to come. The show went from bad to worse to completely awful, and even the bottle of "fine French champagne" left a bitter taste in my mouth. The combination of basic and uninspired choreography, many of the dancers being completely out of rhythm much of the time, the cringe-worthy lip-synched renditions of songs such as "*I Will Survive,*" and the blatant animal cruelty of the performers parading around frightened Shetland ponies left us both shaking our heads in utter disappointment. The romance, the magic, and the French cancan dancing were nowhere to be found.

The show ended after a completely undeserved final encore, and before the last note had sounded, we were headed out the door in a rush to be in the front of what we figured would be a long line to retrieve our camera.

We walked out shelled-shocked by the torture we had just endured. Devoid of excitement and glamour, the Moulin Rouge was nothing but a tourist trap that preyed on naive and curious tourists.

"Stupid French," was all I could mutter as Sarah and I walked down the street in the warm night, feeling as though we had just been robbed by a troupe of singing and dancing French clowns. A long line of tourists stretched down the sidewalk, waiting to get inside for the midnight show. They all had the same giddy look on their faces that Sarah and I had had just a few hours before. Shortly, they would have their cameras taken away from them, would be drinking champagne that tasted like spoiled apple juice, and would slowly but surely realize that they, too, had just been robbed by the Moulin Rouge. I wanted to tell them to run, to get as far away as possible, but I knew they would not believe us.

It took me a couple minutes, but I began to notice that something seemed much different about Paris—and it was not the atmosphere of all the adult bookshops surrounding the Moulin Rouge in the Montmartre Quarter. It felt as though the city was holding its breath in anticipation of something big. The streets seemed to have cleared of all cars, and the only people on the streets were tourists. We passed a small bar that was filled beyond capacity, with all eyes peering up at a small television in silence. I looked through the open front door and squinted up at the television. My heart skipped a beat at what I saw.

"Come on, Sarah. Hurry up," I said, as I grabbed her hand and almost carried her down the street.

We found a half-empty restaurant and joined the dinner patrons, waiters, and bartenders, whose eyes were glued to the television set. You could actually hear the city and surrounding bars count down in unison—"Five, four, three, two, one"—as France upset the mighty and star-studded Brazilian team 1–0 in the World Cup.

We exited the restaurant as waiters scurried off to fetch bottles of champagne to cater to the guests' new celebratory mood. We jumped on the metro train, which had turned into a moving party, resounding with joyous cries of "*Allez les bleus!*" ("Let's go, Blues!")—the nickname of the national soccer team. When we got back above ground near the Eiffel Tower, the streets had filled with cars honking their horns and waving the French flag while strangers hugged each other. The citywide celebration was one of the largest since the end of World War II.

Sarah and I sat down on the grass next to the Eiffel Tower, basking in the light of the tower and out of harm's way from the massive celebration, appreciating the significance of that moment in time. It was such a great ending to a disastrous evening that should have been filled with romance.

"Kiss me now or lose me forever," Sarah whirled around and said to me in a playful and spontaneous mood. I hesitated for a moment, because I hated the feel and taste of the sticky lip gloss she was wearing. Sarah noticed my apprehension. "Do you think we girls enjoy wearing lip gloss? No. I hate it, but I do it for you," she said with a slight pout.

"But ... " was all I could get out.

"You think I like to wear nylons? Hell no! They are a pain in the ass, but I do it for you," she said.

I started to wonder how long her rapidly expanding list of "I do it for you" would be.

"And don't even get me started on high heels. Do you even know what lipstick is made of?" she asked accusingly.

"No," I said.

"Bat poop!" she yelled.

I was really starting to have second thoughts about kissing her. But I had no choice. After all, it was her birthday, and twelve million Parisians had just shown up to celebrate.

- Chapter Twenty-Seven -

Love–15
(More Minutes of Sleep, Please)

✦

The morning sun was starting to creep through our bedroom window as the sound of angels slowly pulled Sarah and me out of deep sleep. Even though the beautiful voices emanating from a CD appropriately titled *All Angels* announced the morning's arrival from our alarm clock, because it was sitting on the dresser on the other side of the room and required one of us to get out of bed to turn it off, we usually listened to tracks one through five before one of us managed to get up and silence the heavenly chorus.

"Time to get up. We really have to get moving fast," Sarah said, sounding quite unangelic.

The word "fast" was mostly incomprehensible to my brain before seven o'clock in the morning.

"Come on, Sarah. It is only five o'clock in the morning. Please, just one more hour," I said.

"One more hour and it will be too late," she said.

Sarah was what you would call a morning person. If, for some reason, I decided that I should get a paper route to help us earn some extra money, Sarah would most likely be the one out delivering the papers each morning, while I stayed in bed for some extra sleep. I loved nothing more than to sleep in and would often sacrifice breakfast before work each morning just to spend fifteen more minutes in bed.

"This is so not funny. We have to make the first train, or we will never get tickets," Sarah said.

Usually, that was the moment in the process of trying to wake me up when she would pull all the covers from the bed and then all the pillows. But it was so hot that I preferred to sleep without any covers, and while the loss of my fluffy pillow was painful, it was not enough to get me out of bed.

"Come on. This is your dream, too," she said.

"There is no way we're getting in. Go back to sleep!" I shouted, with one eye open.

"You suck! I hate you!" Sarah yelled in frustration, crossing her arms obstinately like a pouting child. Sarah did not really hate me, but she did hate my attitude between the hours of five o'clock and seven o'clock each morning. "You suck! Suck, suck, suck, suck! You're the suckiest suck who ever did suck! Supreme Suckeroni! *See you later, sucker! I'm going by myself!*" came the angry onslaught. She stormed out of the room.

Somewhere in my wedding vows, I believe the phrase "I promise not to suck" was spoken somewhere in between "to have and to hold" and "till death do us part," so to hold up my end of the bargain and "not suck," I managed to roll myself out of bed.

The Earl's Court Tube station was empty except for the ten or so tourists milling about and waiting for the first District Line train of the morning. It was obvious they were American tourists because they kept fidgeting with their security wallets tied around their necks and tucked into the fronts of their shirts, producing awkward-looking bulges that protruded from their chests.

"Who is going to pickpocket them at five thirty in the morning on a completely empty train?" I said to Sarah as the train pulled up and we waited for the doors to open and let us in. "For some reason, their paranoia about being pickpocketed so early in the morning on a train almost makes me want to walk over and try to pickpocket them myself, just so I can hear them say to each other, 'Good thing we had these trusty security wallets tied around our necks. That petty street criminal didn't stand a chance.'"

We rode the Tube for ten minutes and got off at the Southfields Tube station.

"So, where do we go from here?" Sarah asked, as we both looked up and down the empty street.

I reached into the small backpack I had slung over my shoulder and pulled out a beautiful brochure printed on expensive glossy paper—*A Guide to Queuing for the Wimbledon Championships*. In true British form, there actually is an official and extremely helpful thirty-two-page color guide to queuing for the mother of all queues—the one for match day tickets at Wimbledon. I opened the guide and, after reading lengthy paragraphs on "Queuing Code of Conduct" and "Queuing Procedures," I figured out where we needed to go.

After a short walk down Church Road through a very nice, residential area, we came upon a group of well-dressed, clean-looking people standing along a sidewalk. The long line had the look of a group of individuals hoping to break the Guinness World Record for waiting in line at a bus stop.

It was only five forty-five in the morning. The first matches of the day would not start for another six hours.

Wimbledon was the only major sporting event that offered the chance to purchase some of the best seats on the day of play—but only if you were willing to "go the extra mile." Camping out overnight or arriving early in the morning to claim a place in line could earn you the right to purchase a ticket prior to the start of the tournament and the opportunity to experience firsthand the Wimbledon Tennis Championship without having won the ticket lottery.

While looking down at my watch to see what time it was, I noticed the date: July Fourth.

"Hey, Sarah. Did you realize today is July Fourth?" I asked.

"No. It definitely does not feel like the Fourth of July," she said. "But it does feel like we are standing on the sidewalk waiting for a Fourth of July parade to go by any minute," she said, smiling at her own joke.

"I guess the Fourth of July is not as big of a deal here in England as it is back home in Chicago," I said.

Sarah picked up on my lame Fourth of July attempt at sarcasm, but the people standing in front of and behind us did not; they quietly shook their heads while most likely thinking to themselves *Ignorant Americans*. The joke was probably reinforcing some American stereotype in their minds, but I did not let it set in for too long. I used the joke as an opening to introduce us to our fellow Wimbledon queuers, whom we would be getting to know quite well in the next few hours.

There were two sides to the queue on Church Road that both eventually led into the Wimbledon grounds entrance via Gate 3. It was all but impossible to decide which queue line was shorter, since the ends of both were miles apart. When Sarah and I joined the queue, we were each handed a queue card by one of the honorary stewards, who greeted us with a warm "Welcome to Wimbledon," providing a small teaser that we would indeed get tickets. The official Wimbledon queue cards had the date printed on them and the numbers 0250 and 0249. We had read that only 250 tickets would be put aside each day for queuers, and there was also another long line in the other queue with just as many people. I felt as if there were no chance of getting the tickets we dreamed so much of having. Grounds tickets, which provided access to all the public areas of Wimbledon except for the show courts, were sold each day. However, Sarah and I felt that the Wimbledon experience was not complete unless you witnessed a match on one of the show courts: either Center Court or Court No. 1.

The queue cards had been introduced in 2003 to bring complete order to the line and prevent queue jumpers who joined friends already waiting in line. The queue line was long and filled with thousands of people from all over the world, and within six hours, we felt as though we knew half of them. I had never really understood how queuing for tickets for Wimbledon could be fun. Life was miserable for the thousands of people standing along the sidewalk for hours at a time, but conversations eventually started, and random acts of kindness—such as sharing a camping chair, passing on an already read newspaper or magazine, or making a coffee run—sprouted up. When word made its way through the line that ticket sales were cash only and no credit cards were accepted, I was amazed by how complete strangers offered to lend each other money on the simple promise to repay them in the near future, even though show court tickets were close to $100 each.

At nine o'clock in the morning, we all watched the skies for Hector the Hawk, who was released for one hour each morning to chase the pigeons away from the grounds. We talked to the volunteer honorary stewards who walked up and down each queue, answering questions and making small talk with everyone. It seemed that the only job requirements to become an honorary steward were to be the nicest person in the world and to be able to tackle a queue card thief.

The queue was made up of people from all over the world, and we all had one thing in common: each of us had dreamed of one day enjoying firsthand the complete Wimbledon experience. Over and over again, we heard people saying to each other, "Wimbledon is on my list of things to do before I die. I can't believe I am here doing this today!"

By ten o'clock, word had spread that the honorary stewards were making their way through the queue and had started passing out colored bracelets that would allow each person to purchase either a Center Court ticket or a Court No. 1 ticket. Half an hour later, the stewards were within sight. They appeared to have a fair number of colored bracelets in their hands, as they continued to place them on the wrists of people waiting in line.

There were multiple factors on our side. The first was that it was an extremely hot day and many people had decided against queuing for tickets. Even though I had thought that the line was very long, I had been told that it was not as bad as it usually was. It was also a women's game day, meaning that the majority of the matches on the show courts that day involved women players. Even though the women's games were just as entertaining as the men's, many people wanted to see the men's star players more. The last bit of luck on our side was that a popular Australian men's player would be playing on Court No. 1 later that day. Even though England was experiencing a severe drought, Wimbledon always seemed to always be behind schedule because of rain. That year was no exception, and the tournament organizers were trying to catch up. A large group of queuers were Australian, and even though Center Court was the grandest of all tennis stadiums around the world, the Australians were opting for the Court No. 1 tickets rather than Center Court tickets.

The moment finally arrived when the stewards reached us; they were still holding a few more colored bracelets.

"Would you like Center Court or Court No. 1?" the steward asked us with a welcoming smile.

Sarah and I had a sudden urge to hug the grandfatherly looking honorary steward.

"We will take Center Court tickets, please," we said, as excited as teenagers buying tickets to a concert.

The steward reached out and placed green-colored bracelets tightly around our wrists. Even though the bracelet cut off the blood flow to my hand, I did not care; I just looked down in amazement.

"So, this means we will sit in Center Court today?" I asked the steward, with a feeble voice, waiting for the catch.

"Yup. Welcome to Wimbledon," he said, as another steward placed a small, round sticker—with a strawberry and the words "I queued for tickets at Wimbledon" printed on it—on the front of my shirt.

It took another two hours to make our way through the winding and twisting line until we could show our bracelets at the ticket window, pay for two tickets to Center Court, and walk into the 120th Wimbledon Tennis Tournament. Upon walking onto the grounds at Wimbledon, we were greeted by a large tournament bracket sign and the smell of Pimm's, strawberries, and flowers. During the tournament, 150,000 glasses of Pimm's and seventeen thousand bottles of champagne were poured. Sixty thousand pounds of strawberries from Kent and 1,500 gallons of cold, fresh cream were dished out. Twenty-five thousand petunias and geraniums had been planted to decorate the grounds for the tournament and complete the atmosphere. According to the tournament bracket board, Maria Sharapova was scheduled to play fellow Russian Elena Dementieva on Center Court, followed by the Belgian player Kim Clijsters against China's first-ever Wimbledon quarterfinalist Na Li.

It was only eleven o'clock in the morning, and the show court matches would not begin for another two hours, allowing us plenty of time to enjoy our first strawberries and cream while we walked the grounds together, occasionally peeking in at some of the matches on the smaller outer courts and soaking in the English summer, garden-like atmosphere.

After enjoying our delicious and expensive treat of strawberries and cream, we purchased some souvenirs to send back home and continued to walk the grounds. We came across Aorangi Terrace, which was more commonly known as Henman Hill, named after the British, formerly number-one-ranked player. The large, grassy hill was a popular area for gathering with friends to sit and watch the ongoing play on a large television screen that had been set up there. The hill had been a hugely popular meeting place to watch Tim Henman play from during his tournament appearances. In the near future, the hill could be temporarily named Mount Murray, after the young, rising United Kingdom tennis star Andy Murray. But the renaming of the popular spot to Mount Murray was probably a long shot because Andy Murray was actually Scottish, and when asked who he would be supporting in the World Cup soccer tournament as Scotland did not qualify, his reply had been: "Anyone but England."

Only two Englishmen had achieved the status of Men's Wimbledon Singles Champion—Fred Perry being the last way back in 1936. British women had fared slightly better; Virginia Wade had won the singles crown in 1977.

Because of the severe drought and the heat, the green grass had turned a dusty brown color and the hill was empty during the day. At night, when the temperatures cooled off, the hill would be filled with after-work drink celebrations.

As the match time approached, we made our way to the Center Court stadium. We walked in and handed our tickets to the usher, expecting to turn and climb up the stairs to the top seats or the worst seats in the stadium. Instead, he turned to his right and walked down toward the court. Sarah and I looked at each other with increasing amazement, each step taking us closer and closer to the court. Surely this was some sort of mistake. Finally, the usher stopped and announced, "These are your seats. Enjoy your time here at Wimbledon."

As the usher walked away, Sarah and I looked around and surveyed our good fortune. Just a few hours ago, Sarah had been begging me to get out of bed. We were sitting along the grass court of Center Court in the *third row*.

"Glad I got out of bed for this!" I said. That was my way of thanking Sarah for her persistence.

Wimbledon was often described as a magical and special place. The atmosphere was a mix of tradition and modernity clashing together in an elaborate and pompous spectacle that was quintessentially English. The tournament had endured the test of time, because it had not strayed from many of its traditions, such as the strict dress code, which mandated that competitors be dressed predominantly in white. Andre Agassi, the American tennis star who had made a name for himself out of his wild, rebellious image on and off the court, had refused to play in Wimbledon from 1988 to 1990 because he thought it was too stuffy and did not want to have to change his colorful on-court appearance just to please the traditionalists.

The tournament had always been played on grass and was the only grass court tournament of the four major tennis tournaments. On the hallowed grounds of Center Court, very little advertising could be seen. The tournament had embraced the modern game—the last wood racket had been used in 1987—and technological advances had been incorporated to assist in calling balls in and out.

As we waited for the players to emerge onto the court, we waved at all the new friends whom we had met while queuing for tickets; they also had seats very close to the court. The grass court was starting to look worn and was fading from its pristine green color to a light hay color. In the run-up to the tournament, there had been discussions as to whether or not Wimbledon would be exempt from the ban on watering lawns and gardens due to the water shortage. It was suggested that, for the first time, the courts might have to be painted green to look better on television.

Our seats were at the middle of the court and close enough to see clearly that the tradition of placing two shots of brandy under the umpire's chair to steady the hands of nervous players on Center Court if needed was not being kept up. As Maria Sharapova and her opponent, fellow Russian Elena Dementieva, walked through the players' door and onto Center Court, the packed crowd let out a polite round of courtesy applause for the two women. A light warm-up between the two players lasted ten minutes before the match began.

Both players, dressed all in white, walked back to their respective baselines and got into position for the match's first serve. The crowd sat in complete silence while Maria Sharapova the tall, blond Russian tennis star and part-time model, bounced the ball against the grass a couple times before tossing it high into the air and smashing it toward her opponent, who patiently waited for it. The beautiful silence of the Center Court crowd lasted only a split second. The silence was then replaced by a loud, grunting shriek every time Maria Sharapova hit the ball. There were no specific rules that addressed players grunting, and it was up to the discretion of the umpire to decide what too much noise was, but rarely would a judge give a player a warning. Maria Sharapova's shriek every time she hit the ball had been known to reach a level as high as 101.2 decibels, which is slighter higher than the level of a pneumatic drill and just below that of a propeller aircraft taking off. One would think that the additional energy spent letting out such a loud shriek would only tire a player out, but in Maria's case it was part of the total game that had helped her become a Wimbledon women's singles champion.

The match was turning into a one-sided affair. Maria Sharapova quickly took a commanding lead and put on a clinic at her opponent's expense. The spectators so far had really had nothing to cheer for and were looking for something to get excited about. But, the excitement that soon arrived was far from what we had been expecting. As Sarah and I waited in silence for the serve of the next point, a loud, growing roar from the crowd began building behind us. As we looked over our shoulders to see what was happening, a man—who was completely naked except for his socks and shoes—leapt onto the court and danced around, attempting a cartwheel or two. The streaker, a Dutch DJ and the third male streaker ever at Wimbledon, came within ten feet of Maria Sharapova before she turned and walked away from him while security quickly rushed onto the court with a large blanket and took the man away to loud and raucous applause from the crowd. The scene was definitely not what we had pictured as part of our Wimbledon experience, but it provided a great souvenir when pictures of the streaker dancing on the court appeared on the front pages of many newspapers the next day—Sarah's face and large grin were visible in the crowd behind the streaker.

Maria Sharapova went on to win easily, and the next match was also mostly a one-sided affair; China's first-ever Wimbledon semifinalist let her nervousness get the best of her and lost 4–6, 5–7. I had always enjoyed playing tennis and watching it on television, but I had never been to a tennis tournament as a spectator. During the second match, my neck muscles actually began to ache from moving my head to track the movement of the ball. I experimented with holding my head straight and just moving my eyes back and forth, but that did not seem to help—it just made me feel dizzy. I tried only watching one side of the court, but the person sitting to my right came extremely close to head butting me every time she turned her head to the left to follow the ball each time it crossed the net. I also found that if I did not turn my head back and forth with each shot, it became hard to concentrate on the ball, because the thousands of people sitting directly across from us on the other side of the court were all moving their heads back and forth in perfect unison with each stroke of the ball. I tried to explain my problem to Sarah, but she did not understand.

Sarah and I were sunburned, tired, and ready to pack up our Wimbledon memories and head back home when the second match ended and the two women curtseyed toward the royal box before walking off the court together. We were still wearing our "I queued at Wimbledon stickers" as a badge of honor as we rode the train home. The day had been everything we could have hoped for and more. We both agreed that if we ever decided to go again, we would never try to buy tickets; instead we would earn our way in and once again join the small fraternity of individuals who had successfully queued at Wimbledon.

- Chapter Twenty-Eight -

When Irish Eyes Are Smiling

✦

There are friends who come into your life, stay a little while, and then quietly fade away into a distant memory. There are also friends who come into your life and never leave—Mike was one of those friends. Destiny had brought Mike and me together when we had been paired up as roommates during a four-month, college study abroad program.

It was already early August, and I had not seen or had the chance to talk to Mike since Sarah and I had moved to London, but in a few hours, Sarah and I would be meeting up with him and his wife Mary at the Dublin Airport to relive a portion of a trip that Mike and I had experienced together in Ireland ten years prior. It would be a weekend retelling story after story of memories of times spent together that had had a lasting impact on both of our lives as friends. After the weekend, Sarah and I would fly back to London, and Mike and Mary would join us in London a few days later. Then Mike and I would eat and drink together at all our old favorite places and continue torturing Sarah and Mary with more tales of alcohol-fueled immaturity of youth from our four months together in London.

The Dublin Airport felt much bigger than I remembered it being, and it took a little while to find Mike and Mary. After a quick stop to pick up the rental car and a polite argument over who should sit in the front passenger side, we finally resolved the issue so that three of us did not all end up in the backseat, because we really did want one another to enjoy the front seat first. We exited the rental car parking lot and began our drive from Dublin to County Clare in western Ireland for the weekend.

As we drove through the streets of Dublin, Mike and I used the opportunity to retell Mary and Sarah the story of how we had traveled together to Dublin during our study abroad semester to attend the college football game between the University of Notre Dame and the United States Naval Academy at Ireland's famed Croke Park. Croke, pronounced with a silent *k,* was a history-filled, Gaelic sports stadium where all "British" sports, such as soccer and rugby, were absolutely banned. Since American football was not considered a British by-product, the doors were opened for the two American colleges to take the field and battle it out.

Notre Dame beat up on the United States Naval Academy, but the real entertainment of the experience took place outside of the stadium on the streets and in the pubs of Dublin, where the locals had come out to see why ten thousand Americans wearing baseball caps and sweatshirts had invaded their city for the weekend. The locals were amazed by the two eighty-five-member football teams, 125 uniformed marching band members, twenty-five short-skirted cheerleaders, and most of all, by a short, bearded man dressed in a long, emerald coat with matching green hat and a large golden buckle who brought to life the school mascot—the University of Notre Dame Fighting Irish leprechaun. The locals did not know what to make of the dancing mascot that played off the stereotype that the Irish were all red-headed, freckled-faced, and fearless people who were always looking for a good fight.

I had never understood how the University of Notre Dame had come to be known as the Fighting Irish, because Knute Rockne, the legendary coach who had built Notre Dame into the college football giant that it was, was an immigrant from Norway.

Sarah and Mary began to tire of hearing countless stories of sleeping in train stations, losing ATM cards, and finding cheap eats from our travels throughout Europe and were relieved when we pulled into the hotel parking lot. We were staying in a large and recently built hotel near the coastal village of Doolin, a small village that was best known as the place to find great traditional Irish music each night at one of the three charming and authentic Irish pubs. The town was also close to the first tourist stop of the weekend, the Cliffs of Mohr.

The last time I had visited the majestic Cliffs of Mohr, it had been a cold, wet day and there had been barely another person in sight. Mike and I, along with our good friend Ben, had hiked the misty, muddy pathway alongside the cliffs, daring one another to take a peek over the edge, where powerful waves crashed far below and looked like miniature waves splashing up on a beach. It had been a day in my life that I would never forget.

We arrived at the cliffs, paid the admittance fee, and proceeded to walk up to the newly built viewing platform that looked out over the breathtaking Cliffs of Mohr and the Atlantic Ocean. Then we joined an endless progression of tourists and southern European schoolchildren on an official school trip over the worn walking path that ran dangerously alongside the edge toward the remains of O'Brien's Tower. We took turns nervously taking pictures of one another as we penguin-walked to get as close to the edge as possible to snap a quick "look, I've been here" picture and then quickly crawl away from the edge for fear of being another tourist who was tragically killed by accidentally slipping over the steep and unforgiving edge.

As the afternoon turned into evening, we stopped back at the hotel to change into dry, mud-free clothes and began the half-mile walk down the street to one of the three small pubs in the village of Doolin to enjoy some pub food and a couple of cold pints of Guinness beer, while treating our ears and souls to wonderful traditional Irish music for the evening.

As we approached McGann's Pub, we began to think that dinner might not be as close as we had thought. The place appeared to be packed with a large crowd of pubgoers who spilled out and into the small street with pints of beer in their hands. We stuck our heads into the pub to see if we could find a hot meal. To our delight, the pub had a few open tables. Ireland had recently banned smoking inside pubs, and most of the patrons preferred to stand outside in the street to enjoy the freedom to drink and smoke amongst friends.

We enjoyed our meal and toasted each other with a shot of Jameson Irish whiskey. Mike and I then re-toasted each other with the two still-full whiskey shots that Sarah and Mary refused to drink. Then we waited for the five musicians who were setting up their instruments to begin playing for the crowd of picture-snapping tourists.

I placed my arm around Sarah and pulled her a little closer to me, still enjoying the effect of how being apart for a long period of time made the heart grow fonder. I took in the full atmosphere of the moment with Sarah and two dear friends near. As we spent the night sipping pints of Guinness and listening to the music, which changed as musicians came and went throughout the night, altering the sound slightly with each addition or subtraction of an instrument, I could not stop thinking about the enormous change that Ireland had experienced since I had last visited with Mike and Ben. It was not just the change in smoking laws or that morning's newspaper's report that the Irish band U2 was moving to the Netherlands—or at least their "corporate shell" was moving to the Netherlands to avoid paying millions of dollars of royalties for their music sales to the Irish government. The change that I could not believe was the tremendous growth in just about everything: roads, airports, homes, hotels, cars, and even the Cliffs of Mohr, which had somehow managed to grow in size and no longer had the appearance of an untouched, uninhabited magical place where you could just walk right up to the edge and hang your feet over. The site had been augmented by the additions of a large, stone observation deck, an expanded visitors' center with a panoramic restaurant, and an enlarged parking lot built to accommodate the huge influx of visitors traveling in large tour buses on widened roads and sleeping in new, modern Holiday Inn-type hotels. Even some of the pubs that Mike and I had loved for their uniqueness and charm had tripled in size and were mostly decorated with wall-to-wall flat screen TVs and staffed with employees who were not Irish. The magnificent, green, rolling pastures along small roads that barely allowed two cars to pass each other had been replaced by widened roads that seemed to be littered with small pitch-n-putt golf courses that catered to tourists looking for additional activities to spend their money on.

All these changes had been driven by the enormous technology boom that the country had experienced. No longer was agriculture, once the heart of Irish communities, the choice among working-age citizens. Farms were starting to disappear as the younger generations turned down the family farm life and moved to urban areas where good technology jobs could be found and fortunes could be made overnight in the booming real estate market. To fill the huge demand for low-skilled laborers needed to help cook, clean, and maintain many of the newly built hotels, restaurants, and office buildings, immigrants from eastern European countries were allowed in to fill the need.

Except for the clerk at our hotel, it was difficult to find another worker who was actually Irish. Time eventually brought change, and it was obvious that time had not stood still since I had last visited, but I could not help but be saddened by the thought. The Ireland of my memories—with endless green pastures and thatched roof cottages sprinkled far off in the distance— was slowly disappearing.

Our night ended with a discussion of what musical instrument we would want to play if the four of us suddenly developed musical talent and decided to form a band that would play traditional Irish music—Mike picked the Bodhran drum; Mary picked the harp; Sarah picked the tin whistle; and I picked the fiddle. We made a final toast to good friends with our nearly empty pints and walked out the door.

As we walked back to the hotel in the starry night, I retold Sarah and Mary the story of the proudest moment in Mike's life—when he had received an unexpected phone call at a pub while we were traveling through Ireland and how big the smile on his face had been when the bartender hushed the conversations of the packed pub and yelled over everyone's heads, "Is there a Michael O'Connor in the pub this evening?" Mike's Irish relatives had tracked us down to invite us to dinner by calling all the pubs in the county to ask if a young American tourist by the name of Michael O'Connor was in their pub.

The next day, we decided we needed a little adventure and drove over to the local harbor to see when the first ferry would leave for the nearby Aran Islands in the northern area of the Galway Bay. The morning sky was overcast and dark grey; it felt colder than it was because of a slight breeze blowing in from the water. Looking out over the harbor, it was tough to tell how rough the seas actually were.

Seasickness occasionally snuck up on Sarah, and she wanted to know how rough the boat ride would be before committing to the expedition. The woman selling tickets for the ferry promised us that, despite the grey, overcast skies, it was actually a beautiful day to be out sailing the ocean waters, so we boarded the small, deep-sea fishing trolley that had been converted to a ferry boat. We enjoyed a different perspective of the Cliffs of Mohr as we looked up at the fog rolling over the top, hiding the tiny ant-like line of tourists making their way toward O'Brien's Tower.

Ten minutes into the journey, we discovered that we were victims of the saying "One man's paradise is another man's hell." The water that had been calm in the harbor became choppy, and the small boat began to sway slowly back and forth and up and down the farther we traveled into the open waters. To be fair to the woman selling the tickets, I should say that a seasoned deep-sea fisherman would probably view the day's conditions as a walk in the park.

As the boat continued to sway back and forth, we all held on tightly to the nearest railing and looked straight ahead over the bow of the ship for the first indication of dry land, hoping it would arrive sooner rather than later. The loud engines on the boat finally pulled back, and the choppy water seemed to come to an abrupt end as we slipped through the edge of the soupy, wet fog and entered a magical world of warm, cloudless skies with the islands directly in front of us and within swimming distance. A few passengers had gotten hit with seasickness, but Sarah had made it through with her cheeks still rosy and red as she walked off the boat and back onto dry land, proud that she had survived.

On the island, we had two choices of transportation: a guided horse-drawn carriage or a simple bike. We picked the bike option, because it gave us the freedom to explore the island at our own speed. We were on the smallest of the three islands, Inisheer, which was a mostly flat island with a few small, gently rolling hills that provided occasional views of the distant coastlines. The other highlights of the island included a lighthouse and a large, rusted boat that had shipwrecked on a rocky beach that tourists seemed to be instantly drawn to. The island's landscape was unique because of the tall, grey, stone-stacked walls that were all connected and made up a system of small, mostly square-shaped animal pens to keep livestock separated.

With the bright sun shining down on us and clean, cool air hitting our faces, we could not help but smile and feel like kids again. The four of us riding along together on our bikes looked like actors in a television commercial for the Irish tourism department as we slowly rode up and down the hills of the island, enjoying the weather, the landscape, and the company of friends. "Come to Ireland if you dare. A magical place where the air is clean, the Guinness is perfectly chilled, and the smiles are free" was what I imagined the voice-over saying in an accent from Cork & Kerry. The camera would then swoop over our heads and show a large panoramic shot of the landscape and the four of us riding happily into the sunset.

The island had no large hotels, just a few small bed-and-breakfasts. There was barely a car in sight, and many of the houses still had thatched roofs. I felt like I was at an outdoor museum that was preserving the memories of the Ireland that I remembered. That was my Ireland.

After running out of places to explore on the island, we returned our bikes and stepped into a pub where a group of locals was watching a Gaelic football game on the small television. We sat down and repeated a process that was becoming our daily routine; we ordered four bowls of Irish stew and two full pints and two half pints of Guinness. The men watching Gaelic football next to us let out a loud roar in appreciation for their team's performance. Their excitement was contagious, and while Sarah and Mary found something other than sports to talk about, Mike and I tried to make sense of the rules of Gaelic football. We began watching the match with the men. The sport seemed to be a cross between soccer and rugby and was incredibly entertaining with its fast-paced action, high scores, and tooth-loosening, full-contact tackling.

The sun was starting to set, and it was time to rejoin the many familiar faces from the morning ferry ride for our journey back to the hotel. We were late to board the ferry, so the best seats—or at least the seats that passengers felt offered the best chance of not causing seasickness—were already taken. Fortunately, the water had calmed, and with the last bit of sun still setting, the boat ride back was enjoyable and relaxing and nothing like the morning's adventurous sail to the island.

The weekend went by fast, and it was time for Sarah and me to head back home to London. Our good-bye to Mike and Mary at the Shannon Airport was simple and short, because we knew we would see each other again in just a few days, when Mike and Mary would fly to London—or at least we thought we would see them soon.

Please Don't Let Them Win

The day would have felt like any other normal morning if it were not for the feeling that the sky was falling. Hysteria had quickly engulfed London after the morning's announcement that the police had arrested a group of twenty-five men in London and the surrounding areas in what was being described as the final planning stages of the group's detailed plan to detonate liquid explosives on numerous transatlantic flights in midair as they traveled between England and North America. Flights were cancelled or severely delayed, causing a hurricane-size headache for air traffic controllers that would take days to fix. Unprecedented security measures were instantly put into action around the world. Passengers were severely limited in carrying any liquids or creams onboard.

The telephone rang, and instantly my heart skipped a beat. Mike and Mary were scheduled to fly to London later that day, and it did not look good. I picked up the phone on the fourth ring. My guess was correct—it was Mike calling. We briefly discussed the unbelievable events of the morning before Mike got to the point of his phone call—they were no longer coming. I wanted to tell Mike, "Please don't let the terrorists win. Do whatever it takes to get to London. Take the ferry or swim to England if you have to. Just don't let the terrorists win." But I couldn't. Mike and Mary had an infant child back at home, and at that moment of confusion and hysteria, they wanted nothing more than to get on the first available flight back to Chicago, even if it meant cutting their trip short. I could not blame them for feeling the way they did. There would be no London pub crawl or trying to sneak back into our old dorm to see what had changed. The terrorists were winning.

Weeks later, you could have made a strong case that the whole episode had been an exercise in fearmongering and that the actual threat had been greatly exaggerated. None of the alleged suspects arrested had purchased plane tickets or built any bombs, and most did not even have passports.

Since arriving in London, it had been difficult not to be aware of the constant reminder of the threat of terrorism. We wondered not if it would happen again, but when. When Sarah and I first heard the breaking news of the tragic London Tube bombings, we were both at work in Chicago.

We had discussed the event over AOL Instant Messenger; each of us made simple statements like "I can't believe this" and "This is terrible" before I finally got the courage to type the words I wanted to ask her: "Do you still want to go?" I looked at the flashing cursor, waiting for Sarah's reply to show up on my computer screen. Her response was taking some time while she thought it over. Before she replied, I typed another message: "I still want to go." Her reply a few seconds later was, "Me, too!"

The next day, as more details became clearer, I sent an e-mail message to the university I would be attending in a few months and told them that I would still be coming and a few coward terrorists were not going to stop me. The next day, the school posted my message of support on their Web site, in the hope that it would help build support from other students who were considering withdrawing from the program.

After the initial headlines reporting the events of August 10, 2006, had faded, new headlines replaced the initial shock headlines; they all had the same message: "Get Britain flying again." I was amazed at how the country did not sit in shock for a long period of time but rather seemed to shrug off the entire episode quickly. After all, the country had experienced the nightly bombings during the Blitz, the IRA atrocities, and more recently, the London Tube bombings. Each time, the country had simply gotten up off the ground, dusted itself off, and gone about living life just as it had before.

During the next few days, we came home to find messages piling up on our answering machine from friends who had been planning on coming to visit us in London. They were calling to say that they were sorry but that they had decided to cancel their trips. Sarah and I felt as though we were fighting a war against the terrorists, who were fighting to stop our friends from visiting London. The terrorists were winning easily.

- Chapter Twenty-Nine -

Land of the Free and Home of the Whopper

✦

Dr. Samuel Johnson once said, "When a man is tired of London, he is tired of life, for there is in London all that life can afford." I could not agree more with the man, but I was looking forward to a week-long trip back to Chicago and to my parents' home for a baptism, some birthday celebrations, and a wedding. All we needed was a funeral and a graduation party, and then we would just about have an entire life cycle of events covered during our trip. We landed at Chicago's O'Hare International Airport, where for once, Sarah and I actually had the privilege of standing in the shorter, citizens line versus the much longer noncitizens line that we had to stand in to clear customs whenever we flew throughout Europe.

For the special trip back home to the United States, I had reverted to wearing white socks with running shoes—something my friends in Europe would never be caught dead doing. With my white socks, running shoes, khaki J.Crew shorts, white Gap polo shirt, blue eyes, and blond hair, I breezed through customs with little more than a quick glance from the eyes of the on duty United States customs officials.

Looking over my shoulder as Sarah and I walked past the United States customs desks, I could not help but notice the long lines of foreigners answering question after question and being asked to provide their fingerprints. The voices of friends and strangers who had said to me, "Do you know how I am treated when I first enter your country? Like a criminal," were as clear as day in my head, and I had a better understanding of the feeling and the experience that they were talking about.

It is true that we are not winning many friends with our new welcome-to-America,-now-explain-why-you're-here attitude at our international airports, but in this post-9/11 world, the general harassment at customs is most likely a necessary evil until a better way can be found.

It felt good to be back home in the good old United States of America and in Chicago, but something was missing—our four-legged friend Sydney. It was a strange and slightly uncomfortable feeling to think that Sydney was thousands of miles away in London.

Our return trip home to the United States started off rather painfully—for me at least—because the first thing on my to-do list was a visit to the dentist. I walked out of the dentist office with my teeth feeling clean and shiny again, turned the corner, walked into one of my favorite Mexican restaurants in Chicago, and immediately ordered a large chicken burrito. I devoured it in seconds.

One of the most commonly asked questions by friends and family back home was "What did you miss the most?" There was not too much that I had missed, but if there was something, it was Mexican food. You can find types of food from all over the world in London, but if there is one shortcoming on the list, it's Mexican food. Not only did I miss chicken burritos the size of my head, but I also missed chili dogs, pizza, cheeseburgers, milkshakes, and pancakes with maple syrup. During the first few days at home, friends and family said I looked like I had lost a little weight. I did not hear that comment again five days into my fat-filled Oh,-but-it-tastes-so-good! favorite food binge while in the United States.

Sarah and I had traveled back to Detroit to visit our families and attend the baptism ceremony of my brother's daughter Anya, whom we had gotten to spend time with just a few months before in London and Norway. The following day, Sarah traveled back to Chicago for work while I stayed in Detroit for a couple more days of Mom's cooking and to catch up with some old friends.

The last time I had driven a car was when Sarah, Sydney, and I had first arrived in London. We had sold our car just before we moved to London, so I did not have easy access to a car during the week. I could not wait any longer, and as we Americans say, I announced, "I'm going for a ride." Just as I had when I was sixteen years old when I had first gotten my driver's license, I shouted up the stairs to my parents, "I'm taking the car," and quickly snuck out the door before they had time to say anything.

As I backed out of the driveway, I caught a glimpse of my mother standing in the doorway as she often did when one of her three sons left the house. I gave her a quick wave, and she smiled back. I pushed down the accelerator with much more force than was necessary, causing the car to speed away, just like I had when I had first gotten my license and was still really learning how to drive.

I changed the radio station from my parents' preset oldies station and found some driving music. I really did not have anyplace I needed to be, so I just drove. Strangely enough, or possibly subconsciously according to plan, I ended up at the nearest Starbucks. With my coffee in hand, I continued on with my drive.

Upon returning home to the United States for the week-long visit, I was surprised by how much reverse culture shock I was experiencing in my own country. It had actually started when we had first arrived in Chicago and I went to Starbucks for my morning coffee. My usual caramel macchiato tasted different. I told the friendly barista that I thought something was wrong with my drink. She kindly made me another one, but it still tasted different. It took me a minute to realize that milk in the United States tastes different than it does in the United Kingdom. My taste buds had adjusted to the slight variation in the taste of milk in the United Kingdom.

Everything also seemed so much larger. Cars, homes, roads, expressways, and food portions all seemed so much bigger than what I had become accustomed to. Waitresses, bank tellers, and store clerks seemed so out-of-this-world friendly. Air-conditioning was in abundance and everywhere. Like a reborn television addict, I found myself in awe at endless numbers of television channels available.

Reading the newspapers and watching the nightly news, I looked for international news and stories, which seemed to be such hot topics in Europe, but they were nowhere to be found on the nightly news in the United States. Instead, celebrity news, gossip, and divorce proceedings were sprinkled in with the weather, sports, and business news of the day, leaving no, or very little, airtime for international news. The only international news that seemed to make the final cut was, more often than not, about a horrific natural disaster in a third-world country or news about an American soldier's death in Iraq.

As I passed by a heavily concentrated strip of American car dealerships with American flags hanging from every available space, God sent me a message via the radio. As I channel surfed the radio dial, a song caught my attention. It was the famously patriotic Lee Greenwood song, "God Bless the USA." Without skipping a beat, I joined in at the chorus, and as loud as I could and completely out of tune, I sang along to the words "I'm proud to be an American, where at least I know I'm free."

As the music played on, an enormous red, Ford pickup truck zoomed right past me on my left-hand side. On the back of this hulking red truck were two bumper stickers. The first was a bumper sticker of a cartoon of a small boy who was wearing a cowboy hat and peering over his shoulder as he peed on Toyota's logo. The second was an American flag with the words "These colors don't run." I could not help but laugh out loud as I opened up the sunroof, turned the radio up a little bit louder, and continued to sing along to the song.

Riding the Rails

When it came time to make my way back to Chicago, I needed a one-way ticket to get there from my parents' house. Without access to a car to drive myself back to Chicago, I was left with the choices of flying, taking a train, or a taking a bus. If I was back in Europe, I wouldn't hesitate to take a train or would even consider traveling the three hundred miles by bus. But since I was in America, my first choice was always to drive or fly. Out of curiosity as to how our current rail system would stand up to those in Europe and Asia, I decided to ride the Amtrak train back to Chicago from Detroit.

In all honesty, I knew that taking the train was not going to be nearly the experience that Sarah and I enjoyed in Europe when we traveled by train, but how bad could it be? My parents waited with me at the small, nondescript Amtrak station in downtown Detroit. As we waited for the train to arrive, my parents told me about the old Michigan Central Station, which at a time in history had been a magnificent and crowded train station in Detroit. Built in 1913, the large beaux arts, classical-style building was located in the Corktown District of Detroit. The main waiting area of the train station had been built to resemble an ancient Roman bathhouse with expensive marble used to create the look and feel. Doric style columns adorned a long hallway filled with shops and restaurants. In 1988, the historic building had watched its last Amtrak train pull away from the station.

The old Michigan Central Station building is another example of the ongoing urban decay that has plagued many rust belt cities in the Midwest. Detroit has been no exception, and it was desperately searching for a way to reinvent itself. I truly hope it succeeds someday. The grand old Michigan Central Station building had been stripped of its marble, copper wire, and anything that illegal "urban miners" had deemed to have some sort of value. The depressed and decaying building could also be viewed as a symbolic victory of the automobile over the train as Americans' preferred choice of transportation.

My train pulled slowly into the station fifteen minutes late. Any urgency to board the train was not felt by fellow passengers who were boarding or by the train employees. I quickly kissed my parents good-bye and got onto the train, only to sit there for another ten minutes before the train closed its doors and slowly crawled out of the station.

The train was sparsely filled, and I had an entire car to myself. I tried to find the window seat that had the cleanest window so I could enjoy the view along the way. The train's interior had a 1970s feel to it, and even though the outside of the train desperately needed a bath, the interior was clean. For the first half hour of the ride, the train never seemed to pick up much speed as it switched tracks and navigated its way toward the next station in Jackson, Michigan.

Forty-five minutes into the journey, the train came to a halt and sat still for fifteen minutes. A train employee walked down the aisle, and as he passed by me, I asked him why we had stopped.

With a warm smile, he said, "We're waiting for tracks to clear up ahead. We should be moving shortly."

Just about every developed country has an efficient, high-speed rail system, with the United States as one of the few exceptions. Through blood, sweat, and now tears, we Americans aggressively competed with the Japanese and European car companies. But when it came to building the fastest, safest, and best trains and railway systems in the world, we have waved the white flag. While the Europeans and Japanese, and soon the Chinese, have built trains that come close to rivaling the speed and travel times of planes, the United States has ignored the need for national railway improvements. It is true that we lived in a country where breakfast, lunch, and dinner were all being served at the same time but in different time zones, and train travel for distances over five hundred miles had a difficult time competing with the airlines.

We Americans love our highways. We have built an incredible network of efficient, safe, and memorable highways and roads that have earned pop culture status, such as Route 66. You can debate that McDonald's would not be the huge global conglomerate it was if not for the extensive highway system that stretches literally from coast to coast, and along which McDonald's has claimed much of its real estate stake just off exit ramps.

After the third episode of sitting motionless, waiting for the tracks to clear ahead, or moving slowly through a slow zone of deteriorating tracks, the train started picking up speed again. The rhythmic sound of the train's wheels made me feel relaxed and tired, and my mind began to drift. I did not have any reading material or any sort of electronic distraction with me. It was the first time in a long time when I was without a cell phone in my pocket. It was just me and my thoughts.

During our time in London and Europe, Sarah and I were learning so much about ourselves, our marriage, and the world outside of our own country. Each and every day in Europe, we learned or experienced something new. We never imagined we would be in a time or place that would change how we felt and how we looked at the world differently. Unexpectedly, I found myself learning more and more about what it meant to be an American.

We Americans are proud to be Americans, but at the same time, we secretly admit to complete strangers that we are not like other Americans. I guess it is true that we are all unique and different, which makes what it means to be an American a constantly changing and evolving definition that is impossible to describe accurately, as I found out when trying to tell my European friends what being an American means to me.

We are a culture that "shops till we drop," where consumer spending and consumption drives our economy, making us the workhorse of the world economy. We are criticized as a materialistic culture and, at the same time, blamed for global slowdowns when we don't buy enough televisions, automobiles, and other factory-type products, which are now mostly made outside of our borders. Our economic stimulus plans can be considered a Hail Mary football pass with the distribution of tax rebate checks. After 9/11, George Bush told us it was our civic duty as Americans to go out and spend the tax rebate checks: "Don't pocket the money. Spend it. Spend it to create jobs."

As Americans, we live an active lifestyle. We are a fast food nation that does not have time to rest or eat, which makes me wonder why we Americans are so fat. Contrary to the *New York Times* best-seller, titled *French Women Don't Get Fat,* they do, but at a much lower rate than Americans. Some 40 million of us each year move houses as easily as we update our wardrobes. And we are constantly engaged in the never-ending pursuit of happiness; we purchase some $700 million worth of self-help books each year.

We Americans have created unparalleled college experiences on vast and scenic campuses filled with research and academic facilities that the world dreams of having. We also pack more than one hundred thousand spectators into stadiums during college football season, while millions more tune in to watch.

As a society, Americans are extremely generous, if not the most charitable people in the world, based on citizens giving more per share of GDP than any other country. It is also extremely difficult to criticize us for our willingness to provide foreign aid. But it is also true that we don't always take care of our own, as friends in Europe like to point out in reference to terrifying images that were sent around the world after Hurricane Katrina crushed New Orleans and to the lack of basic health care for so many Americans.

Statements such as "If you can find the time and money to kill people with bombs thousands of miles away from home, why can't you find the money to help people who live next door to you?" became routine when discussing America with European friends. "You are the richest country in the world; shouldn't you have the healthiest people, too?" And finally, "You know, you are the only industrialized country that does not have universal health care" more often than not completed the list.

The United States spends more on health care per person than any other country, but at the same time, the United States does not rank high in overall quality of health care compared to far less wealthy countries. Politicians have failed the American people when it comes to health care reform, and it is quite sad. My only defense when discussing the issue with friends was to rely on the argument that Europe does not have a real military and the United States has been paying for Europe's defense for many decades. You can have a universal health care program, or you can have a military. Use of that defense opened the door for the counter of "We Europeans would rather invest in babies, not bombs." Ouch!

Americans seem to come in only two different colors—red or blue. Often I was asked what kind of American I was. At the same time, I also overheard many Americans apologizing for the mess we had created and insisting to total strangers whom they had struck up a conversation with, "We're blue Staters. Don't blame us."

We may all love our country dearly, but a majority of us had come to find deep fault in our recent president's leadership. While Bill Clinton could tour through Europe with the status of a rock star for things he "did in his office rather than while in office," George W. Bush was public enemy number one throughout Europe. George W. Bush, the uncultured shoot-'em-first,-ask-questions-later, Texan, oilman, gunslinger of a president, was a gift to European caricature artists. "How could Americans be so stupid to elect and then reelect him?" I dreaded hearing that question because, not only did I vote for George W. Bush the first time around, I also voted for him the second time. When I came clean with that truth, some people were utterly shocked. How could an American who traveled outside of the United States and was tuned in to world events make the mistake not once, but twice? I explained that I did not feel that George W. Bush had won the election; I felt that his opponents had lost the election. I found it difficult to properly explain to Europeans that Americans usually voted with the best interests of their pocketbooks in mind and not based on foreign affair concerns.

George W. Bush had been the scapegoat for everything that had gone wrong since 9/11, and his you-are-with-us-or-you-are-with-the-terrorists statements had been burned into the minds of angry Europeans. Hearing how passionate Europeans were about how much the United States' image and reputation had been damaged or lost because of George W. Bush really was leaving a lasting impression on how others then viewed America. It was remarkable to hear people say to me, "I wish I could vote in your election. I need to vote in your election, because the decisions your government makes affect my life more than my own government's decisions do."

We Americans are also a nation of worriers. We have made it a habit to toss and turn during restless nights as we worry about paying our mortgages, paying rising college expenses, saving enough for retirement, and keeping our loved ones safe. Even though our employment is at a level that Europeans can only dream of, we live in fear of losing our jobs, since losing our jobs usually means the loss of health insurance for the family. "Have a safe trip!" is a common phrase that we share with one another as we part ways.

We Americans live in fear of terrorist attacks. While Europe looks inward to explain why Islamic extremists have made the European continent such a favorite and easy target, the United States has not had a repetitive problem on a large scale. Surprisingly, because it is the United States that is considered public enemy number one by Islamic extremists because of the multiple wars waged within Muslim countries by the United States.

In America, we often hear the saying "If we don't fight them over there, we will be fighting them over here" as a rally cry for the United States' go-it-alone military strategy. With two large oceans and a no-fly list, it is much easier geographically for Islamic terrorists to travel to Europe to train for, recruit for, and carry out attacks. The argument of fighting them in the Middle East versus the United States is difficult to substantiate. I cannot help but think that we Americans might be misguided in our thoughts about Islamic extremists walking our streets. Since 9/11, fortunately, the United States has not suffered another catastrophic terrorist attack.

We might not have Islamic terrorists openly walking around in our schools, but we do have disturbed teenagers and adults with chips on their shoulders walking our streets, schools, and even our churches seeking to shoot, kill, and harm as many people as possible, often leaving behind some sort of "media kit" to be played over and over on YouTube and on the nightly news. We Americans might view terrorists as an external threat to the country, but really we should be much more concerned about the terrorists walking the high school and college campuses and church aisles among our friends and children.

Living in Europe has taught me how much the United States has lost its cool and confidence in the eyes of much of the world. Our position as a moral and political leader for the rest of the world has been severely tarnished by military, economic, and political decisions, and this loss weighed heavily on my mind, because much of the world has caught up to us or is quickly catching up. We may no longer be the world's factory, but it is not too late to become the world's biggest factory of ideas, collaboration, and political peace agreements that move everyone forward.

America was built on the idea of entrepreneurship and has been thought of as the land where ideas are nurtured, financed, and made possible through group collaboration. America truly is a place where business risk-takers are appreciated. Game-changing new technological ideas and businesses, such as Google, eBay, and Yahoo, were all started by individuals born outside of the United States but who launched their businesses here.

The American attitude that we can do anything seemed to have lost its way in much of the world, and it was time to reverse the trend. As the world continues to face larger and more complex challenges and uncertainties, the American attitude that any problem can be tackled needs to resurface and lead the way again. Many of the Europeans I have had the opportunity to get to know seemed to find comfort when I told them that the United States population was made up of a large and diverse society, there were large groups of people representing both sides of controversial issues, and all Americans did not have the same feelings toward health care, guns, the death penalty, and politics.

I was brought back from my thoughts as my train arrived in Chicago an hour and a half late because of the many unplanned stops the train had had to make to wait for other passenger and freight trains as they passed us or cleared the tracks ahead of us before we could proceed. Even though I judged the experience to be a complete letdown, the employees on the train could not have been any nicer. I suspected that they had taken on a laid-back and relaxed attitude of "We'll get there when we get there," because it suited them best when they often arrived at the destination late.

- Chapter Thirty -

Like a Candle in the Wind

✦

School had taken on a slightly different look and feel since the previous semester, because many of my close friends had recently graduated and moved on to jobs throughout Europe, where they would be eligible for ten weeks' worth of vacation from day one. There were still some familiar faces, but it was easy to spot students who were part of the incoming class of nervous, first-day MBA students.

I spotted Lukas, an Austrian friend of mine who was starting his second semester at the school, and I took a seat next to him. With many of my friends leaving London, Lukas and I began spending more time together. Lukas was younger than I, and as a result, I had developed a habit of treating him like a younger brother. It was a good thing he let me get away with it, or I don't think we could have ever become such good friends. My early morning coffee time with Denis had been replaced with early morning tennis matches with Lukas. Neither of us had played tennis in years, but we quickly picked up the sport again and our matches had become very competitive.

Sarah returned to London the following day, and after picking Sydney up from Meridith and Petter's flat, where Sydney had spent the week while we were back in the United States, we were once again all together as a family and walking to our favorite place in London, Kensington Gardens.

It was early September, and the heat and drought had yet to soften. Unless a severe cold front decided to visit London and make itself at home for a few months, meteorologists were predicting that the year would be the hottest on record since 1730. The usual green grass of the park was still a baked, golden brown color. Many areas of the grass had been allowed to go uncut and had grown tall, giving many parts of the park the look of large fields of golden

221

wheat swaying back and forth in the wind, taunting the park groundskeepers to come and harvest it.

Every time Sydney jumped into the deep, two-foot-high grass, she blended right into the wheat color, making it difficult to see her. She was happy to be there and repeatedly poked her head out from the edge in paranoia to make sure we had not decided to abandon her for another week. We followed our regular route of walking through Kensington Gardens, into Hyde Park, and around the Serpentine Lake before finally returning to Kensington Gardens and completing the counterclockwise loop.

While Sarah and I had been back in the United States for a week, London had slipped past another unfortunate milestone anniversary. Reminders of the event, along with small pieces of paper with handwritten notes, blew in the wind and across the park. The trail of litter became more and more prominent as we walked leisurely over to peek at the thousands of withering and dead flowers that had been placed at the black, ornate, wrought iron gates outside Kensington Palace, just as they had been ten years before, when it had been announced to everyone's shock that Diana, the Princess of Wales, had been killed when the car she was traveling in had hit the thirteenth pillar in the Pont de l'Alma tunnel in Paris. Her companion Dodi Al-Fayed and the driver had also been killed in the accident. Her death was one of those tragic moments in life that left a clear and unforgettable impression in your memory of exactly where you were when the news hit you.

It had been ten years since Princess Di had been taken from the world, but she continued to fill an excessive number of pages in tabloids and newspapers. Lately, it had been coming from three fronts. The first was that of the conspiracy theories, primarily driven by Mohamed Al Fayed, owner of the world-famous Harrods department store, whose son had also been killed along with Diana. He honestly believed that British secret service agents, acting on the instructions of Prince Philip, had orchestrated the crash. The second was that of gossip tales of a cover-up and that Diana had been scandalously pregnant at the time of her death, a rumor that refused to be buried. The third front and recently the biggest page-filler of them all was that of the royal bumbling and ongoing bickering over who would be invited to the anniversary memorial church service—Al Fayed was out, along with Diana's butler, who was making a living off of selling Diana memorabilia; Camilla, Prince Charles's new wife, was also out so as not to cause any controversy.

Tabloid and newspaper publishers were well aware that any reporting on Princess Di dramatically increased sales, no matter how crazy or unverifiable the news sources were. I routinely kicked myself for being sucked into buying tabloids because of teaser headlines about Diana news that, more often than not, was pure garbage and made me wish I had never purchased the tabloid.

Many Americans were still wildly crazy about the late princess and viewed her as "saint-worthy." We still couldn't get enough of her and continued to talk about her style, the way she had presented herself, and most importantly, her use of her celebrity status to make the world a better place for all. In America, it was all but impossible to find someone who had anything negative to say about her.

But in England, as the ten-year anniversary of her death approached and the media coverage of her life was ratcheted up, I was surprised to hear some people openly share a degree of negativity about her. Everyone had an opinion to weigh in with on the matter. One side blamed her for being so naïve, and the other blamed the Royal Family for the mess. The two vastly different ends of the spectrum of how the British felt about Diana once again provided an interesting insight into the different feelings that Americans and the British have about royalty and the Royal Family.

The hysteria from the wake of the London transatlantic terrorist scare had subsided, and many of our friends had decided to rebook their trips. First up was my childhood friend Bryce, who had grown up just down the street from me. Bryce was the type of friend I could go months without seeing or talking to, but the minute we reconnected, it seemed as if time had never passed and we were still teenagers pushing the outer boundaries of our parents' patience, trust, and understanding. Bryce added much of the color and content to my high school memories, and if it was true that the best years of your life were the four years you spent in high school, then it was Bryce that I had to thank for some of the best years of my life.

Bryce had never been to Europe before and would be visiting us with his wife Christa. I had suggested to Bryce that they visit London and Paris, so that Bryce would be able to experience the vast differences between the two great European cities. Sarah and I had also been saving a special weekend trip specifically for their visit, and we could not wait to take them there.

To reach our special weekend destination, Sarah and I felt it was best to rent a car so we would have the freedom to explore on our own schedule and at our own pace; that would also make it much easier for Sydney to travel along with us. I wanted to get an early start on the weekend, so I picked up the rental car a day early. I also hadn't wanted to go get the car during the Friday morning rush hour traffic.

Since we were still keeping a close eye on our budget, I searched for the best rental car deal out there. I was impressed with the deal that I had found and was starting to think that we should rent a car every weekend, because it was so cheap. Once I picked up the car, my weekend car rental dream was dashed as I discovered the true cost of driving a car in London. I declined the incremental insurance, hoping that it was actually true that my credit card company covered it and wishing that I hadn't been so lazy and had checked. I also discovered that the advertised car rental price did not include the congestion toll or the gas, which quickly quadrupled the price of the car and made the weekend car rental scheme an absolutely unnecessary luxury.

In 2003, Central London had introduced a toll for every car driven into the city. Cameras had been placed on each road entering the designated area to capture the license plate number of each vehicle entering the zone. Every time a car entered the congestion area, the driver was required to pay a toll of between ten and twelve dollars within a twenty-four-hour period or risk facing fines that escalated quickly if not paid. The controversial tax had been viewed as a success because of the thousands of cars that no longer entered the area each day, reducing the number of cars on the roads. Cities around the world were considering similar plans. The money generated from the tolls has been put into improving trains and buses for commuters and individuals looking to travel to the area. In essence, the plan had priced the poorer people off the road and put them on a bus or a train.

The congestion charge might be another annoying cost of owning a car, but the largest annoyance of driving in London and Europe by far was the sky-high cost of gasoline. While Americans fret over rising gas prices at the pump, Europeans have had to endure eight-dollar-per-gallon gas costs for years. More than half of the cost was due to taxes, while in the United States taxes make up just pennies on the dollar, which was miniscule compared to Europe's tax.

As a result of the high cost of gas, you could make the argument that Europeans were more "green" than Americans when it came to driving, not because they chose to be more environmentally responsible about the amount of driving they did, but rather because they had to drive less because the high gasoline taxes had forced them into seriously thinking twice about driving long distances or driving at all.

Americans loved their cars. Walking was not for us Americans. A car meant freedom, and just about everyone could afford them or had access to one. Almost every American household had one car; many families would be unable to imagine life without having two cars parked in the driveway. Memories of our lives were often recounted by including the type of car we were driving at the time. We sang songs about our cars, made movies and TV shows about them, and sold them with emotional and patriotic themes mixed together with catchy songs. Most Americans even had their first sexual experience in a car! We wanted cars that could not be mistaken for any other and often thought of them as an extension of our personality and who we thought we were or the person we wanted to be. Because of that, we demanded a huge range of shapes, sizes, colors, and makes to choose from, and when that was not enough, we customized them with vanity license plates or put stickers on the back that told the people driving behind us a little trivia. When we got a new one, we felt as though we were truly saying good-bye to a good, loyal friend.

Not only had the sizes and weights of cars increased dramatically over the years but engine horsepower had as well—even in smaller cars—aiding the overall decrease of cars' average miles per gallon. Americans had moved farther and farther out into suburbia and drove an eye-popping household average of twenty-seven thousand miles per year. Along with being obese from overindulging in fatty food, we were just as guilty when it came to gasoline overindulgence from cheap, all-you-can-consume-priced gasoline. Ted Koppel once said, "Try and separate us from our automobiles, and you will know where our national interest lies."

I truly believe that all cars on American roads will eventually look and feel more like the cars in Europe today. We will eventually have to cast off our emotional attachments to our automobiles and view them as just a way of getting from point A to B, if not as a luxury and far from a necessity. The start of this trend had already begun in the United States and would continue to grow. The site of the minuscule, two-passenger Mercedes-Benz-built Smart Car may turn heads now, but in the future, it may be as common as the pickup truck on our streets and roads.

The Heart of England

I was nervous driving the four of us and Sydney, but I tried my best not to show it. The sound of a random car horn pushed me closer to the edge of insanity. *Are they honking at me? What am I doing wrong?*

The rental car I was driving was a four-door, French model sedan with a stick shift. It was an odd feeling to be changing the gears with my left hand, while concentrating on which side of the road I needed to drive on. The car was also a diesel car with very poor pickup compared to what I was used to, but it got an incredible forty miles to the gallon. Half of the cars in Europe ran on diesel, which gave them incredible gas mileage but also made them pollute much more, which was why many states such as California had banned them.

Bryce and Christa told us about their experiences of fine dining, people watching, and shopping on the cosmopolitan streets of Paris while we drove down the highway, giggling like teenagers every time we came upon a roundabout and attempted to navigate through it without heading off in the wrong direction.

With the city fading into our rearview mirror, we were getting closer to a place where time seemed to stop, where long walks were encouraged, and the soft sway of the leaves on the trees told the ever-changing story of the season. Honey-colored stone mansions and cottages of splendor and elegance lined the sides of winding, clear, trout-filled streams in a magical place in the English countryside known merely as the Cotswolds. The spot had been designated as an official area of outstanding natural beauty because of its rolling hills, which looked down on charming villages and picturesque green valleys. It was often referred to as the "Heart of England."

We pulled into our hotel parking lot to "oohs and aahs." The peak tourist season had ended weeks prior, so hotel prices were much more affordable, and we decided to splurge on a night's stay at a small luxury hotel. When I had made the reservation, the receptionist had inquired whether we would be arriving by private helicopter. I had told her we would be driving, but out of curiosity, I asked her if it would be a problem if we decided to travel by helicopter. She said it would certainly not be, because the hotel had numerous landing sites and she could provide the coordinates if we changed our minds and needed them. She had also informed me that the hotel offered chartered helicopters to take guests to and from Paris for an afternoon of shopping if the urge struck us.

We checked in and all made our way up to our rooms to change and drop off our bags. The room Sarah and I had been given was appropriately named the "Sarah Suite," as indicated by the elegant, cursive, gold sign hanging on the front door.

"Did you ask for this room?" Sarah asked in amazement.

Not letting an opportunity slip by, I said, "Yes, yes, I did request it," but I could not hold back my laughter long enough for Sarah to believe me.

Each of our rooms had king-sized beds with heavenly pillows and comforters begging to be napped in. Stone mullioned windows offered sweeping views of the perfectly manicured grounds, and the bathroom was the size of our entire flat in London. We tried a quick snuggle in the heavenly bed before opening our bags to retrieve a secret weapon that we had specifically purchased for the trip.

Where's My Wellie Boots?

For three full weeks leading up to my birthday, a midsize box wrapped in birthday paper had sat patiently in an empty corner of our living room. The only attention that it had received was from Sydney occasionally sniffing it before deciding it was harmless and laying down next to it for an afternoon nap. I knew exactly what was in the box, and when my birthday finally arrived, I tore it open. In it was a pair of navy blue Hunter Wellington Boots, or wellies.

Wellie boots came to life on St. James Street in London in 1817, when the Duke of Wellington, who had just returned from kicking Napoleon's butt at the Battle of Waterloo, requested calf-length boots to wear inside his pants. A few years later, after Charles Goodyear figured out how to vulcanize rubber, the boots had evolved into the more modern-looking rubber boot.

It was impossible to find another boot in the world that even came close to matching the history of the Wellington boot. Over the years, the boots had touched almost every segment of society, from soldiers wearing them in the muddy trenches of both World Wars to farmers who were able to put food on the table without getting stuck in the mud to fashionistas such as Madonna, Kate Moss, Angelina Jolie, and even the Queen (who preferred hers in dark olive green), who have made the boots a must-have fashion item for a rainy day.

Wellie boots had helped to define the English countryside and were considered a quintessentially British institution, mostly because they were the perfect complement to the muddy, wet climate of the United Kingdom. Princess Diana had helped to jump-start interest in the boots and elevate them to a classic style icon when she was courting Prince Charles and was photographed at the Royal Family's Balmoral Estate sitting alongside Charles, wearing a pair of green wellies with the classic, oblong, red-on-white Hunter brand label clearly visible on the front of them. After the photograph of Diana wearing wellie boots was published in numerous papers, sales of the boots skyrocketed.

The high labor cost of manufacturing the boots in the United Kingdom had forced the Hunter Rubber Company, maker of the Hunter Wellington Boot, into "administration" (the British word for bankruptcy), and the company was in the process of "redundancies" (the British equivalent of "layoffs"). The ongoing struggles of the company were another example of an old, established company having to quickly adapt to the new global economy or ultimately perish. The simple boot was unable to compete because of high labor cost and would most likely need to follow other United Kingdom companies who had had to move manufacturing and production to third-world countries, where the boots could be made by employees who got paid a tiny fraction of what they paid employees in the UK for doing the same work.

The color of the boots said a lot about the person who wore them. Sarah had purchased a red pair, communicating to others that she was mischievous, fun, and unpredictable. Sarah had purchased me a blue pair, telling other passerby, fellow wellie-wearers that I had traditional, emotional, and introspective values.

Before the weekend trip to the Cotswolds, Sarah and I had enjoyed wearing our boots to break them in while walking through the parks with Sydney; we were delighted when we woke up to wet and rainy conditions. The first time I wore my pair to the park on a rainy day, I received the official approval of the early morning, dog-walking group of old ladies, who were all wearing dark green olive wellies just like the Queen. They all smiled and nodded in a sign of approval as I passed them, walking far off the gravel path and through the deep, thick, wet grass.

Another time while Sarah and I were wearing our boots and walking Sydney together, we said hello to an English couple that had also been walking through the park. Right after we passed them, we heard the husband lean over to his wife and say a little bit too loudly in disbelief, "That was two bloody Americans wearing wellies!"

"Bring yer wellies! It's wet outside" I leaned over and said to Sarah, who was already putting her pair on.

She smiled and said, "You're lucky I love you so much, or I would think you were just plain weird."

We met Bryce and Christa, who were already standing outside the hotel and were not really sure what our afternoon's activity would be. The two broke out into instant laughter at the sight of the two of us marching out the door hand in hand in our Hunter wellies. Sydney greeted them both and began running wildly back and forth like a puppy, wagging her tail in uncontrollable excitement. Sydney had quickly learned to associate the putting on of our wellies with going for a long walk through muddy, wet places—a favorite activity for light-colored dogs.

The saying that "the journey is the destination" was perfectly suited for the Cotswolds, because a long afternoon walk was one of the best ways to experience and enjoy the distinct beauty of the area and was easy to do by following a specially planned walking path. We spent the afternoon exploring parts of the Cotswold Way walking path, a one hundred-mile-long path that had small signs to mark the route. The trail connected the small fairy-tale villages, which had names like Circencester, Stow-in-the-Wold, Chipping Campden, Tetbury, Moreton-in-Marsh, and Bourton-on-the-Water. Huge, castle-like homes perched perfectly on the tops of small hills and overlooking the valley below could be seen from the trail.

The area got its name from the Cotswold stone that had been discovered in the surrounding land. With Cotswold stone in abundance, it had been cheap and easy for landowners to enclose their fields with tall walls made of the same honey-colored stones that had been used to build the cottages and large homes—a key ingredient to the beauty and uniqueness of the area. With an artist's touch, ivy pushed its way up and spread over the stone walls and sides of homes; the ivy had recently changed color to a magnificent deep red, reminding us that fall had arrived. It was truly a beautiful time to be in the Cotswolds as we listened to the rustle of the leaves and basked in a light, warm fall breeze, walking along together waiting to see what surprises were waiting for us around every new bend.

We took turns snapping pictures of one another sitting on top of a whitewashed "Kissing Gate"—or waist-high, hinged gate often used on the walking paths between two fields that allowed people to safely pass through without letting the livestock escape. The name "Kissing Gate" came from a tradition in which the first person passing through the gate requested a quick kiss from the person behind him in exchange for letting her pass through; it was a tradition well suited for parents and their kids or affectionate couples, but it was probably not as popular between two farmers passing through to tend to their sheep.

At each small stream we crossed, Sydney paused to splash in the shallow water, occasionally sniffing at the water, confused by the sight of her own reflection. The area seemed so perfectly planned out that it was almost as if we were at a theme park created by Walt Disney in an attempt to recreate the stereotypical English countryside. Every tree, stream, stone wall, and cottage was perfectly placed with not a single detail overlooked.

After a long day of exploring the Cotswold footpath, we had built up an appetite, so after a long nap, we made our way down to the small but elegant restaurant in the hotel. We enjoyed a sampling of local Cotswold lamb, venison, and duck, along with wild mushrooms and macadamia-crusted goat cheese.

When we finished dinner, we retrieved Sydney from the "Sarah Suite" and spent the rest of the evening sitting next to a gigantic roaring fire in the cozy hotel pub, drinking glasses of red wine and relaxing in the atmosphere of the intimate private pub. Outside it began to rain, pelting the windows with soft raindrops, creating the perfect mood to grab a blanket, curl up on the couch in front of the fire, and let the stress of life roll off our shoulders. Sydney also enjoyed the quiet and tranquil moment and quickly fell asleep in the corner, dreaming of someday catching one of the many sheep that she had encountered during the day. The weekend was everything we had dreamed it would be in the company of good friends, enjoying great food and wine in the English countryside.

The World's Oldest Billboard

One of my earliest introductions to Europe came through the 1985 film *National Lampoon's European Vacation,* starring Chevy Chase and Beverly D'Angelo. The movie was a continuation of the slapstick misadventures of a suburban Chicago family (the Griswolds) as they embark on a whirlwind tour of Europe. Numerous European landmarks had starring roles in the film, including the Lambeth Bridge roundabout, Big Ben, Parliament, Buckingham Palace, the Tower Bridge, Rome's Coliseum, Paris's Left Bank, and Stonehenge, where Clark Griswold accidentally reverses their rental car into one of the huge stones, causing a domino effect and knocking down the entire monument before driving away, clueless about what he has just done.

On our way back to London, we took a side trip so Bryce and Christa could see Stonehenge themselves.

The prehistoric monument was one of the Seven Wonders of the Medieval World that most people can actually name, along with the Coliseum, the Leaning Tower of Pisa, and the Great Wall of China. Most, including me, were unable to complete the list by naming the Catacombs of Kom el Shoqafa, the Porcelain Tower of Nanjing, and the Hagia Sophia Mosque.

Most Americans who visited Stonehenge unfortunately left disappointed, not because visitors were no longer allowed to walk among the stones like in *National Lampoon's European Vacation* but because of the proximity to the A303 highway that was literally a slingshot throw's distance from the monument. The closeness to the heavily traveled highway gave the appearance that the monument was a large billboard or "tourist trap" that had been built on the side of the road.

The majority of the photographs and videos taken at the site for documentaries and movies was filmed with the camera facing away from the highway to give the impression that the monument was in a quiet field. For many years, the government had discussed moving the highway, which probably should never have been built there in the first place, in order to help preserve the stones and enhance the visitor's experience. Due to the high cost of rerouting the section of the highway, the plan had been scrapped and the world-famous medieval monument would continue to live on at the side of the highway like a tacky billboard fighting for drivers' attention.

Sarah and I walked Sydney around the sheep-filled fields next to the monument, because we had both seen Stonehenge before, and we did not want to pay the high admittance fee. You had to see it to believe it, or in that case to believe why people left disappointed. I really did not want Bryce to end his trip on a disappointing note, because Europe had yet to disappoint Sarah and me.

- Chapter Thirty-One -

A Good Cup of Tea

✦

Sarah had been saving a special experience for the arrival of her good friend Julie, who had flown in from Chicago for a few days to experience London for the first time and have some fun with Sarah.

Thank goodness my personal flaw of occasionally procrastinating on important matters had not reared its ugly head; for once, I had actually listened to the multiple warnings that Sarah had given me and booked the special experience—a table for three for tea at The Ritz—months in advance.

Since we had arrived in England, many of the e-mails and phone calls from friends jokingly included the question of whether or not we were following the English tradition of enjoying a "cuppa tea" each and every day. The truth probably would have shocked them—no, I was having Starbucks candy coffee every day. With a Starbucks within a five-minute walk of just about anywhere in central London, I found myself agreeing with the occasional slow news week headlines that claimed that "Starbucks was killing the British Tea Hour." It was true that tea sales had dramatically dropped off in the United Kingdom, while coffee sales had skyrocketed, but anyone making a reservation at The Ritz wouldn't know that; you still needed to book months in advance for tea there. The English had become slightly more American in their need for more time in the day, and the tradition of entertaining friends over tea had been reserved for the weekend. Weekday coffee on the go was a better, more time-friendly fit.

As soon as my last class of the day ended, I rode the Tube over to The Ritz hotel, where I found Sarah and Julie waiting for me in the lobby. There were four daily sittings for tea, and we had picked the five thirty sitting, because it had worked best for our schedules, and we hoped that we could also get away with calling it dinner.

The Ritz had a strictly enforced formal dress code in many of its public areas of the hotel, and gentlemen were required to wear a jacket and tie. Because I had come straight from class, I had had to wear my coat and tie to class. I did not have the courage to tell my friends or classmates that the reason I was really dressed in a coat and tie was because I was having tea at The Ritz after class. The truth probably would have earned me praise from British professors but ridicule from my fellow students.

I am certainly not the first to say it, and I will not be the last, but tea at The Ritz was an institution in itself. The tea was served in a two-step, raised area of the hotel called the Palm Court. The slightly elevated room gave the area a feeling of a small stage where customers could see as well as be seen.

The three of us sat down at a small table in the middle of the room. Sarah and Julie admired the feminine, flower-filled, cream-colored Louis XVI decorations with oeil-de-boeuf windows, multiple hanging chandeliers, coved cornices, and gilded trelliswork.

Great care had been given to perfecting the lighting in the Palm Court. Supposedly, the light had been designed to make your skin's reflection look fabulous.

I savored the moment for its historical significance, because the likes of Charlie Chaplin, Sir Winston Churchill, and countless other historical and celebrity figures had experienced what we were about to.

Sarah wore one of her favorite dresses—a white, pink, and grey flowered dress—and Julie wore a black dress with small green and white flowers that complemented her black hair and brown eyes. Neither of them needed the help of the soft, glowing light of the room; they both looked great.

Sarah and Julie were thoroughly enjoying being called "madam" by the white-gloved men who opened the doors for them and tipped their hats as well. The hostess and the French waiters were dressed in black jackets with red vests underneath.

When it came time to order, I picked the Earl Grey, because the menu description of "delicately bergamot scented tea, famous for its exceptional lightness and fragrance" sounded good, even though I did not fully understand it.

After the waiter took our order and walked away from the table, I told Sarah and Julie that I had read that the average British citizen drank close to forty-seven thousand cups of tea during his lifetime. I could tell the girls were not listening. They were too busy scanning the room for celebrities.

The atmosphere was warm, inviting, and a perfect example of what the English referred to as "civilized." A few minutes after we had placed our order, a three-layer serving plate was brought to our table by our waiter. He described each layer in great detail with fine showmanship. The bottom layer was filled with various types of finger sandwiches: finely cut smoked salmon, cucumber, cream cheese, and chicken and mayonnaise. The middle layer was filled with an assortment of freshly baked scones that waited to be smothered in clotted cream. The best was saved for last—the top layer held pastries and cakes begging to be devoured.

The waiter poured our tea through a strainer and into our tea cups, which looked like they should be displayed in a museum. I was relieved that the waiter had taken charge and was pouring the tea for each of us, because I could not remember if the rule was to bring the tea to the water or to bring the water to the tea.

I fought off the temptation to start eating from the top of the serving plate down, and instead of straying from tradition, we began with the finger sandwiches on the bottom.

The service was amazing, and the French waiter even gave us an "I thought you would never ask" reaction when we asked if he would be so kind and take a picture of the three of us, sitting at our table and enjoying the experience. Sarah and Julie had loved every instance of "Madam, more cakes?" from the passing waiters as they noticed that our platter's offerings were running low.

The murmur of pleasant conversations from each table in the packed room relaxed me, and I enjoyed the moment, even though Sarah and Julie had finished their food and tea and had turned into giggling teenagers. The source of their giggles? They were leaving the next morning for Amsterdam for a "girl's weekend" together—God help me!

- Chapter Thirty-Two -

Meet Me in Spain

✦

My final days as an international MBA student were quickly drawing to a close. I desperately wished that time would slow down, because completing my MBA studies meant a final return to the United States and to the real world of office work. Unless I decided to pursue a doctorate in "Only God Knows What," my last days of sitting in lecture halls, debating, laughing, and arguing with my fellow students would shortly be over.

But before the final push of the semester would begin, I was awarded one last gift of a week-long, study-free, fall semester break to enjoy before the mad dash to the finish line. Sarah and I were not letting the opportunity to collect another stamp in our passport pass us by, and we had planned a trip to Spain with some friends who had decided to throw caution to the wind and were flying to Europe from the United States for a "babymoon" vacation—a trip that first-time expecting parents took to enjoy life a little before the sleepless nights and constant diaper changes that followed the baby's arrival.

As the last class of the week before the break ended, my fellow classmates and I discussed how we would be spending our week off from studying. While talking to an Italian student whom I did not know too well, I graciously accepted his attempt at a compliment when he said to me, "Wow, you're not like other Americans. You really do travel and visit other countries." With just a smile and a "Thanks," I had watched as he walked out of the classroom. I had decided to let his comment go—actually, I had to, since he had just walked out of the classroom—but while riding the Tube home later that night, I could not stop thinking about what he had said.

I always enjoyed hearing the comment because I had a great rebuttal, and I was kicking myself for losing the opportunity to use it once again. When pressed by friends and other students with the observation that we Americans never left our country and hardly any Americans had a passport, I enjoyed responding to their comment by telling them, "Well, I left the United States all the time when I was a teenager. In fact, I visited another country almost every other weekend while I was in high school."

The statement usually left the person with a confused look on his face, and then I would finish the story by telling him, "You see, I grew up in the Detroit area, which borders Canada, and as soon as my friends and I could drive, we left the country all the time to go over to Canada, where it was much easier to pass for nineteen than twenty-one and therefore easier to sneak into a bar."

My sharp-witted story never seemed to win any points and always evoked the response: "Canada doesn't really count."

I would counter with, "Go tell that to all the Canadians traveling around Europe. It's easy to spot them; they all have Canadian flags stitched on the backs of their bags, because they don't want people to mistake them for Americans."

We Americans got a bad rap for that, but I always found it interesting that most of the people who brought it up had never been to the United States or even traveled out of Europe—or quite possibly the worst were the ones who had just visited New York City for a few days and thought they were experts on all Americans.

The truth was that we Americans were some of the most mobile people in the world. On average, we moved houses every five years, and we jammed into the airports and clogged the highways during long holiday weekends. Just because we couldn't get into our cars, drive five hours, and pass through four countries didn't mean we didn't travel.

The average American was not nearly as wealthy as most Europeans thought we all were, and even though most Americans would love to travel to Europe, they simply couldn't afford the expensive flight not to mention the hotel and food cost. It's just not feasible for the vast majority.

Many Americans were lucky to even get two weeks of vacation time during the year, and it was all but impossible to take two consecutive weeks off, so we looked for cheaper and much closer destinations. With the six-hour or more time change from the United States to Europe, it took three days, upon first landing in Europe, before a traveler felt as though his head was finally out of the clouds and he could get out of bed before the noon hour. Just as he started to adjust to the time zone, he had to fly home three days later.

With the numerous inexpensive vacation options in Mexico, Canada, and the Caribbean Islands, as well as the thousands of miles of pristine, sandy coastline beaches in the United States, many Americans were able to easily afford vacations to those close but "foreign" destinations. With new rules requiring Americans to travel to and from those destinations with a passport, the number of Americans who have a passport should rise dramatically.

Hostel or *Hostal?*

Fall had worn out its welcome in London, and many of the days were gloomy, cold, and wet, so the opportunity to pack our shorts and T-shirts into the suitcase one last time for some warm weather was a good feeling.

"Sorry, Sydney, but we are flying solo on this trip," I said, breaking the news as gently as I could. Sydney always got nervous when she saw the suitcases come out, because she never knew if she was coming with us. She often sat by the door and tried to sneak out with us and get in the car as quickly as possible, in the hope that "Once I'm in the car, that means I'm going, too."

Our friends Steve and Heather had flown from Detroit a few days earlier to spend some time in London before we all flew to Spain together for the week. Heather was five months pregnant, but the excitement of the "babymoon" trip had helped her to push aside the aches and pains of pregnancy, even when she had to spend a couple of nights sleeping on an air mattress in our living room. She had a great attitude.

Steve and I had spoken over the phone a few weeks prior, when it was late in the evening London time and Steve was at work. Neither one of us was in the mood to chat on the phone, and as guys will do, we thought it would be fun to not make any hotel reservations and just wing it.

"It's October—the hotels will have plenty of room," I remembered saying, adding to the validation that our decision to "see where life takes us" was the right one.

The British loved Spain in the same manner that we Americans loved Mexico. The weather was warm for most of the year, the food was great, and it was only a few hours' plane ride away. Spain was not only one of the most popular countries for the British to plan a holiday visit but also a common destination choice for purchasing a second holiday home.

Steve had spent some time in Madrid and Spain during a college study abroad program, and between the four of us, his Spanish-speaking skills were the best, so he was our unofficial tour guide for the trip. Steve's promotion to tour director status had not bothered me in the least bit, because for once, it was nice that I could sit back and just follow the group.

Steve and Heather had been married for three years and had first met while they were both living in Chicago. At the time, Steve had been one of my two roommates. I had always appreciated the time that I had lived with him, getting to know him like a good friend. I had also been grateful for being there right from the start when he and Heather had first met and started dating.

They were both tall. Steve had brown hair, Heather had blond, and how they looked together truly complemented both their personalities and appearance as a couple.

Upon landing in Madrid, we took the train into the city center, and Steve guided us, beginning a long process of working the rust off of his Spanish. The majority of the people we encountered along the trip spoke English, but somehow, relying on Steve's limited fluency made the trip more of an adventure.

Since we did not have a hotel booked, the only place we could go to was a restaurant, which suited Heather well, because she was hungry and looking to get off her feet. We picked a restaurant close to the Puerta del Sol Square in Madrid, an area brimming with hotels that catered to backpackers and tourists. Upon finishing our lunch, Steve and I left Sarah and Heather behind while we ventured out to find us a hotel room for two nights.

Surprisingly, the girls had not given us too much trouble about our decision to find hotels as we traveled, but the results of our initial search only confirmed that our decision had been reckless. Hotel after hotel that we walked into gave us the same response, indicating that no rooms were available, shrugging their shoulders, and saying, "Maybe mañana?"

We finally did find a room and then traced our steps backward to the small restaurant where we had left our dear wives sitting for a much longer period than we planned to.

Steve and I deflected questions about the hotel as we carried the suitcases down the newly paved brick street, until we came to the section of the road where new bricks met an old, worn, and cracked section waiting to be repaved; we were right in front of a *hostal*. As the girls looked on in horror, Steve quickly explained to them that the four-story, apartment-looking building was not a "hostel," but a "*hostal*." "A" instead of "E"—and there was a big difference between the two.

It took a few minutes, but the girls finally accepted our explanation that *hostal* was really Spanish for "lodging" and was much different from a hostel, because a *hostal* was known as being family run and nicer than the dorm room-style hostel. Using the word "upgrade" somehow seemed to help sell the plan to the girls or at least to get them through the front door.

The news they received upon entering the *hostal* did not get any better. Not only were we staying there, but we had to share a room. At that moment, Steve and I had honestly expected to be punched by our lovely and hopefully soon-to-be understanding wives. It would get much worse, because they had yet to discover that the only reason why the *hostal* had rooms available was because the repair of the street twenty feet below our room's only window required eight to ten hours of constant, ear-piercing jackhammering; the only break in the noise was during the three o'clock to five o'clock siesta period, before resuming until nine o'clock at night.

The girls finally accepted the less-than-ideal and far-from-romantic sleeping conditions and arrangements, and we walked out the *hostal's* front door and carefully tiptoed our way around the army of men wielding bone-smashing jackhammers.

We began our afternoon with a nice walk through Madrid's main park, the Parque del Buen Retiro ("Park of the Pleasant Retreat"). After the morning stress of the flight, compounded by the mad dash to find a place to stay for two nights, it was nice to just stroll through the park past the large pond, stopping to take pictures of each couple seated on the steps in front of the monument to Alfonso XII.

A large thunderstorm snuck up on us, and a heavy rain poured down; it was time to find someplace dry. London did not really get thunderstorms, and even though the loud, crashing thunder over our heads made us a little nervous, I realized how much I had missed thunderstorms. We decided there was no better time than then to make a stop at one of the world's greatest museums, the Museo del Prado, because it was so close to the park.

We were not the only ones who had had the idea of visiting the museum during the rainstorm, and the squeak of the wet shoes of all the tourists also seeking shelter in the museum echoed throughout the colossal hallways. The nasty turn in the weather had put as all in the mood to be inside enjoying the massive collection of European masterpieces. The only problem was that we had only a single afternoon to explore one of the world's finest collections of art and we really needed three days to get through it.

As we explored the various collections of the museums, I was surprised by the actual size of Hieronymus Bosch's *Garden of Earthly Delights*; I had only seen the painting flat in a book instead of on its original three-sided canvas. Even though the painting was small in scale, I could have stared at it for hours, amazed by the hallucinatory, dreamlike scene.

I was touched by the sheer power of Francisco Goya's *The Third of May* and basked in the glory of the opportunity to actually stand close enough to the canvas to see firsthand the stigma, which Goya had snuck into the painting, on the soon-to-be-victim's right hand.

I was frightened by Goya's *Saturn Devouring His Son*, which provided my psyche with material for future nightmares. Goya enjoyed home field advantage in the museum, because he was Spanish, so a visit was not complete without viewing both the nude female and the fully clothed *Maja* painting, which were displayed next to each other in the museum. Goya had not given in to the controversy that the original nude *Maja* painting had attracted. Instead of conceding to the demands of critics and painting clothes on the model, he had left it as it was and simply painted an exact replica of *Maja*— but fully clothed.

"You're so immature," Sarah said to me, when I pointed out the fact that if I closed my left eye I could only see the nude Maja painting, and if I closed my left eye and opened my right, I could see just the clothed Maja painting. Quickly opening and closing alternating eyes provided the effect of the unknown model being clothed then naked, clothed then naked. Sarah walked away in embarrassment.

The normal afternoon siesta time was between three o'clock and five o'clock, which meant that Spaniards usually did not think about dinner until at least nine o'clock. To fill the long period between the end of work and dinner, bar hopping in search of tapas, or small, appetizer-size plates, was the norm. Many bars and restaurants catered to the demand and offered a wide selection of tapas. During our trip we enjoyed octopus, *patatas bravas,* and a selection of olives as some of our favorite tapas.

When it finally came time for dinner, we usually ordered a heaping, family-style plate of seafood paella, the country's national dish, which was a combination of rice, vegetables, and beans, topped with seafood, served hot in a wide, shallow, round pan, and placed in the middle of the table.

During our first dinner in Madrid, we tried to do as the locals did and sat down to dinner at a completely empty restaurant at nine o'clock. By the time we finished our large pan of seafood paella at ten o'clock, the restaurant was packed. Sarah and Heather got up to go to the bathroom, which required them to pass a long table of twenty businessmen dining together, who all turned their heads and stared as the girls passed by. Some of them almost fell out of their chairs trying to get one last look as Sarah and Heather rounded a corner. When they came back to the table, the same attention and response came from the table full of men, and some decided to whistle the second time.

In America, the unabashed and overly obnoxious behavior would have been considered offensive, but in many parts of Europe, especially southern Europe, the practice was considered a compliment. Steve and I held our heads up, as if to say, "Yeah, those girls are with us," before turning our attention back to the impromptu play we were acting out on the table, using the disgusting lobster-like prawn heads as the characters, making the prawn heads kiss each other.

After dinner, we returned home to our *hostal*, passing through the Puerta del Sol Square, where many young *Madrileños* stood in lines for clubs that would not open for at least another hour. Their night was beginning just as ours was ending.

The first stop the next morning would not be at a coffee shop, museum, or anywhere remotely fun; it would be at a smelly, smoke-filled Internet café to book hotels for the rest of our trip.

- Chapter Thirty-Three -

The Rain in Spain
Stays Mainly in the Plain

✦

Toledo, Spain, was a little over an hour's drive from Madrid if you were a local; if you were four tourists in a small rented car, it took two, if not three, full hours to get there. With Madrid finally far off in our rearview mirror, we pulled into a parking spot on a steep incline in the shadow of the Alcázar of Toledo.

The plan was to not stay the night in Toledo but continue driving to the city of Seville. But, we arrived much later than planned, and a sense of urgency to see the sights and get back on the road was the prevailing attitude during the side trip to Toledo.

Surprisingly, or perhaps not, Toledo, Spain, was a "twin city" or "sister city" for Toledo, Ohio, in the United States. I was sure that Toledo, Ohio, was a great city, but if I had to guess which city could probably lay claim to the well-known and used exclamation of surprise, "Holy Toledo," I think Toledo, Spain, would be the winner, because of its beauty and the numerous churches.

After fulfilling the desire to see enough of the city to say "We saw Toledo," Steve put a damper on the day's fun when he asked the three of us, "Does anyone remember where we parked the car?"—not the words that a pregnant woman wanted to hear after she had been walking up steep, narrow streets, climbing church bell tower stairs, and having to walk a little faster than normal in order for her husband and his friend (me) to adequately feel as though we had "conquered" Toledo.

By the time we could see the lights of Seville in the distance, it was nighttime and a steady rain was falling. The four of us questioned the origin and meaning of the phrase "The rain in Spain stays mainly in the plain." Steve was the smartest one in the group and the unofficial tour leader, so we all felt he should have known or at least made up something that sounded interesting. Later, I discovered that the "The Rain in Spain" was used in a song in *My Fair Lady*.

We had to park the rental car a few blocks away from the hotel, because the entire boulevard outside the hotel was completely closed; a deep crater from ongoing road work made walking to and from the hotel lobby an adventure. The loud, sprawling road work project was probably the main reason why the hotel had still had rooms available. I was starting to suspect a trend in our choices of last-minute hotel bookings.

After a good night's sleep, we got up early—or, more accurately, we were awakened early by the sound of bulldozers and cranes in the deep crater below the street—and set out to explore the city. The sun was still rising, and the afternoon heat was hours away, making it the perfect time for a visit to the Plaza de España. The plaza was a huge semicircle building with beautiful tiled alcoves running along the lower semicircle walls. It featured a small moat filled with water, the only purpose of which seemed to be that it allowed the architects to show off by also building romantically detailed bridges that tourists loved to take their pictures on. The center of the square focused on a large fountain that seemed like an afterthought in the architect's mind.

We did as all the other tourists did and snapped pictures of ourselves on the bridges, in front of the fountains, and on the upper balcony walkway looking over the plaza.

No Bull

Call it stereotyping or just being a tourist, but it seemed like a trip to Spain would not be complete without a visit to a bullfighting ring, and there might not be any better in Spain than the Plaza de Toros de la Maestranza, home of one of the world's best bullfighting events in the world, the Feria de Abril.

The romantic and adventurous writings of Hemingway had softened the edges of the animal brutality involved in bullfighting in many Americans' minds, but even in Spain it seemed like the sport had divided the nation. Depending on whom you ask, the sport was either on the rise or on the decline.

I couldn't remember where I had heard or possibly read it, but a supporting argument for the sport had placed the brutality of the spectacle a notch lower than fox hunting, the rationale being: "We are not like the English, who have a dog do the killing of innocent foxes; the English have no right to complain." I didn't know if the tactic of "Don't blow on my candle so yours can burn brighter" was best used in the argument to defend the practice, but love it or hate it, you might not really know until you actually went to see a bullfight on the grand stage.

Unfortunately, that day was not the day that Sarah and I would find out, because the bullfighting season had recently ended. I was kind of relieved, because I think I would have actually cheered for the bull to win.

Even though the season was over, we were still able to tour the grounds of the stadium and learn a brief history of the sport. I had made up my mind about the sport as soon as we learned that the mother of a killer bull was also killed so she would not be able to produce any more "super human-killing bulls," ending the blood line. I thought, *Well, that isn't fair. Just because a bull actually wins for once, they kill it as well as its coach and trainer—aka the bull's mother!*

None of us would openly admit it, but we were all suffering from "church fatigue" and were getting tired of touring the grand churches of Spain. But since we found ourselves on the steps of the Cathedral of Seville, the fourth-largest Christian church in the world and the largest Gothic church in the world, we felt we had to see it, so we stepped inside.

We explored the large cathedral, wearing headsets like all the other tourists in the church; we pushed corresponding buttons to hear what the narrator was saying. I walked right past a large, square tomb, and was intrigued by the four towering, deathly looking men holding up a coffin. I was fascinated to discover that the tomb was the resting place of possibly the greatest explorer of all time, Christopher Columbus.

Even in death, Christopher Columbus continues to travel farther than most people living travel. After his death, he had originally been interred in Valladolid, Spain, in 1542, but then he had been moved to Seville; Santo Domingo in the Dominican Republic; Havana, Cuba, in 1795; and then again to Seville in 1898. I could not resist the temptation and started singing the song I had learned as a child:

> *In fourteen ninety-two*
> *Columbus sailed the ocean blue.*

> *He had three ships and left from Spain;*
> *He sailed through sunshine, wind, and rain.*

> *He sailed by night; he sailed by day;*
> *He used the stars to find his way.*

We stepped outside the cathedral and decided it was time for lunch. Next to the cathedral, we found a restaurant that had plenty of outdoor seating and a postcard view of the church.

Lunch took much longer than planned, but since we were happy to be sitting and enjoying a cold glass of wine out of the hot sun, we were in no rush to leave. When the bill finally arrived at our table, Steve and I, who had rarely argued as roommates, had one of the biggest arguments we had ever had over one silly, little gesture—leaving the tip.

In the United States, tipping was a culturally accepted custom, and the practice was never questioned. Even the cheapest Americans knew and understood the importance of leaving a tip and accepted it as an unwritten law, because many of us Americans, at some time in our lives, had worked in an industry in which we relied on and were thankful for tips.

We tipped waiters so they would bring our food hot and fill our glasses in a timely manner; we tipped taxi drivers so they didn't pad the bill with a longer-than-necessary route; and we even tipped at the barbershop and beauty salon so we wouldn't walk out with a chop job. In the United States, great customer service was expected. But without the tip ingredient of the recipe, the incentive to provide the above-and-beyond customer service would, most likely, not exist.

Steve was arguing that he thought it was right to try to make a good impression, especially since America's standing in the world had been taken down a few notches in recent years. I agreed with him that we wanted the Spanish to like us, but I argued that leaving a generous tip was not the way to do it and only added to the expectation that an American should tip. The waitress had only brought one menu for four people; she had brought us a fish replacement that was four times as much as what we had wanted and had never told us of the price difference, and she had spent more time smoking cigarettes than filling our glasses—"To get the tip, you need to do the work!"

When Sarah and I had first arrived in Europe, it had felt strange to not tip taxi drivers and restaurant servers. Depending on whom you asked—an American or a European—the expectation of good customer service at a restaurant varied dramatically. Learning not to tip, or barely tipping, became routine over time for Sarah and me when eating out or ordering drinks. If I found the process of tipping or not tipping difficult in Europe, I could only imagine how awkward Europeans must have felt when they visited the United States.

Steve's play-it-safe attitude when traveling was not a bad attitude to have, and I let Steve have his way. "At least wipe your armpits with the money," I jokingly suggested as a compromise, but I did not get my way, and a king's ransom was left behind on the table for our deadbeat waitress.

The farther south you traveled in Spain, the warmer the weather seemed to get and the more obvious the Moorish influence in the country was. When we called ahead for directions to our hotel, we were advised to park the car just outside the El Albayzín district in the city center of Granada and take a taxi or walk the remaining distance because the district was made up of narrow streets, and cars were not permitted. After parking the car and listening to Steve remind us, "Let's all try to remember where we parked the car," we picked up our bags and looked for a taxi. After twenty minutes of not a single taxi passing us, we went to Plan B: walking the distance to the hotel.

First-time visitors to Europe learned very quickly that it was not always chic to be a pedestrian on many city streets, given the way Europeans drove and the number of Vespas or motor scooters on the road. The 1953 movie *Roman Holiday,* starring Audrey Hepburn and Gregory Peck, had introduced Americans to the charm and romance of the scooters. It was true that the scooters were charming when you were riding one in Europe, but they were annoying when you were not. Automobiles were not allowed in the narrow medieval streets of the El Albayzín district, but scooters seemed to be welcome, and in the pecking order of the streets and sidewalks, pedestrians were dead last at the bottom of the list.

The hotel we had booked was tucked away in a small courtyard, making it even harder to find. More importantly, it was in an ideal part of the district, close enough to the small and interesting shops and restaurants and within a short walk of the famous Moorish citadel and palace, the Alhambra.

The hotel was in a nondescript building that lacked any interesting detail or architecture, but the inside was anything but plain. The building had originally been built in the sixteenth century and had received many careful and detailed renovations in recent years. The lobby, rooms, and dining areas looked like those of a nice hotel you'd find in Casablanca, Morocco. Our room was decorated with interesting and finely crafted rugs, furniture, lamps, and oddities like those we had seen in the small shops close to the hotel.

Sarah wanted to shower before dinner, so I decided to go explore the rest of the hotel and wait for her in the lobby. After asking the hotel clerk way more questions than he wanted to answer about the history of the hotel, distracting him from the soccer match he was watching on a small television, I passed the time by accepting the hotel clerk's offer of an English-language newspaper to read and sat down on the couch.

An article about a school in Pisa, Italy—where the schoolchildren had been exchanging letters for ten years with a Texan man who was about to be put to death for hiring a hit man to kill his adoptive parents—caught my attention. The school in Italy had requested that it receive the condemned man's remains upon his death so the school could bury him in the town.

Even though the death row inmate had been labeled "pure evil" during his prosecution, the school had seen some good in him and felt they should somehow honor him upon his death.

Starting in 2000, the Coliseum in Rome was illuminated every time a death sentence was lifted or commuted anywhere in the world. The death penalty had become a bigger point of difference between Europe and America, and it was pointed out to me several times that the United States joined countries such as China, Saudi Arabia, Iran, and Iraq as the few countries that allowed the practice of capital punishment. My joke—"Europeans have used capital punishment for years, and we are just catching up"—never went as well as I thought it would.

When asked "Why does America still use the death penalty?" I answered by saying that the United States was a democracy; each state had the right to decide whether it wanted to use the death penalty as a jury sentencing option or not. When discussing it, I occasionally received the reply, "So, do Americans consider this when they decide which state they want to live in?" I found the question funny, but at the same time, I wondered if some Americans did consider it.

Far more states do not use or no longer use the death penalty as a sentencing option, but about twelve states still did. The State of Texas had become ground zero for the European debate and received an enormous amount of press when a prisoner was put to death. Arnold Schwarzenegger, the Austrian-born actor turned politician and governor of California, had also found himself heavily criticized for not stepping in and stopping executions carried out in the State of California. I did not believe in the death penalty, because I felt like life in prison with no chance of being let out—no matter the age or health of the individual—was a far worse punishment.

We Americans got angry at European countries that refused to extradite murder suspects, because the suspect claimed some kind of dual citizenship and fled to the Caribbean islands governed by the French government. The European country in charge of the local government often said that they would try the suspect themselves, but even if found guilty, the suspect only received fifteen to twenty years maximum. Strangely enough, it seemed the number of United States citizens supporting the death penalty continued to decrease, while some polls in Europe showed the trend reversing in Europe, with support for it increasing.

After dinner, the girls gave Steve and me a free pass to go out and have some fun together. Like two teenagers who had just snuck out of their parents' home, we did not waste a minute of time, and the bar tour of Granada had begun. Over the next few hours, we sampled numerous bars in the area. The atmosphere ranged from us being the old, creepy guys in a bar packed with American college study abroad students to us being the two gringos sitting in the corner. The night was fun, and around midnight, we decided that a nice bed sounded much more appealing than a crowded, sweaty bar.

The next day, the lack of sleep slowed me down, and along with pregnant Heather, I was happy to ride a small, cramped bus up an enormous hill to the entrance to the Alhambra, the former palace and fortress of days past when the Moors ruled Granada; it was a reminder that much of Spain had once been Muslim.

The Alhambra architecture was beautiful, and its color constantly changed with the movements of the sun. Fascinating stories that lingered behind every twist and turn in the gardens, hallways, and courtyards could fill an entire textbook with history. The gardens and fountains and the stone and marble details, topped off by the exquisite views of the city far below, left each visitor with a complete understanding of what a jewel the place was.

Like all great journeys, it was a little sad when it came time to head back home, but not before one last taste of adventure. Steve had done much of the driving on the trip, but I was given the honor of chauffeuring us all to the airport.

Southern Europeans might live a slower-paced life, but they made up for it by driving as fast as they could. Many northern Europeans were shocked by the complete disregard for basic traffic laws and etiquette toward fellow drivers from southern Europeans. Even if the light was red, I could never be sure whether drivers would stop at the light or only take the red light as a suggestion to stop if they had the time.

We were driving on the two-lane expressway, paying close attention to the signs so as not to miss the airport car rental exit. Once the time came to merge into the right lane to exit, I checked my rearview mirror, and with three car lengths between my car and the car behind me in the right-hand lane, I started to merge. Noticing what I was trying to do, the car in the right-hand lane sped up and closed the gap. Our eyes met in the mirror. I had only two options: act like a gringo, slow down, and let him have his way; or do as the locals do, merge into his lane, and let him decide if he wanted to hit us or back down. I made my decision, and to emphasize it, I saluted him with the reversed V-sign (or flipping him the "European Bird"). With a smug look on his face that said "well played," the driver backed down and let me into the lane.

Lesson learned: Do as the locals do, or you'll never get where you want to go.

- Chapter Thirty-Four -

A Routemaster's Last Ride

✦

Twenty years ago, if you had told your wife you were sending her to cooking school or giving her a vacuum cleaner for her birthday, you most likely would've earned yourself a night on the living room couch. In today's times, tell your wife you're sending her to a cooking school in Italy or giving her a beautifully designed and engineered Dyson vacuum cleaner, and you might be considered the world's best husband in her eyes.

I wanted to thank Sarah for all her hard work, for putting up with me and not giving in to the temptation to leave me at a bus stop and drive away, so I decided to surprise her and send her to an Italian cooking school in the heart of Tuscany to learn how to cook recipes that had been passed down through the generations—"recipes worth their weight in gold," the school claimed. Being an avid cook, Sarah could not have been happier with the news. I loved Sarah's cooking, and I viewed the trip to the cooking school as an investment in future delicious and scrumptious dinners.

One of my favorite moments of the year had come when I walked through the front door after class as Sarah was about to bend a cooking sheet over her knee in frustration. I asked her what was wrong.

"It's this stupid spotted dick recipe. It's driving me crazy!" She was never able to successfully make spotted dick, which I eventually learned was a steamed pudding dessert. The "spotted" portion of the name came from the raisins sprinkled in it, and the "dick" was a corruption of the word "pudding."

Sarah had always had an open mind when it has came to food, and without my trust in her, I would not have appreciated the great food we had experienced in England and throughout Europe. Her interest in cooking had helped me get past the stereotype that British food was awful, and I had discovered that it was not that bad—I just needed to open my eyes and look past the British icons of the English breakfast, fish and chips, and bangers and mash, and see that a revolution had taken place in the culinary options available and could be seen in the many gastropubs, Marks and Spencer takeaway meals, and British celebrity chefs, like Jamie Oliver and Gordon Ramsey, who had both opened amazing restaurants and were filling up the cookbook sections in bookstores all over the world.

One of my favorite meals during the year was the traditional fall Sunday roast, or a smaller-scaled version of the Christmas dinner, served at gastropubs. It consisted of slow-cooked, roasted meat, mashed potatoes and gravy, vegetables, and Yorkshire pudding. The fall-time, hearty meal on Sunday, roast tradition came from the belief that the meat could be left to slow cook on Sunday morning while families were in church, and by the time they returned home in the afternoon, the meat would be ready to eat.

Finally, a trip to London was not complete without a walk through the Borough Market, where you could literally rub elbows with celebrities as you looked at, smelled, and tasted the offerings and enjoyed the unique food experience of the market. You might not spot the former French president Jacques Chirac eating in a London gastropub anytime soon, especially after his famous remarks: "The only thing they (the English) have ever done for European agriculture is mad cow," and "You can't trust people who cook as bad as that." But I had no complaints about the food.

Sarah had flown to the Italian cooking school in Tuscany the day before. She woke me up early with a phone call to tell me how wonderful and beautiful the Cyprus trees, olive groves, and vineyards of the Bertini Hills area, where the cooking school was located, were and how much she loved the old Tuscan country farmhouse she was staying in, with its terra-cotta floors, vaulted ceiling, original stonework, and wooden doors. With a quick "I love you so much for doing this," she was off to meet up with her classmates and enjoy heaven on earth for the next few days.

I was awake and could not fall back to sleep, so I decided to treat Sydney to an early morning walk through the park.

Halfway through our walk, as Sydney was getting ready to make our usual turn around the Serpentine in Hyde Park, and I continued walking straight along the horse rails and toward Hyde Park corner. Sydney sat down in protest and watched as I kept on walking. Her "but we always go this way, not that way" protest lasted a full minute before she reluctantly came to the conclusion it was best to stop and follow me instead.

We crossed into Green Park and began walking through it. I reached into my pocket to see if I would be lucky enough to find some money to buy tea at the small kiosk in Green Park. I wasn't, but I did find a disposable camera and wondered how long it had been in there. With the camera in my hand, inspiration struck, and I once again changed course and headed toward St. James Palace.

Near St. James Street was a small entrance to St. James Palace. Posted outside the tall security wall was a guard from the Queen's Guard regiment, whose responsibility was to guard the Queen's royal residences of Buckingham Palace, St. James Palace, Windsor Castle, and the Tower of London.

It was still early in the morning, and other than the Queen's Guard and myself, there was no one else within sight. The guard, dressed in his grey winter overcoat, stood in silence, looking straight forward. I took Sydney off her leash and tried to get her to sit as close to the standing guard as possible. The Queen's Guard had yet to even flinch, and Sydney, not sure if the guard was a person or a statue, sniffed the air in caution. I finally managed to get Sydney to sit within five feet of the guard and got the camera ready to snap the picture. Just as my finger found the correct button to push, the Queen's Guard lifted his right foot into the air, held it steady for a second, and then crashed it down on the ground, making an unexpected loud noise and sending Sydney running down the street.

I convinced Sydney to come back and sit within ten feet of the guard. As I rushed to step back and snap the picture, the guard lifted his right foot high into the air again and held it there.

"Come on. Is that really necessary, now? Just one quick picture and I'm off," I pleaded my case to the guard, who was standing at attention with a large gun slung over his left shoulder.

I snapped one picture, but I was not sure if Sydney had moved her head, so I took another quick one, and then another. The guard quickly noted that I had failed to keep my promise as I snapped picture number three, and pounded his foot against the ground, once again sending Sydney scurrying down the street.

"Thank you!" I yelled back at the guard as I ran off to retrieve Sydney.

I dropped Sydney off at home, and with time to kill before my first class of the day, I headed back out the door to visit one of my favorite museums in London. It was a place where the official motto was *Omnia Omnibus Ubique,* or "All Things for All People, Everywhere"—the largest, grandest, and finest department store in the world, Harrods.

Officially, Harrods was not a museum, but when you couldn't afford most of the items in it and had to follow the look-but-don't-touch rule (because you couldn't afford it), it might as well have been. Harrods was a remarkable place with an endless list of one-of-a-kind facts, such as, it had its own fire brigade.

As Harrods was located on Brompton Road in the Knightsbridge area and only walking distance or a quick Tube ride away from our London apartment, I liked to stop there on my way to class just as the store was first opening its doors at ten o'clock in the morning. I could enjoy twenty minutes in the mostly empty store to explore and discover and feel like the store was only open to me.

My standard routine began on the first floor, walking through the Room of Luxury, where the residents were Gucci, Burberry, Dior, and Louis Vuitton. Then I'd walk through the perfume section, where the gorgeous young perfume girls were still shaking off the morning's hangover and perhaps wishing that they did not work in the perfume section at the moment. Next came the amazing food halls stocked with fish from all over the world, hundreds of different scents of cheese, and fifteen different types of bacon. I always walked out of the food halls wondering if people really did all their all grocery shopping there; the store had actually started out as a grocery store.

After leaving the first floor behind, I would then ride the elevators to the upper floors, admiring the Egyptian-themed columns and architecture. That early in the morning, there was no live opera singer or piano player perched on a small balcony, singing to the customers as they passed by on the escalator. I would then walk through the fine art section and admired the works of art, where one could actually purchase a real Picasso, Renoir, Salvador Dali, Warhol, or works from many other masters of the art world.

The next stop was always in the electronics department, where I had to spend at least a full two minutes admiring the world's first seventy-one-inch, gold-plated flat screen television. "It is a favorite of Saudi royalty," the Harrods customer service representative had once told me, while I had stood there admiring it. My final stop was always in the children's area to admire the kid-size $50,000 Lamborghini Countach and the other out-of-this-world kid's toy displays.

On my way out, I overheard a customer (the only one I had seen since first walking in) ask a saleswoman, "How do I know it is not fake? I have heard the fake ones look just like the real ones." She held a leather wallet in her hands. The saleswoman seemed surprised by the question and assured the woman that it was the genuine article.

Harrods had survived through good times and bad, through wars and tragedies and controversies, and it shows its scars to prove it. Just outside the fourth door was a plaque acknowledging the 1983 IRA bombing of the store, which had killed six people and injured ninety-three. Harrods had prided itself as a place where anything (as long as it's legal) could be purchased, including multimillion-dollar helicopters and, more controversially, fur coats. If you look hard enough, you could see a faint yellow line painted on the sidewalk, thirty feet from the edge of the store; the line wrapped around most of the sidewalk along the store and was legally the line that fur protestors were not permitted to cross when protesting. For a few years, Harrods had stopped selling fur, but the store had quietly resumed selling it again years later, and the protestors had once again shown up outside the store.

The largest and latest controversy of the store was the Diana and Dodi Al Fayed Memorial, located in the basement of the store just outside the elevator. The son of Mohamed Al Fayed, Harrods' owner, had been tragically killed alongside Diana. To honor them, Al Fayed had erected a memorial comprised of two large photographs of the two, lipstick-smudged wine glasses, and an engagement ring that Dodi had purchased the day before he had been killed, which he was supposedly planning to give to Diana.

The popular in-store memorial just did not seem appropriate, and it was possibly a little creepy, with the lipstick-smudged wine glasses enclosed in a glass case. It was almost as if the store's controversial owner Mohamed Al Fayed was making a political statement using his son's death, in response to Mohamed's unsuccessful bid to gain British citizenship, because the government felt that he was not of good character.

I walked out through the front doors of Harrods and onto Brompton Road. I turned around to admire the huge window display of an oversize model of the man-made archipelago being built in the shape of a world map just off the coast of Dubai. Harrods was even selling pieces of the dream.

There's My Bus!

My first class did not start for another half hour, and as I walked toward the Tube entrance, fate intervened again as a large, open-air, double-decker tour bus, which allowed tourists to hop on and hop off as it drove around many of the city's great tourist sights, crossed my path.

I had experienced the London Big Bus tour just about every time friends had visited, and I knew the tour well enough that I thought I could probably narrate most of it. Unexpectedly, I found myself caught up in the feeling that, soon, the great wonders of London would no longer be just a quick train ride away; the feeling was compounded by the exhilaration of playing hooky from classes for the day. Strangely, I found myself stepping onto the sightseeing bus.

I paid the driver for a ticket, accepted his offer of a map, acknowledged that I understood that I needed to keep my receipt to get back on the bus if I decided to get off, and took a seat upstairs in the open-air portion of the bus. The sun was shining, but it was still a brisk and cool fall day. With the wind in my hair and a devilish smile on my face because I had decided to skip class, I sat back and took in the magnificent sights of London as the bus pulled away from the curb.

The bus traveled down Cromwell Road past the Victoria and Albert Museum and the Natural History and Science Museum, stopping briefly to let a couple of passengers on and off the bus. We drove down Queensgate Road, and the tour guide, microphone in hand, explained how the Boy Scout movement had started in London before it had become a worldwide program. The live commentary switched to the history of the Royal Albert Hall as the bus stopped at the rounded brick building to let passengers in and out.

The tour bus turned right onto Kensington Church Street and headed toward the Notting Hill Gate area. With nothing of historical value within sight, the tour guide filled a few minutes, until we came upon something of more interest, by telling the passengers about the Great Smog of 1952, when a typical London weather event had become a tragedy. What was thought at the time to be iconic London fog "that dreadful day on December fifth, was the beginning of a great tragedy," the commentator whispered with a scary voice.

She continued by describing the details of the events and why Londoners had not panicked at the time; they had thought it was fog. But the fog, which was really smog from burning coal to heat homes, had made it impossible to drive, had seeped into homes and buildings, and had left its mark on history. Four thousand deaths had been attributed to it at first, but weeks later, the depth of the tragedy came into focus when the death toll was raised to eight thousand. The guide stopped using the scary voice and transitioned into a newscaster's voice and ended the story by saying, "The tragedy set in motion the political movement of Clean Air Acts by the government."

The bus got stuck in a small traffic jam on Bayswater Road. The tour commentator needed some filler material to last until the bus started moving again and continued with a tale that fit nicely after the Great Smog of 1952. "In Victorian times in London," she had said, "it was quite common for young boys to be employed as chimney cleaners, because they could easily fit down the narrow chimneys and clean them. But they were eventually replaced by the invention of the chimney brush because of public outcry over the deaths of many young boys who choked to death on soot while trying to scrub clean the chimneys."

When the traffic finally cleared, the bus turned left at Lancaster Gate and continued down the road until it reached the next stop on the tour, Paddington Train Station. When the station came into sight, the tour guide looked at a group of Japanese riders and asked, "Do you know the Paddington Bear story?" After waiting for an answer that never came, she asked the rest of the bus the same question. I did know the story—it was one of my favorites—but I was unaware of the inspiration behind the idea of leaving the Paddington Bear at the station with a note attached to his coat that read "Please look after this bear. Thank You." The tour guide finished the story by telling us how the author, Michael Bond, had gotten the note idea from his knowledge of the train evacuation of children during the war. Many children had stood around the train station with suitcases filled with a few possessions and notes wrapped around their necks on strings.

When the bus made its next stop near the Marble Arch monument, I got off to walk for a little while and spent some time visiting an area where I had completed a college internship; I had not visited the area in quite some time. To get to where I was going, I had to first walk through Grosvenor Square, which was home of the United States Embassy.

Security in the square and at the United States Embassy had been heightened following 9/11 and attacks at other United States Embassy buildings around the world. It would be tough to miss the ugly, nine-story building, which looks like a building you would find on a community college campus, because of the large statue of General Eisenhower in front of the embassy and an oversize, gilded bald eagle with its wings stretched open wide adorning the top of the building.

The land that just about every United States Embassy was built on was owned by the United States and considered United States soil, but along with the embassy in Japan, the United States did not own the land on which the United States Embassy in England stood. Instead it leased the land from the Duke of Westminster.

Rumor has it that when the United States government approached the Duke of Westminster to inquire if he would sell the United States government the land, he had said that he would not sell it to the government, but he would kindly give it to the United States, provided that, in return, the United States gave back all the land in America that had been illegally taken from his family during the Revolutionary War—a very unlikely scenario.

Another rumor that had been floated in the press after 9/11 was that the United States had wanted to move the embassy and staff to a more remote and safer location; the Embassy had looked at Kensington Palace as a possibility, but supposedly, the Queen had said no.

I zigzagged my way down the streets until I entered Berkeley Square, a beautiful and very posh area of London with many offices, high-end car dealerships, and desirable residences that all surround a long and narrow park in the middle of the square.

During my three-month college study abroad program in London, I had interned at a large, well-known advertising agency whose offices had been located in the square at the time. I had looked forward to walking through the park in the square each day, and I had loved my internship.

One of my responsibilities during the internship had been to put out all the small fires that routinely broke out in garbage cans and desks surrounding my desk; the fires started when a lit cigarette was left unattended by a colleague who had rushed off to another part of the building and left his burning cigarette in an overfilled ashtray or, worse, had dumped his ashtray into the garbage can with hot ashes still smoldering.

After a nice reminiscing trip through the square, I walked back toward the bus route and got back on when the bus pulled up in front of one of the world's largest toy stores, Hamleys, which was located on Regent Street.

As I took a seat on the open-air top deck of the tour bus, I looked to see if I had caught up with the same bus I had been riding before, but I hadn't; the guide providing live commentary to the tourists on the bus was not the same.

The bus pulled away from the curb and entered Piccadilly Circus, the famous rounded intersection, recognizable by the large illuminated advertising billboards for McDonald's, Sanyo, Samsung, and Coca-Cola that clung to the sides of some of the buildings located between Shaftesbury Avenue and Glasshouse Street. The large, rounded, iconic area with the funny name often referenced in pop culture had gotten half its name from the Latin word *circus,* meaning circle.

We continued down Haymarket Street onto Trafalgar Square, dropping off a few riders at the National Gallery to take pictures of themselves in front of the fountains and in front of one of the four large lion statues that guarded the base of Nelson's Column.

After a couple new passengers took their seats, the bus moved on to Whitehall Street, slowing down so passengers could get a quick glimpse of one of the most famous doors in the world—the Number 10 Downing Street door, the door to the home of the prime minister.

For a time, you could actually walk up and knock on the door, but after an IRA attack in the early '90s, the street had become closed to the public and was heavily guarded by a machine gun-carrying guards and a menacing iron gate. The simple, six-panel, black oak door with an iron knocker in the shape of a lion's head had often been described as a "masterpiece of understatement," because of its modest entrance to a place of immense world power.

Sensing the frustration of the tourists on the bus because they could not see the famous door well enough to snap a picture of it—the bus was not permitted to stop in front of Downing Street—the guide diverted the group's attention by pointing to a row of red telephone boxes, where tourists on the street were taking turns snapping pictures of themselves in front of each one or pretending to talk on the phones inside.

The guide explained that the color red had been picked for the phone booths to help make them easier to spot, even in the fog. However, the phones were slowly becoming tougher to find, because the wide use of mobile phones was making them unnecessary. With labor cost to fix and maintain them quickly increasing, their path toward extinction seemed certain, and in the future, the phone booths might only be found as a display in a museum.

The bus turned left and drove over the Westminster Bridge. My fellow tourists and I cranked our heads backward for one more view of Big Ben and the Parliament building, as the live commentator told us that the bell tower was really called St. Stephen's Tower and the large bell that can be heard but was hidden inside and out of view was actually Big Ben.

The bus turned left onto York Road, giving us all a quick glimpse of the top half of the London Eye, a giant, futuristic-looking Ferris wheel, with curved glass passenger capsules, that had been built along the river and opened on December 31, 1999, to both positive and negative reviews. Since London was pretty much flat, the thirty-minute ride on the London Eye provided one of the best views of the city.

We crossed the River Thames for a third time, but this time by way of the Waterloo Bridge. We slowly drove down Fleet Street toward St. Paul's Cathedral. The bus became stuck in traffic on Fleet Street. The tour guide was out of interesting stories about the days when Fleet Street had been the home to the British press and not close enough to tell interesting facts about St. Paul's; the guide filled the time by entertaining the riders with the history of perhaps London's most iconic symbol, the Routemaster double-decker bus.

The Routemaster double-decker bus had first taken to the streets of London in 1956 and had lived a long and prosperous life until it had been taken out of service on December 9, 2005.

When the news became official, many Americans had mistakenly thought that it was the red double-decker bus, which was found all over London, that was being taken out of service, but the Routemaster double-decker buses were just being replaced. The difference between the old and the new was that the Routemaster buses had been known for their open platforms that had allowed passengers to run down the street and jump onto the platform at the back of the bus while the bus was driving down the street. The old buses had needed two operators—one to drive and another to collect tickets and assist in pulling up passengers who leapt and missed the moving platform. Because the buses were not handicap accessible, increased labor cost, and badly polluted the air, the decision had finally been made to take them out of service. The Routemaster service ended, but a few still remained, mostly to please visiting tourists, and were used on two heritage routes.

After a stop at St. Paul's Cathedral, we turned left past the Bank of England onto London Bridge and crossed the River Thames for the fourth time. I had been waiting for that moment, and I eagerly awaited the live commentary. As we reached the halfway point of London Bridge, the story that I had anxiously waited to hear began with the guide asking, "Has anyone here heard about the silly American who bought London Bridge, mistakenly thinking he was buying the Tower Bridge?" When the guide mentioned the Tower Bridge, she waved her hands to her right as if to unveil the much more ornate and beautiful Tower Bridge. As expected, the tale received a few chuckles, and someone even said out loud to the tourists sitting around him, "What an idiot!" The guide explained that when the original London Bridge was sold, it was dismantled piece by piece, carefully packed up, and shipped to the United States, and a new London Bridge was built in the exact same spot.

I had lost track of the number of times I had heard the tall tale about how the wealthy businessman Robert McCulloch had thought he was buying the more desirable Tower Bridge and had instead received the plain, old, boring London Bridge. I guess I had finally gotten over how crazy it made me when I heard the story told and had come to accept that it was a much more entertaining story than the truth. I thought, *What harm did it cause to entertain tourists by telling it?*

Just as the children's song "London Bridge Is Falling Down" says, there was actual concern that the bridge might fall down, and the city had felt the need to replace it and put it up for sale. The truth was that Robert McCulloch had come along and paid close to $2.5 million for London Bridge, well aware of which bridge he was purchasing. In 1968, he had the bridge reconstructed at Lake Havasu City, Arizona, at an English-style theme park development that he had owned. He had successfully turned it into one of Arizona's biggest tourist draws.

After crossing the River Thames and riding down Tooley Street, the bus turned left and crossed the river for a final time when we drove over the Tower Bridge. As we crossed the bridge, I relived the feeling that I had experienced when I had run over the Tower Bridge during the London Marathon. With the wind blowing through my hair, I felt as though I was running over it again.

We crossed the bridge in silence, but just as we were back on land and in sight of the Tower of London, the tour guide's microphone turned back on, and the guide asked the bus, "Do we need to drop anyone off at Traitors' Gate? No?" She paused a second before explaining that Traitors' Gate was an entrance, which faced the river, to the Tower of London. Many high-profile prisoners had passed through Traitors' Gate before being executed. The guide went on to tell the riders about the long list of famous prisoners who had been held or executed there, the last being Joseph Jakobs, a convicted German spy who had been executed by firing squad in 1941. In its nine-hundred-year history, the Tower of London had been a prison, a palace, an arsenal, a mint, a jewel house, a place of execution, and a zoo.

I had been on my spontaneous London sightseeing trip for over three hours, and as the bus pulled up at the Embankment Pier to let passengers on and off again, I decided it was time to get off and end my tour with a walk through Parliament Square and one last stop at Westminster Abbey to say hello to someone who waited there for me—or, to be more accurate, rested there.

- Chapter Thirty-Five -

Great, Great, Great ... Grandpa Longshanks

✦

First-time visitors to Westminster Abbey were often confused as to whether the building was a church or a cemetery. It's actually both. The monumental, Gothic-style church in the shadow of Parliament and Big Ben (or St. Stephen's Tower, if you wanted to take the fun out of it) could also be called a multiuse development. Traditionally, it had been a cathedral, a site of Royal Coronations, and a memorial and burial site for hundreds of distinguished individuals. Add in the gift shop just outside the abbey doors, and it could also be called a retail development. Technically, the place was a Royal Peculiar, which was a place of worship under the leadership of the British monarch and not a diocese.

I entered Westminster Abbey through the front doors, walked around the memorial for the Unknown Warrior, and continued along the edge of the building. I had not come to admire the Gothic architecture, visit Poets' Corner, or listen to the choir practice. Instead, my visit was a personal one. I continued to navigate through the maze-like floor plan of the abbey until I found what I was looking for—a large, simple, square, stone coffin that looked as if it could fit a refrigerator. Inside the simple stone coffin was a relative of mine, King Edward I.

To be honest, I did not know much about Edward I, or "Longshanks," as he was more famously known in pop culture. The good: He was king. The bad: The way he treated the Jews to increase his popularity. The ugly: The portrayal of him in the riveting but historically inaccurate, Academy Award-winning movie *Braveheart*.

When Edward's father King Henry III had died, Edward had ascended to the throne at the age of thirty-three and ruled until his death in 1307. He had left his mark on history through his attempts to conquer Wales and Scotland. The throne on which British monarchs still sat during coronation ceremonies, known as King Edward's Chair, sat not too far from his coffin. Edward I had had the wooden chair built specifically to fit perfectly underneath the Stone of Scone.

Edward I had obtained the stone from its previous owners, the Scottish, and for hundreds of years it had sat under the chair in its designated place. In 1996, the English, in a symbolic gesture, had returned the stone to the Scots under the condition that it be returned and placed back under the chair for use in future coronations.

After Queen Elizabeth II, whose bottom would sit in the chair next while the coronation stone was underneath it was anyone's guess.

The Royal Descent
Edward I, King of England
Elizabeth de Bohun
Margaret de Courtenay
Edward de Courtenay
Sir Hugh de Courtenay
Margaret de Grenville
William Grenville
Thomas Grenville
Sir Thomas Grenville
Sir Roger Grenville
Sir Richard Grenville
Sir Bernard Grenville
Sir Bevil Grenville
Elizabeth Grenville Prideaux
Sir Edmund Prideaux
Peter Prideaux
Susanna Prideaux Evelyn
Charles Evelyn
Phillippa Evelyn
Frederick Evelyn Houghton
Lydia Houghton O'Brien
Theresa O'Brien Day
Nellie Day Custer
Blanch Custer Ryan
Delbert Ryan
Thomas Ryan
Garrett Ryan

- Chapter Thirty-Six -

Auf Wiedersehen

✦

(Until We Meet Again)

Sarah and I could not help but feel bad for missing Denis and Jenny's wedding, so we had decided that the best way to make it up to them would be a long-weekend visit to their new home in Dresden, Germany, to hear about the wedding and see the pictures. School and studying were taking up much of my time, and it had been awhile since Denis and I had had the chance to talk and catch up on what was going on in each other's lives. I was really curious to hear all about his new job as a wine export manager for a small, family-owned wine importer and exporter and to see their new home.

Our flight to Germany would only be a couple of hours, but we had learned through experience that the art of budget airline travel throughout Europe took patience and more patience, so we arrived early at the airport to prepare for anything. Instead of sitting and waiting for our flight to board, we used the time to browse through the airport bookstore and duty-free stores with more of a purpose of passing the time than of buying more stuff that we did not need.

When we heard the flight boarding announcement, we casually walked to the gate. By the time we made it there, the majority of the passengers had already boarded the flight. We had taken our place in the back of the line when a familiar voice from behind us caught us both off guard.

"Hello, Garrett and Sarah. I was starting to think that you might not make the flight." Standing there behind us, enjoying the surprise he had been waiting all morning to spring on us, was Denis.

"Wow! You Germans really are efficient. Are we already in Germany?" I asked Denis, pushing his extended handshake aside and giving him a hug.

"Very funny, Garrett," he said. Denis had never appreciated my German efficiency stereotype jokes, but I could not resist the opportunity to lay one on him—it had been awhile. Denis had flown into London the day before for a work meeting. He apologized for not calling us, but since his business meetings were in the London suburbs and he was also staying at a hotel outside London, he would not have time to see us.

Denis introduced us to his boss, who had been told ahead of time of Denis's plan to surprise us. The boss commended Denis on the execution of his plan. Denis had never spoken kindly of his new boss and had previously described him to me as a "Porky Pig"-type fellow who only had his job because his family owned the company. His boss was about ten years older than Denis, and his chubbiness and kid-like demeanor made me kind of agree with Denis's "Porky Pig" reference. The four of us boarded the Ryan Air flight and found our seats. Denis sat near the front of the plane, and Sarah and I sat in the back, one row behind Denis's boss.

Ryan Air had been called the IKEA of the skies, because of its cheap fares, its no-frills service, and most notably, its in-your-face blue and yellow airplane color scheme, which was identical to IKEA's. Ryan Air was famous for offering one cent fares on some of its routes, which I had written off as a marketing gimmick until I booked our flight to Germany and was able to purchase two one-cent fares for our flight back to London from Germany. Another Ryan Air marketing promotion had included being entered into an on-flight, free flight sweepstakes drawing if you purchased a drink during the flight. Denis's boss ended up being the lucky individual holding the winning free flight ticket, and he waved it high in the air and shouted like a child on Christmas morning when the flight attendants called out his winning number.

As we flew high in the sky over Europe, I was amazed by the number of planes I could see crisscrossing through the sky as they passed a few thousand feet above and below us. The skies of Europe were filled with many shiny new planes, because low-cost airlines had transformed Europe. Closed military airfields had been taken over by discount airlines, and new routes to once-sleepy destinations in Europe had caused tourist and property booms in places that had once not been easily accessible. Most of the old military airfields being used as discount airline hubs were located far outside of the city, and travel to and from them often cost passengers more than the flights themselves.

Looking further down at the ground, I could also see large wind farms producing clean and "green" energy for Europe. The many recently built wind farms were a great step forward for Europe as it strode toward meeting its promises of reducing carbon emissions in the coming years. But the huge environmental cost of the additional discount airline flights filling the skies as they traveled along newly formed routes throughout Europe left a big carbon footprint, and that could make it impossible for Europe to meet its goals.

Our flight landed on a tiny airfield in a lush green field without a building larger than one story in sight. Alongside the runway were midsize airplane hangars built into the side of a small, grass-covered, man-made hill, which camouflaged the hangars from high above in the sky; the camouflage was a relic of past wars. Our plane was by far the largest at the airport, and I had the feeling that after the plane refueled and took off back to London, the airport workers could go home for the day and wait for the next discount airline flight to arrive in the next day or two.

We picked up our bags from the luggage carousel and walked out of the tiny, one-room airport terminal. Jenny was outside the airport, waiting anxiously to see how surprised we had been to see Denis at the airport in London. Sarah and I had been practicing a greeting in German during the flight, but in the excitement of our arrival, I could not correctly remember the line: "*Guten Tag, Jenny! Wie ist es Ihnen denn so ergangen?*"—or "Good day, Jenny! How have you been?"—and instead garbled out the bits of it I could remember. Jenny politely smiled and played along as if she had understood me; even though I was positive that she did not understand one word of the German I had said, she played along.

"It is wonderful that you can now speak German, Garrett."

Denis still had some work to attend to, so he headed back to the office with his boss while Jenny was left in charge of showing us the sights before taking us to Denis's offices for a tour of the wine bottling facility. Sarah and I placed our bags in the trunk and climbed into the familiar two-door Volkswagen. Even though the car had broken down during the move from London back to Germany, it still had a little life left in it. Denis was no longer frustrated by driving Jenny's beaten-up white Volkswagen, because he would shortly be receiving a brand new Volkswagen company car to use.

The airport was located an hour's drive from Dresden, an hour's drive that was very scenic and beautiful. During all of my travels through Europe, I had never traveled on the high-speed German highway, the autobahn. Jenny pushed the gas pedal down as far as it would go in the small Volkswagen car, which reached a top speed of seventy miles per hour and began to shake ever so slightly in protest. Sarah and I had arrived ill prepared for our first autobahn experience, as BMWs, Porsches, and Audis whizzed right past us as if we were standing still. Even though Jenny's car was not the fastest on the road, it was getting us to where we needed to be—or at least, we hoped it would.

Our first destination of the day was the small city of Meissen, which was located on the banks of the Elbe River. Jenny looked at me suspiciously to see if I was "pulling her leg" —another English idiom that I had tried to explain to Jenny, similar to teaching her the phrase "keep your eyes peeled to the road"—when I told her that Sarah and I had heard of the city of Meissen before.

When we arrived in Meissen, Jenny parked the car, and we all walked down the street toward the entrance to the Meissen porcelain factory. Jenny was still not sure if she was the victim of some sort of joke; she was surprised that not only had we heard of the city of Meissen but we had specifically requested to make a stop at the Meissen porcelain factory.

My parents enjoyed collecting small, decorative, blue Meissen porcelain plates, which they liked to display on various walls throughout their home. Sarah and I could not think of a better Christmas gift for them than a plate purchased directly from the factory. Our only concern was getting the plate back home without breaking it.

Jenny, Sarah, and I browsed through the factory store display cases. The salespeople ignored us as we leaned over the glass display counters to try to get a glance at the price tags. Since we were half the age of the next-youngest customer and far from the demographics profile of the average customer, who usually walked directly off a tourist bus and straight through the front doors, the salespeople did not bother to ask us if we needed any help.

I explained to Sarah that the blue crossed sword signature logo found on the backside of the Meissen porcelain plates was one of the oldest trademarks still used today and dated all the way back to the 1720s.

"Is it in bad taste to pick out something that we like since your parents will probably leave it for us in their will someday?" Sarah asked; it sounded half like a question and half like a statement. I laughed out loud at the joke, but honestly, I found myself agreeing with her. We finally made our choice and surprised the salesperson when we told her we wanted to purchase a plate.

We spent the rest of the afternoon walking around the Albrechtsburg Castle in the center of the city. Instead of learning interesting historical facts about the city, we walked and talked about how Jenny was frustrated with her job search. Jobs in the area were hard to come by, and the few available jobs were predominantly focused around the tourist industry. With her extensive work experience in film production, she was better suited to be living in a city like Berlin than in a city like Dresden. Jenny also told us about a form of discrimination that I had never heard of. She explained that East Germans didn't always like to hire Western Germans, an indication that long after the

Berlin Wall had fallen—or the change had happened, as Eastern Germans liked to say—some work still needed to be done.

The afternoon was turning into early evening, and it was time to drive over to Denis's workplace to take a tour and drive him home. We got back into the small Volkswagen car and drove toward Denis's office, some twenty-five minutes away. I sat in the backseat, and as Sarah and Jenny talked while we drove down the autobahn, my eyes slowly closed for a quick nap.

I was wakened suddenly by Sarah tapping on my leg.

"Garrett! Wake up! Wake up,"

"Oh, no. Denis is going to kill me," Jenny said as she slapped her hand against the top of the steering wheel in frustration.

It took me a full three seconds to understand what was happening; the cars that had been zooming past us at a high rate of speed were now moving past us as though we were standing still. The small Volkswagen had run out of gas.

Jenny had managed to get the car to the side of the road, about a hundred yards away from the closest highway exit ramp. Jenny was scared, frustrated, and mad all at the same time, so her slowly thought-out English came out in short, incomprehensible fragments. I could not tell for sure, but it sounded like she was trying to tell us that you got a big fine in Germany for running out of gas on the highway. Other motorists liked to inform the police of your mistake and tip them off about your whereabouts so the police could come ticket you.

I got out of the car and told Jenny to put the car into neutral. I pushed as hard as I could, and the car started moving. It gained speed as I pushed. Jenny rolled down her window and yelled back at me, "Wow, Garrett, you are very strong!" Jenny had failed to notice that the road sloped downward, and I really did not even need to push the car.

The car rolled all the way to the exit ramp, but our momentum ended when the road sloped severely upward. We got out of the car, and in the distance we could see the bright lights of a gas station. Jenny instantaneously apologized to us for the predicament we had found ourselves in, and she was on the verge of tears.

"Jenny," I said, "we don't care about running out of gas. We are just so happy to be here with you walking down this road. You may find this hard to believe, but Sarah and I are having a great time."

It was true. Sarah and I loved every minute of the adventure, and eventually Jenny began to believe us and the smile that we loved so much came back to her face. We purchased a gas canister, filled it with gas, and walked back to the stranded car.

The event caused us to show up at Denis's office an hour late. Denis immediately apologized to us while simultaneously cursing at Jenny in German for her carelessness. Even though I could not understand what Denis was saying to Jenny, I could see that it was not good news. I interrupted him and told him that we did not care, and we were having so much fun just being there with the two of them. It took Denis a few minutes to believe us, but he finally did.

With everyone happy again, Denis handed us all blue lab coats, hard helmets, and safety glasses and took us on a tour of the wine bottling plant behind his office. I was transfixed by the large, fast-moving machinery that precisely filled each bottle, then shot a cork into the top, and finally perfectly placed a label on it. The entire production process for each bottle was completed in just under ten seconds.

After the tour, we all piled into the Volkswagen car and headed home to Denis and Jenny's new home, a second-floor apartment in a three-story, white stucco building with brown wood trim. It had a slight Bavarian feel to it. Enormous, beautiful, black—and working—gas lamps lined the streets, giving the area a romantic and old-time feel. As we walked up the stairs to their apartment, I asked Denis who his neighbors were.

"No, Garrett, we do not know them. We are not American. We do not barbeque with our neighbors every weekend," Denis said, making fun of me and my fellow Americans.

Their two-bedroom apartment was enormous. The kitchen could easily fit a cocktail party with thirty guests and another twenty guests comfortably standing in the massive attached bathroom. The place was clean and orderly and held many familiar objects that I had seen in their London apartment.

Denis opened a bottle of wine, and the four of us sat down for a nice candlelit dinner of vegetables and various raw meats cooked on a hot stone.

"Is this wine from your company?" I asked Denis, as he filled my glass to the top.

"Garrett, I wouldn't even serve a dog that stuff we pass off as wine," he said.

"Denis, be nice," Jenny said, before backing him up: "Actually, Denis is right. It is not nice stuff."

After dinner, as Jenny shared Sarah pictures from their wedding, Denis and I poured ourselves another glass of wine and talked. I often liked to serve up a question to Denis and just sit back and listen to him talk. For this occasion, I decided to ask him about his work travel experiences, since he had given me bits and pieces through e-mail messages and quick phone conversations.

Denis was the most junior of the salespeople at his new job and had been given a sales territory with the smallest chance of making a sale as he "earned his wings." Instead of places like France, Spain, or Italy—mature wine-consuming markets—Denis found himself in places like Mongolia, Kazakhstan, and Russia, where wine—even cheap wine—was not the first choice of alcoholic drinks.

Since he worked for a wine company, it was expected that wine would be drunk with the prospective buyers that he traveled to see, Denis explained. However, the amount of wine that Denis ended up having to pay for, as well as dinners and nightly entertainment, had not been expected. Often business was conducted during late dinners, where his hosts ate indulgent, expensive meals and then drank themselves near death, often ending the evening with some of the businessmen disappearing into the night with strange women.

Of course, Denis was always left to pay the bill. Many times the prospective buyers could not even remember what had been discussed or promised the previous night, and as Denis said good-bye and drove to the airport, he was told that they would get back to him. Denis was smart, and he was well aware that this meant that he would not hear back from them again.

"So, Denis, how do you fill out a work expense report when your clients stick you with paying for their evening entertainment?" I held up my hands and put air quotes around "entertainment."

"Luckily, Garrett," he said, "the people at my office have traveled to these miserable places, and they know what these good-for-nothing wine import people expect me to pay for during a full evening of discussing business."

Motor City Spies

The next morning, we enjoyed a relaxed breakfast, sitting at the table and talking about the day's plans. After showering and getting dressed, we got into Jenny's Volkswagen car and drove off toward our first destination—the Volkswagen automobile factory in Dresden.

The Volkswagen factory was known as the *Gläserne Manufaktur*, or "factory made out of glass." In English, the factory was called The Transparent Factory. The English name made sense, because just about every wall, including the exterior walls, was made completely out of glass. The factory looked more like a museum than a working car assembly factory. Canadian maple wood floors covered the entire assembly line area and complemented the glass wall interiors nicely. It would have been fair to say that the factory had been designed with the purpose of appealing to tourists and car buyers who could actually watch their cars come to life.

The factory was not much of a factory; it was, more accurately, an assembly plant. There were no noisy industrial machines or strong-smelling paint chemicals. All the "dirty" components of the car creation process were completed someplace else and shipped to the factory for final assembly. Since it was a Saturday morning, no workers were in sight and the assembly line was at a standstill.

We joined a tour group of fifteen other people and waited in a semicircle for the tour guide to speak. When our guide began her welcome speech, she talked and talked and talked—in German. Denis leaned over and quietly whispered to us, "Sorry, Garrett and Sarah, but the tour will only be given in German." We decided we would still take the tour and kept listening.

The tour guide, a middle-aged woman with long, pulled-back black hair and wearing a sharp blue business suit, started to walk as the group followed her. She abruptly stopped and appeared to give the group a stern, quick lecture.

"What was that all about?" I asked Denis.

"She just told the group that no pictures or filming are allowed inside the factory. No exceptions," he said.

"Should we not tell her that we are Americans originally from the Detroit area?" I asked.

"No, it is fine. She will say thank you for buying our German cars," he said.

What we could not understand with our ears, because it was in German, we could see with our eyes. The factory was home to the Volkswagen Phaeton sedan and the Bentley Continental Flying Spur. The Volkswagen Phaeton had been introduced to the American market in 2004 and had quickly failed. The American car consumer was not ready or willing to pay $80,000 for a Volkswagen sedan, preferring the $20,000 Volkswagen Jetta instead. To my astonishment, every third car on the assembly line was a Bentley Continental Flying Spur. I was amazed that, with a few adjustments, they could produce a car that was mostly made of Phaeton car parts but could be sold for close to $300,000.

Since we could not understand the tour group leader, and Denis was getting tired of trying to translate everything, we silently snuck away from the group and walked around on our own. We stumbled upon—or it was possibly perfectly planned out in the flow of the factory tour—a gift shop and a virtual reality driving experience for the Volkswagen Phaeton near the exit.

After a brief argument over who would go first in the car simulator, Denis and Jenny insisted that Sarah and I should go first. Sarah got into the driver's seat, and I jumped into the passenger's side. The ride operator gave us a brief set of instructions, shut the door, and started the simulator. A large wraparound monitor on the front windshield lit up with what looked like a test track. The car appeared to accelerate and decelerate as Sarah pushed down the gas pedal. The car shook slightly, replicating the feeling of driving off the road.

I had never had a problem with motion sickness, but just two minutes into the ride I had to close my eyes, because I was feeling sick. Screams of "*Fahrvergnugen*! "*Fahrvergnugen*!" blasted from the car speakers; Denis and Jenny had managed to talk the simulator operator into letting them yell at us through an intercom system, while he stood by and laughed at the whole spectacle. Five minutes into the ten-minute ride, Sarah and I both agreed to hit the emergency terminate ride button, because we were on the verge of throwing up our morning's breakfast.

The ride came to an instant stop, and the interior lights came on. We both exited the car holding our stomachs. Denis laughed at us for feeling sick.

"It's because you don't know how to handle a German car," he joked. Denis and Jenny took their turn and got into the car with Jenny driving and Denis in the passenger's seat. Three minutes into the ride, the emergency terminate ride button was pushed by Denis and Jenny, and they also exited the car holding their stomachs and feeling severely dizzy.

The four of us exited the factory in far worse shape than we had entered. We all agreed that we could never buy the car, because it would remind us of how sick the ride had made us feel. It would take close to an hour of fresh air and walking at a slow pace before we all felt good enough to continue our day.

The afternoon was spent experiencing the many magnificent gardens, churches, and historic buildings of Dresden. It was such a beautiful city but it was not a city that Denis and Jenny loved. Being a young couple, there just was not enough for them to do. They deeply missed living in a larger city like London, Paris, or Berlin.

Dresden was not known by too many Americans. The tragically famous city, had been almost completely rebuilt after the controversial bombing of Dresden at the tail end of World War II, which had been ordered by Winston Churchill. Critics of the bombing said that the action had been unwarranted, because the war was quickly coming to an end and the city was much more of a German cultural landmark than an industrial city capable of aiding the war effort, which made it a very low-level military threat. The bombing by British and American planes in February 1945 leveled large sections of the city and caused massive fires that destroyed other parts of it. Estimates of civilian death tolls of the controversial Allied action ranged from twenty-four thousand to forty thousand.

Our last stop on our tour of Dresden was the world-famous Semper Opera House. The magnificent building, built in the style of the early Italian Renaissance, had been designed by the architect Gottfried Semper and completed in 1841. During the World War II bombings, the building had been reduced to a pile of rubble, but it had risen again forty years later almost exactly as it had stood before the war started. The first opera performed when it reopened its doors was Carl Maria von Weber's *Der Freischütz,* the last opera to have been performed just before it had been destroyed in the 1945 bombings.

As we walked out of the opera house, we were just about run over by a long progression of Trabant cars, also known as the "Trabi," or the people's car of the German Democratic Republic. A German entrepreneur had set up a self-drive escorted tour of the city in which tourists drove around in a group of ten to fifteen cars led by a tour guide in the lead pace car. Three million of the small, two-cycle, air-cooled Trabant cars had been built in East Germany, where buyers had waited up to fifteen years to receive one. Some parents had even ordered a Trabi car when they delivered a baby so that by the time the child reached the driving age of fifteen, they would have a car to drive. When the wall came down, East German residents had ditched their poor-performing and unreliable Trabants for Volkswagens, and production of the car had ended and its place in pop culture had begun.

Later that evening, Denis and Jenny took us to an elegant, white tablecloth restaurant high up on a hill; it provided a beautiful view of the flickering city lights far below in the distance. During dinner, Denis and Jenny described, in great detail, their first date of sitting by the Elbe River drinking wine together. Denis talked about how, when they got engaged, he had worn a commitment wedding band ring, signifying that he was engaged. When they had gotten married, he had moved it to his other hand to communicate that he was married.

At the end of the evening when the bill came, Denis rounded the ninety-five euro dinner to an even one hundred euros. When the waiter saw what Denis had done, he graciously shook all of our hands in appreciation for the gesture. I could not help but shake my head in amazement at how happy he was for just a five percent tip. The waiter had done a great job and made the evening dinner experience exceptional. If Sarah and I had been dining alone, I would have given him a twenty percent tip, and he probably would have driven us all home to show his gratitude. I questioned Denis's judgment when he said that five euros was more than enough, but now that I understood tip expectations in Europe, Denis was right.

We made a final toast to good friends and good times together again in the future. It was a happy and special moment, but it was also sad because I was not sure when I would see Denis again. Sarah, Sydney, and I would be traveling back home for good in just a few weeks.

- Chapter Thirty-Seven -

I'm Thankful for Ben

✦

If you had to dream up one holiday that the entire world could share and celebrate together, it should look something like the traditional American holiday of Thanksgiving. Through the ups and downs of life, there was always something to be thankful for, no matter where you lived. The world did not have to celebrate it on the fourth Thursday of November each year, but just spending a day together with family and friends, celebrating something—anything—that you're grateful for sounded like a good idea to me.

Since Sarah and I could not go home for Thanksgiving, we decided to bring the meaning of Thanksgiving to us by inviting family and friends to join us in our small basement apartment in London for a huge American Thanksgiving experience. My younger brother Greg and his wife Claudia decided to fly to London from Chicago for the holiday, because flights were cheap as most travelers looked for flights to the United States for the holiday versus flying out of the country.

The Thanksgiving feast took days of detailed preparation to pull off, and Sarah was up for the challenge. We decided that Sarah would take care of preparing the food for our guests and I would take care of finding a way to seat them all at one large table in our small living room.

The first step in the preparations was a trip to our local supermarket, where Sarah was delighted to hear "Yeah, we do put out a few extra turkeys for the Americans in the neighborhood this time of the year" from the meat manager, in a voice implying that he understood that Americans like to eat turkey in late November but he did not know why. But Sarah was deeply concerned when she discovered that the turkeys came in only two sizes—super small or super large. We would be serving nine people, so we needed a medium to large turkey. She was concerned that an extra large turkey would not fit into our small IKEA oven, and to make matters worse, the turkeys were frozen blocks of ice. Luckily, she had three days to work on slowly defrosting our turkey.

Through borrowing and stealing, and a little creativity, I was able to create a table large enough for all the food and long enough to fit the chairs, ottomans, trash cans, and boxes that I had collected to seat nine bottoms around the table. The good folks at IKEA would have been proud of my creative use of their products to successfully piece together a table setting for nine that was not only functional but good-looking, too. The morning of the big day, I rode the Tube over to Meridith and Petter's place to borrow a folding card table to complete my Thanksgiving table masterpiece. I had seen many large and strange objects carried on the Tube by fellow passengers, but I had yet to see anyone carry a card table.

As we put the finishing touches to the table and the food preparations, Sarah and I told my brother Greg and Claudia that it really did not feel like Thanksgiving. Outside it looked like Thanksgiving with the falling of the leaves, but it was still not the same. We told them how we had been surprised to have small children trick-or-treating through the neighborhood on Halloween night and how we had kicked ourselves for not having any candy to give to the kids and instead just sat on the front step of the building and watched them parade by.

Three weeks before our Thanksgiving celebration, Sarah and I had experienced Guy Fawkes Night, also referred to as Bonfire Night, when the English celebrated the foiling of the Gunpowder Plot of 1605. Guy Fawkes and a few other Catholic conspirators had unsuccessfully tried to blow up the Houses of Parliament by placing a large amount of gunpowder under the House of Lords only to be caught and hanged for treason. The Bonfire Night celebration was held every November 5, with the burning of bonfires, where "guys," or effigies of Guy Fawkes, were burnt. The bonfires were followed by a large fireworks display. The alcohol-fueled nighttime celebration was fun and different. The celebration had had an even mix of Halloween and Fourth of July feel to it. The holiday kind of filled the void of not having a large holiday to celebrate the month prior to the Christmas holiday.

Our guests were late arriving on Thanksgiving, and I was getting agitated, because none of them seemed to be answering their cell phones. I decided to burn off the nervous energy by making a quick dash for a couple last-minute items that we probably did not need. Sarah had thought of everything, but she relented, and I ran out the door. I picked up some dish soap for the long night ahead of washing dishes, because we did not have a dishwasher, and we would be using nearly every dish, pot, pan, or glass sitting in our kitchen cabinets.

There was nothing more beautiful than looking at a full Thanksgiving Day meal on a hungry stomach. The long, makeshift table was decorated with a red tablecloth, white plates, white napkins, and white candles. A large turkey sat in the middle, surrounded by bowls of mashed potatoes, stuffing, gravy, cranberry sauce, and a freshly baked pumpkin pie.

Our dinner guests included my younger brother Greg and his wife Claudia, Meridith and Petter, Lukas and his girlfriend Taisy, and Max.

"You have to love a holiday where you get to eat your brains out," Max said as we all sat down to eat.

At home, a Thanksgiving was not complete for me without watching my Detroit Lions lose, eating turkey, and standing in a circle holding hands with family and saying one thing we were thankful for in our lives. Petter brought over his computer and pulled up the game so we could watch it on his computer screen, and the Lions did what they always did—lost.

To complete the tradition and help make the day feel a little like Thanksgiving back at home, I made all of our guests hold hands around the table in a circle and tell the group what they were thankful for the year. I started off the tradition by saying that I was thankful for Sarah working so hard and for all the new friends we had made. Sarah said she was thankful for reconnecting with old friends and making new friends.

Our guests thoroughly enjoyed themselves, and we sent them all home with Tupperware filled with three dinners' worth of Thanksgiving leftovers. Even Sydney was stuffed, because our guests could not resist treating her to some turkey as she sat patiently under the table waiting for anything that might fall on the floor or a compassionate hand reaching under the table with a large chunk of juicy, moist turkey for her to enjoy.

The weekend after our Thanksgiving feast, we temporarily said good-bye to Greg and Claudia as we all went our separate ways for the weekend. Greg and Claudia went off to spend the weekend in Paris while Sarah, Sydney, and I rented a car and drove up to the Cotswolds for a weekend of relaxation and countryside fun for Sydney.

We booked an inn that had a small cottage behind the main building and allowed dogs. The late November weather had produced far more clouds and rain than sunshine, so we spent the weekend walking through the tall, wet grass of the five valleys of Stroud. With our tall Hunter wellie boots on and our rain jackets buttoned up tight, we hiked through the green hills until the cold chill had reached our bones. Then we returned to the inn to sink deep into luxurious leather chairs, enjoy a warm drink, and catch a quick nap in front of the roaring fireplace. When we were adequately rested and Sydney's wet fur had dried from the warmth of the fire, we returned back outside and did it again, each time picking a new trail, which led to places with names like Pinfarthings, Minchinhampton, or Littleworth.

We returned from the Cotswolds just in time for the arrival of another visiting friend. Along with Mike, I had met Ben during my study abroad experience in London, and even though he had not officially lived with Mike and me in our small, single dorm room, he had spent so much time there that many of the other students had thought he did.

I was excited for Ben to visit because he did not want to see any of the usual tourist must-see sights; he had already seen them all many times. So instead we could spend his short visit enjoying life and London without an itinerary. We didn't waste any time, and shortly after Ben had dropped off his luggage and taken a shower to help work off the sleepy cobwebs from the red-eye flight, we were off to our favorite pub.

Just about every British citizen had a favorite pub for one reason or another. Ben and I shared a common fondness for the Queen's Arms pub in South Kensington. The pub was hidden down a mews, making it a little difficult to find and hiding from the view of passing tourists. The pub has all the charming features you would expect to find as well as a few unique features that make it special.

In 1393, Richard II had made it mandatory for all pubs to hang a sign outside their doors so the official Ale Taster could identify them. Most of the population at the time had been illiterate, so pub owners had used pictorial signs to indicate that the places were drinking and socializing establishments. The Queen's Arms pub followed the tradition, with a sign hung high over its doors welcoming all those who passed by.

Ben and I had visited the Queens Arms pub together so many times over the years that we have lost count of all the times the pub has redecorated. We remember when the food was bad, then got good, and went bad again, before joining the gastro pub food trend and now served amazing food.

One of the most significant moments in my relationship with Ben had happened during a trip to London that had began at the Queen's Arms Pub. Years ago, Mike, Ben, and I had spent a week-long vacation in London and Ireland reliving our college days together. Early into the trip, Ben had arranged with Mike for just Ben and I to spend some time together one evening while Mike met up with some old work friends from his experience as an intern in London, allowing Ben and me the time to have "a little talk," as Ben had called it.

The evening of the talk had been just like any other visit to the Queen's Arms pub—one round of cold pints had followed another. Ben was not himself that night; he was uncharacteristically quiet. Every time I had gotten up to go to the bathroom, another full pint seemed to be waiting for me, even if I already had a full pint of beer. Somewhere along the night, dinner was skipped, and Ben had stopped buying pints and instead moved on to purchasing shots of liquor. After a good confidence-building alcohol buzz, he finally got the courage to begin his little talk with me.

"Garrett, I don't think I'm ever going to get married," he said.

Clueless to where he was going with the statement and drunk as a skunk, I said, "Marriage is for losers, Ben! Who wants to get married? I just don't get it!" toasting him with one of the three full shots sitting in front of me.

"And I don't think I will have kids, either," Ben said.

"Who needs 'em? They're just a giant pain in the ass!" I said.

Ben became even quieter than before, and with his head slumped, he said, "I think I'm attracted to guys."

It took my brain a few seconds to catch up, because of the temporary handicap that I had placed on it with the amount of alcohol that Ben had purchased us. I shouted my reply over the loud music: "Who wouldn't be, Ben? Guys rule!"

"No, Garrett. I think I'm gay," he said quickly.

I paused for a second or two, waiting for my brain to process the entire sentence. "Well, Ben, then I guess I will be gay, too!" I answered in a joyful and celebratory tone, nearly falling out of my chair but still able to toast him with another full shot. "This is great, Ben. It really is great to be here in London with you again," I slurred, as I reached over the table and gave him an "I love you, brother" hug.

Ben's decision to have "a little talk" with me while bathed in a sea of alcohol had backfired miserably, because I could not take any comment he made seriously and would agree to anything he said at the moment. If an army recruiter had walked by and Ben had thought it would be a good idea to join the army, I might have woken up and found myself in the army.

It took a long, sober talk the next day with Mike and Ben before I finally understood that Ben was trying to tell me that he was, in fact, gay. He had told Mike during a long road trip months before our reunion. During the trip to London, Mike had pressed Ben into finally telling me the news as well.

When all the cards were finally placed on the table, Mike and I had joked with Ben about all those times in London at tourist sites when tour guides had asked where everyone was from, secretly hoping for some tourist from Texas so they could use the line "I hear there are only steers and queers in Texas. Which one are you?" to the chuckle of the other tourists. Mike and I asked Ben why he didn't stand up for himself and say "Well, I'm queer. You got a problem with that?" We had had his back. He just hadn't known it then.

Ben had taught me a lot about life as he had struggled with telling family and close friends. Some had stayed in his life, and others had decided not to when they found out. Ben had been a good friend before he had built up the courage to reveal his secret to me, and he would still be a friend for life. On my wedding day, I was proud to have him standing there alongside my two brothers and some other good friends as one of my groomsmen.

Sarah and I enjoyed Ben's quick visit to London, and we took delight when he told us how impressed and jealous he was when the waitresses at our favorite restaurant referred to us as "regulars" in front of him. I was thankful for the opportunity to catch up with what was new in Ben's life as well as who was new in his life. Sarah enjoyed following Ben's love life, and I secretly enjoyed hearing about it, too, because I wished for Ben to find happiness with someone who made his life as happy as Sarah made mine.

A Ballerina's Big Chance to Take to the Stage

Ben said his final good-byes and headed to the airport to fly back home to Denver. Greg and Claudia would shortly be leaving, too, but we had one last night to share with them before they left, and we had something special planned for the evening.

Lukas had offered Sarah and me the opportunity to watch his brother Johannes, a top soloist for the internationally renowned Royal Ballet Company, perform at the Royal Opera House in Covent Garden. Sarah had grown up dreaming of one day being a famous ballerina, so she jumped at the chance. Through the years, I had grown to appreciate some of the artistic performances that Sarah had always had an interest in, and I attended each event with an open mind. I thought that if she could sit through my ice hockey games, I could sit through an occasional dance performance. But I had discovered that I preferred dance performances that looked more like the singing and dancing in a Gap commercial rather than traditional dances such as ballet.

Greg's wife Claudia also shared an interest in dancing, and I thought she would enjoy the performance much more than I would, because not only were they going to be watching the performance, they would be watching the performance while sitting on the actual stage behind the curtain, far off to the side and out of sight of the audience, but much closer than anyone else. They could even talk to the dancers while they waited in the side wings of the stage until their parts came up.

Greg and I escorted the girls to the stage door entrance, thanked Lukas's brother Johannes for arranging it, and took a quick picture of them standing there before we disappeared into the night to a pub to talk about sports and other "guy stuff" while Sarah and Claudia enjoyed the ballet experience of a lifetime.

Afterward, we all met up to hear about their night's ballet experience over a pint of beer. Sarah and Claudia talked for an hour about how they could see the sweat dripping down the dancers' faces and the tiny, minuscule muscles straining on the dancers' legs as they lifted the ballerinas high into the air with ease and grace. They told us how the dancers had stood on the side of the stage next to them, just inches away, and midway through a sentence spoken to another dancer waiting to perform, they would leap out onto the stage in front of the packed house and perform for a few seconds before leaping back off the stage and finishing the sentence in the conversation.

The experience was as glamorous as Sarah had dreamed the life of a professional ballet dancer in a prestigious dance company would be. I kidded her that that night had been her big chance to live the dream for a few seconds and leap out onto the stage and dance for the enormous crowd, hoping to win over their hearts before being dragged off stage by security. When I asked her why she had not seized the long shot opportunity, she said, "The thought never crossed my mind. I think I would probably pull a muscle before security even reached me on the stage."

- Chapter Thirty-Eight -

All Good Things Must Come to an End

✦

The last bills were paid, the last final exam was scheduled, the last bag would shortly be packed, and the last good-byes would shortly be said, because the time for us to take our lasting memories back home with us had arrived. Since the month of December had first begun, Sarah and I could not make it through a single day without saying, at least once, "This will be the last time we do this." Somehow it made us feel better to add "for a while" to the phrase because it lifted the sadness of leaving by opening up the possibility that we would come back to experience everything that was good-bye-worthy again.

Along with the arrival of December came the holiday season and a wonderful time to be in London. The streets were packed with holiday shoppers, the pubs felt cozier, and complete strangers seemed to make an extra effort at random acts of kindness toward each other. All over the city, the Christmas spirit of Charles Dickens could truly be felt.

Christmas just wasn't Christmas without a Christmas tree, so Sarah and I made sure we arrived early at Trafalgar Square for the annual lighting of the Christmas tree in the square. As a gift of gratitude for England's support during World War II, the Norwegians had been providing London with a full-size, Norwegian Spruce tree ever since. The giant tree was cut down each year from a forest outside of Oslo and delivered to London by ship.

Sarah and I snuggled just a little bit closer to warm up as we stood amongst the crowd in the square, trying to get a glimpse of the crown princess of Norway, Mette-Marit, who had the honor of lighting the tree while the crowd sang Christmas carols together. The only things missing were falling snowflakes, but since snow in London was rare, we had not gotten our hopes up.

My professor reprimanded me for forgetting the rule of keeping one empty seat between students during finals as I sat down. My mind was on autopilot at that moment as I tried to remember all the last-minute facts and figures I had squeezed into my brain.

The final exam began, and I moved swiftly through the test questions as my brain pushed out the facts and figures as quickly as possible, growing ever happier to have more breathing room again. I would not say that I struggled through the final essay portion of the test, but I took my time and ended up being one of the last students to turn the exam in. I did not need to make any last-minute changes to my essay; I had just procrastinated, because turning in the exam meant that my days as a student were officially over.

After a few handshakes, good lucks, and good-byes, I walked out into the cool, brisk London air in Russell Square. All of my good friends were long gone, because many of them had had flights to catch and interviews to prepare for. But instead of heading home, I decided to make one last stop at the British Museum for a final and special good-bye.

I made my way to the Reading Room library inside the British Museum. The sun had set for the day, and the library was illuminated by bright lights, making the baby blue and gold-trimmed domed ceiling look amazing. I walked over to my favorite chair and desk in the library, happy to find it unoccupied, sat down, and pulled out some elegant white stationery that I had purchased and a black pen. I began to write a letter to Her Majesty, the Queen.

It had been such an amazing year, and there were so many people whom I had already thanked for making it so special. But since I could not thank everyone who lived in England, by thanking the Queen, I felt as though I could. Who knew—maybe she would even write me back. By that time, you could even e-mail the Queen, but e-mail just did not seem to have the personal touch that a handwritten letter did. I pulled out my researched note on how to address and write to the Queen and started writing:

Her Majesty the Queen
Buckingham Palace
London SW1A 1AA

Madam,

As the representative of England, its people, and all its glory, I wanted to write Your Majesty this note to express my gratitude for all the parks, museums, celebrations, and traditions that I have experienced this past year that make England such a wonderful place to visit, learn, and live in.

Your Majesty, we have never met, but you have seen my spirit in the eyes of the people that line the streets and proudly wave as Your Majesty passes by with elegance and grace.

England faces many challenges in the years to come, and I look forward to being witness to the many successes and achievements that I'm sure England will achieve, most notably the 2012 Summer Olympics or possibly a 2010 World Cup victory.

This is not good-bye but until we meet again. I have the honor to remain, Madam, Your Majesty's most humble and obedient servant.

Garrett

P.S. My parents say hello and had a great time celebrating your birthday with you!

I sealed the small, white envelope and let out a small chuckle as I placed a stamp with the Queen's picture on it in the top corner of the envelope. Maybe instead of writing the Queen's address on it, all I really needed to do was write, "Please deliver to this woman," with an arrow pointing to the picture of the Queen on the stamp.

With the letter safely in the pocket of my jacket, I made my way to the doors of the Reading Room. I enjoyed hearing the librarian, one last time, shush noisy, camera-snapping tourists who had discovered that their voices bounced off the tall, domed ceiling; shushing them was a nonstop duty of the librarian. Before I walked out, I turned and took in one last view of the great room and quietly said "thank you," before walking out.

I'm Going to Get Your Goat

Saving the last good-bye for Meridith and Petter seemed the most appropriate, because they had been the first friends we had made when we had arrived. They had invited us over for a Swedish Christmas dinner celebration at their home. We ate dinner at a small card table in the middle of the living room. Petter had done much of the cooking, and he explained what some of the food that we were eating was. I was a little apprehensive at first—I was well aware that one of Petter's favorite food dishes was macaroni noodles with nothing but ketchup—but the dinner was great.

While I was overindulging in Swedish meatballs and tempted to jokingly say to Petter that his Swedish meatballs tasted almost as good as the Swedish meatballs they served at IKEA, he explained St. Lucy and the Lucia ceremony. I had never heard about the December Thirteenth St. Lucy holiday that was mostly observed in Denmark, Finland, Norway, and Sweden. Petter described what a great honor it was for the young girl who gets chosen to portray Lucia each Christmas holiday and lead a small procession down the center aisle of the church with a crown full of white burning candles. She was closely followed by other young women, who each held a single candle. The candles were meant to symbolize the burning fire that had refused to burn St. Lucia when guards, who had been ordered to kill her, had tried to burn her. The tradition was completed with the singing of the song *Santa Lucia* as the procession moved down the aisle.

The Swedish social and holiday traditions were interesting, and after many rounds of toasting each other with drinks in hand, the night came to a close. The last good-bye would soon be said, but there was only one question I had for Petter—would the Gävle Goat, or the Christmas Goat, be burned down to the ground this year or not? When I asked Petter the question, he laughed and reached over to pour me a final drink for the night. Sarah had never heard of the Gävle Goat, so Petter told the story from the beginning.

In the 1960s, the Swedish city of Gävle had erected a forty-feet-tall Swedish Yule Goat made almost entirely out of hay as a way to drum up business for the stores in the area during the holiday season. The first year it was built, it had stood tall until midnight on New Year's Eve, when vandals lit it on fire and burned it to the ground. The perpetrators were caught, but a new Christmas tradition of burning down the Gävle Goat had been born.

Since it had been first erected in 1966, the Gävle Goat had been burned down to its steel skeleton more times than not, often within hours of being built. The goat had been run over by a car, had been shot with a flaming arrow, and had Molotov cocktails thrown at it; it had even burned down during a massive blizzard.

In 2001, a fifty-one-year-old American had set the goat on fire. He had been caught and put on trial. His defense was that he had thought it was perfectly legal to burn down the goat and he was partaking in experiencing the tradition. He spent eighteen days in jail and then left the country without paying his fine.

Always looking for something new to bet on, English bookies had even made it possible to bet on whether or not the goat would be burned each year.

I asked Petter why the city kept building the Gävle Goat, which preceded Santa Claus as the bringer of gifts to homes in Sweden. The answer was obvious, and being a newly minted MBA, I could not believe that I had not known the answer myself: word-of-mouth advertising.

Every time the goat was burned to the ground, even with it being guarded around the clock by web cams, police, soldiers, and volunteers, the tradition made the world press and had helped to put the Swedish city of Gävle on the map.

In recent years, the goat had been soaked from head to toe with the same flame-resistant materials used on airplanes to prevent the goat from being burned down or slow down the burning. I had a suspicion that a long run of non-burning years might cause an uproar among the town's citizens, because if the tradition faded from the memory of the world press, the town might fall off the map again.

As the evening came to an end, we decided we would not say good-bye and instead ended the night by saying "Until we see each other again," and giving a final hug and wave good-bye as we walked out the door.

Leading up to our last day in London, Sydney had nervously paced the floor each time another bag was taken out of a closet and overstuffed with clothes and souvenirs for the final trip home. The ritual reached its climax when Sydney's enormous travel crate was reassembled and placed on the floor of the living room, taking up most of the space. Each time I looked at the growing pile of packed bags, I could not stop thinking, "How are we ever going to get all this stuff home?"

Our last night out in London, we ate dinner at Da Mario Pizza Place in South Kensington. We had picked the place because it was unique and close to the Royal Albert Hall, the final evening's entertainment destination. The restaurant had been a favorite of Princess Di, who could sneak over from the nearby Kensington Palace for a pizza at night. Often, she had brought her sons William and Harry. The restaurant had a large painted mural of the owner Mario presenting a pizza to the princess, who was dressed in a stunning red dress. As Sarah and I enjoyed our pizza together, Mario, the owner, came over to our table and offered us two free glasses of champagne from a tray. Then he toasted us: "To love!"

I had wanted Sarah to experience the Royal Albert Hall before we left, and I had thought that there would be no better opportunity than to join thousands of others in the singing of traditional Christmas carols. We stood together on the main floor belting out the tunes of "O Come, All Ye Faithful" and "Hark! The Herald Angels Sing," enjoying the majestic sound of the famous Royal Albert Hall pipe organ.

I had always been self-conscious of my singing in church, and on that night, I was even more so, because I did not want to sound like an American tourist. I did my best to sing the words with an English accent—a nearly impossible task for me.

We walked home from the concert full of the Christmas spirit. We tried to get some sleep, but we just couldn't, and as we sat in the dark silence of the bedroom, the only sound we could hear was the sound of Sydney's heavy panting. She was still nervous about all the bags and her travel crate sitting by the door.

I thought about our first night in London and how stressful the first twenty-four hours had been. We were approaching the same level of stress as we began the final twenty-four hours of preparations to leave London.

When the first sign of the sun appeared through the windows, Sarah and I got out of bed and took Sydney for a final long walk through Kensington Gardens and Hyde Park, before we would make our way to Heathrow Airport. We walked through the wet grass of the park wearing our blue and red Hunter wellie boots one last time. We did not say much, because we were sad to be going home and nervous about taking Sydney on the plane. Animal experts say that dogs can pick up on their owners' feelings, and Sydney, who had been sensing something was not right for the past few days, was not exploring the curiosities of the park like she usually did. Uncharacteristically, she did not leave our side during the hour-long morning walk.

We reached the end of our usual route and stood at the entrance and exit that we had always come in through. Sarah and I said a final "until we see you again" to the magnificent park that we had fallen so in love with during the year.

We had hired a car service to help get us, Sydney, and all of our bags to the airport. Each of the three days leading up to the day of our departure, I had called the car service to remind them over and over again that we needed the biggest car in their fleet. Each time, I had been assured that they would be able to handle it. At the first sight of the car, the frustrated words that came out of my mouth in the tone of an extremely upset English person were, "For fuck's sake!"

The driver thought I was cursing him for arriving twenty minutes late, but when he looked at the amount of bags we had and the size of Sydney's crate and compared it to the size of the small, four-door Mercedes wagon sedan he had brought, he understood my frustration. It took the driver and me fifteen minutes to get all the bags and crate to fit in the car. We looked at the fully packed car with a sense of pride and accomplishment that we had found a way to make it all fit. But making it all fit meant that Sarah, Sydney, and Sydney's large bed all had to somehow fit in the front passenger's seat—an uncomfortable proposition, because the driver smelled like he had not showered for days and he was sweating from lifting all the bags and was deathly afraid of dogs.

With the car packed and ready to go, Sarah and I walked through our tiny IKEA showroom apartment one last time before leaving the keys on the kitchen counter and shutting the door behind us for the last time. Before the door closed, we said a final "until we see you again" to the place that we had called home for the year.

The car did not fall apart from the weight of all the bags during the trip to the airport. Sarah and I did not suffocate from the abusive body odor we had to endure from the driver. Sydney played nice with the driver. So forty-five minutes later, we pulled up to the departures area at Heathrow Airport.

Following the same procedures of traveling with a dog on an airplane, we had arrived at the airport four hours before our flight in order to get Sydney to where she needed to be. Since we had first flown to London with Sydney, the airlines had again changed the fees for flying with a dog onboard, and our credit card was a smoldering mess from all the excessive and oversized baggage fees the woman at the check-in counter gleefully charged away as if the airline's financial well-being depended on getting as much money as possible out of us. Unlike our first trip over with Sydney, our credit card was not handed back to us with two upgraded seats for the flight.

We said good-bye to Sydney an hour and a half before our flight was scheduled to depart, and we watched as her crate was placed on a cart and she was wheeled down a long, dark hallway.

"We'll see you in Chicago, Sydney!" Sarah said, trying to hold back the tears.

We cleared security and customs and found two empty seats at our gate. I focused on lifting Sarah's spirits up by telling her interesting stories from the newspaper I was reading, and to keep myself from worrying about Sydney, too.

"It says here that a woman put her one-month-old grandson through an X-ray machine at Los Angeles Airport, and it was discovered when the X-ray technician noticed the outline of a child's skeleton," I said. She found the story interesting, and I should have stopped there, because she did not appreciate the next newspaper story of jolly Brits flying to New York for last-minute holiday bargain shopping sprees with empty suitcases, returning with them full, taking advantage of the weakness of the dollar. That story reminded her of the small debt we had racked up over the year.

The boarding process began, and instead of being some of the first ones on, we ended up being the last. We were not flying British Airways home to Chicago, and the airline we were flying refused to tell us whether Sydney had been placed on the plane or not. Sarah refused to get on the plane until they confirmed that Sydney was on the flight.

When the airline representative noticed the number of receipts from checked bags and considered the daunting task of having to remove all of our bags from the flight if we did not get on, he felt that was enough motivation to finally look into it and confirmed that a white, soft-coated Wheaten Terrier had been placed on the plane.

We boarded the plane, getting looks from all of the other passengers, who were curious as to why we were so upset with the airline representatives. We took our seats, and the full plane pulled away from the gate and waited in line to take off.

When it was our turn to take off, Sarah and I said a silent prayer to the god of the skies to help Sydney arrive home safely. We didn't have window seats on the flight, so there was no argument over who would get the final look at London when we took off. Stuck in the middle row, we both sat in silence as the plane climbed higher and higher into the air.

New Citizens of the World

After the plane leveled off at thirty thousand feet and boredom crept up on me, I took out a small, blue booklet that I had saved for the flight home: the British citizenship test. I wanted to see if, without studying and while relying only on my experiences from the year, I would be able to pass the forty-five-minute test with a passing grade of at least 75 percent.

Earlier in the year, I had stumbled upon an article describing how a recent survey found that far more Americans could name the five Simpsons family members than the five freedoms guaranteed by the First Amendment in the Bill of Rights.

When I had first read the article, I had panicked because I could easily name the five Simpsons family members, but I could only name four of the five freedoms—speech, press, assembly, and religion—before I fought off the choking sensation and recalled the missing freedom to petition.

The impromptu exercise of naming the five freedoms guaranteed by the First Amendment had made me question whether I could pass a United States citizenship test. I hoped so, because I had lived my entire life in the United States and anyone who had finished the fifth grade in America should be able to.

I found an unofficial, online United States citizenship test and got the easy questions right: "From whom did the United States declare its independence?"; "What are the three branches of government?"; "Who wrote the 'Star-Spangled Banner'?" But I was tripped up by naming all the original thirteen states and the introduction to the Constitution, which was "The Preamble."

I passed the United States citizenship test, but I thought that anyone who dedicated some time studying the answers prior to the test could pass it without really knowing what it meant to be an American.

If I had my way, there would be no study guide, and some of the test questions would include: "What month does the television season begin?"; "Complete the following chant: 'U.S.A! U.S.A! _____!'; "Which direction are NASCAR races run?"; "What does the acronym WWJD stand for?"; and "How many times has Pamela Anderson been married?" (Answers: September; U.S.A!; counterclockwise; What Would Jesus Do; and too many to count.)

I picked twenty-four random questions from the *United Kingdom Citizen Study Guide* and tried to answer them. I breezed through the first four questions: "Who is the head of the Church of England?"; "Where are cockney dialects spoken?"; "Where is the Prime Minister's official residence?"; and "What does the abbreviation 'FA' stand for?" (Answers: the Queen, London, 10 Downing Street, and Football Association.)

But my streak ended there, and as the English say, "I crashed out," unable to answer the questions: "What is the population of Wales?"; "What is the name of the official reports of proceedings in Parliament?"; and "When was the Council of Europe established?" It quickly became obvious that I would not even be close to achieving the necessary 75 percentage rate to successfully pass the test.

I have long-standing criticism that the United States citizenship test does not ask enough questions that everyday Americans can answer without falling back on their sixth grade history lessons. I thought the UK citizens test would be greatly improved if it asked such questions as: "How do you order a pint at the bar?" and "What is a television license fee?" But I did like the FA football question, and it inspired me to add the question "What does the NFL stand for?" to my newly revised United States citizenship test.

I have to admit that I was disappointed that I did not have the right stuff to pass the United Kingdom citizenship test, but what I experienced during that year could never have been measured by a silly test.

Sarah and I had first arrived in London with just a few bags full of clothes. We were leaving with a new understanding of what it meant to wear shorts with black socks or the feeling of wearing Hunter wellie boots in the Cotswolds. We had arrived with a four-legged dog who had often been scared of her own shadow. We were leaving with a dog that had gained confidence and was well-traveled, too. We had arrived not knowing a single person, and we were leaving with a childhood friendship rekindled and some new good friends that we would know for the rest of our lives. We had arrived as a couple that was still learning what marriage was all about. We were leaving with a stronger personal bond than ever before and more respect and love for each other. We had arrived with an open and curious attitude and were leaving with a new outlook on the world and what it meant to be European and American.

We had moved to Europe, in part, so we could better understand the world outside of our own country. Sometimes, you had to leave the comforts of home to really understand what home was all about, because you never truly appreciated another country or your own until you walked on foreign soil. If I could ask for one thing, based on what I learned during the year, I would ask Americans to be a little more like Europeans and for Europeans to be a little more like Americans.

Somewhere over the Atlantic Ocean, I showed Sarah a small gift that I had purchased at Harrods for us. I pulled the item out of the classic hunter green Harrods box and held it up for her to see. It was a tiny, white, baby onesie with the Union Jack flag on the front and the words "Made in Britain" printed on it. We would need it later the next year for the birth of our daughter, Summer Carol Ryan.

Cheers!

Acknowledgments

Special thanks to Sarah for her love, patience and encouragement with the writing and production of this book. I also owe a great deal of gratitude to my parents as well as Jim and Julie for their unwavering love and support.

A big Ryan family hug to; Greg, Claudia, Eric, Ingrid, Anya and Inger as well as our extended Norwegian family Erik and Inger and all those who gratuitously welcomed us into their homes and treated us like family in Norway.

To all those who had the courage to travel across the pond for a visit and a good look around; Jill, Beth, Shamloi, Don, Andrew, Christopher, Julie, Mike, Mary, Ben, Bryce, Christa.

To our new friends who destiny decided to bring us together; Meridith, Petter, Denis, Jenny, Andy, Max, Felix, Christine, Amir and Mona.

To the entire faculty and staff at *Huron University*, especially the honorable Ray Hilditch who I failed miserably to truly capture the magnitude of what a wonderful person and mentor he is.

To Jennifer Kirkland, Rachel Robbins, Mike Pugh and Bobbi Bowers for their editing skills, honest opinions and creative help.

And a *Cheers!* to the fine folks at *Cross Keys* pub, *The Queens Arms* pub, *The Builders Arms* pub and the staff at the *Reading Room* in the *British Museum*.

Made in the USA
Lexington, KY
14 January 2011